Prairie State Books

In conjunction with the Illinois Center for the Book,
the University of Illinois Press is reissuing in paperback
works of fiction and nonfiction that are, by virtue of
authorship and/or subject matter, of particular interest
to the general reader in the state of Illinois.

A list of books in the series appears at the end of this book.

Publication of this book and others in the Prairie State Books
program was supported in part by a generous grant from
William and Irene Beck.

Chicago Stories

Chicago Stories

James T. Farrell

Selected and Edited by Charles Fanning

University of Illinois Press / Urbana and Chicago

© 1998 by Cleo Paturis, Literary Executor
of the Estate of James T. Farrell
Manufactured in the United States of America
P 5 4 3 2 1

This book is printed on acid-free paper.

Library of Congress Cataloging-in-Publication Data

Farrell, James T. (James Thomas), 1904–1979
Chicago stories /James T. Farrell ; selected and
edited by Charles Fanning
p.   cm. — (Prairie State books)
ISBN 0-252-01981-4 (pbk. : acid-free paper)
1. Chicago (Ill.)—Social life and customs—Fiction.
2. Irish Americans—Illinois—Chicago—Fiction.
3. Working class—Illinois—Chicago—Fiction.
I. Fanning, Charles. II. Title. III. Series.
PS3511.A738A6   1998
813'.52—dc21   97-33896
CIP

The world is so full of a number of things,
I'm sure we should all be as happy as kings.

—Robert Louis Stevenson

No sovereign, no court, no personal loyalty, no aristocracy,
no church, no clergy, no army, no diplomatic service, no
country gentlemen, no palaces, no castles, nor manors, nor
old country houses, nor parsonages, nor thatched cottages,
nor ivied ruins; no cathedrals, nor abbeys, nor little Norman
churches; no great Universities nor public schools—no
Oxford, nor Eton, nor Harrow.

—Henry James

For, in reality, the knowledge of an effect is nothing else
than the acquisition of more perfect knowledge of its cause.

—Spinoza

To Fran, Stephen, and Ellen,
and to Cleo Paturis

Contents

Acknowledgments

I am grateful to Cleo Paturis, James T. Farrell's literary executor, for her kind permission to republish these stories. My work on this collection has been aided by Special Research and Summer Research Grants from Southern Illinois University at Carbondale and by a Summer Research Stipend from the National Endowment for the Humanities. I much appreciate this valuable support. For their generously shared wisdom, encouragement, and friendship, my heartfelt thanks to Thomas N. Brown, John V. Kelleher, Emmet Larkin, Lawrence J. McCaffrey, Ellen Skerrett, and Blanche M. Touhill. I have also been blessed at Southern Illinois University with the most congenial and helpful colleagues and critics for whom anyone could wish, and I am especially grateful to Ken Collins, Beth Lordan, Scott McEathron, Dick Peterson, and Anita Riedinger. Special thanks also to the graduate assistants whose intelligence and energy have helped this book in so many ways—Jill Brady Hampton, Ron Ebest, Matt Jockers, and Elizabeth Brymer. As always, I am most thankful for the love, support, and salutary perspectives of my wife, Fran, and our children, Stephen and Ellen.

Introduction:
James T. Farrell and Short Fiction

CHARLES FANNING

In January 1969, at the age of sixty-four, James T. Farrell recalled the primacy of the short story for his career in fiction: "I began not as a novelist, but as a short story writer. For more than two years after I had decided to become a writer, I worked to write publishable short stories. Long before I had completed the first volume of the *Studs Lonigan* trilogy, my short stories had received recognition. Ezra Pound tried to get me a publisher for four of my stories which he himself had selected. Had he succeeded, *Young Lonigan* [1932] would not have been my first book."[1] In his lifetime, Farrell published an astonishing 250 stories, most of them collected in fifteen volumes, from *Calico Shoes and Other Stories* (1934) to *Olive and Mary Anne* (1977).[2] Moreover, his earliest essays about short fiction reveal that he saw the story as a separate genre to which he had something special to contribute.

Farrell's impressive critical intelligence is evident in his "Preface" to the 1937 Vanguard Press single-volume edition of his first three story collections. He offered there a historical overview of the economic and aesthetic constraints that had impeded the positive evolution of the genre in the United States. He began by explaining the market forces driving the demand for "short stories of a certain plot pattern." For many years, such stories had provided "a good living" for writers and "bait for procuring advertisements" for magazine owners. "To use plain language," Farrell declared, short fiction "has often been employed as a kind of literary pimp."[3] Thus conceived, the American short story had become "a business. And just as there are schools to teach accounting, stenography, salesmanship, hotel-keeping, and the like, so are there institutions teaching short-story writing." These included college courses and a plethora of handbooks and guides, replete with charts, formulae, and "cabalistic lore." Farrell then asserted that this mechanistic approach to the creation of literature had had a pernicious effect on the climate of critical opinion. Invariably, "something called *form* is stressed," so emphatically as to expose "the weakness in all approaches to literature that are purely formal. Form becomes a philosophy, a value," and "the material from life on which literature draws is falsified. Inevitably, there is a loss of concern with content. Content is altered—but not to gain that more concentrated effect and meaning which literature strives to achieve. It is changed, pieced together, in order to make it fit into an arbitrary structure. Life is falsified. A literature of hollow and straw men is produced" (xxxvi–xxxvii).

Farrell went on to say that "the content poured into this structure" most often supported a capitalist ideology, by presenting "a simplified view of individualism. . . . If [a character] is a go-getter, if he adheres to the prevailing views of life and the 'worthy' goods of life, if he plays the game of capitalistic struggle, he will advance. He will be a success. Success will bring happiness." In addition, this formula was reinforced by "a hygienic and largely Protestant morality, and a carry-over of the virgin complex that traces back to the medieval cult of the virgin. The ideal of life is success, and the fruits of success are marriage to an American virgin, a home in the suburbs that contains all the advantages, conveniences, gadgets, automobiles, radios, etc., that are to be found advertised in the magazines which have long specialized in printing precisely this type of story" (xxxix, xl).

Much fiction that purported to address working-class or minority experience, Farrell continued, was only a "local-color" subset of this same formula. "In early years, there was the literature of the American immigrant, of first-generation groups, written in an unreal and patronizing vein. The melting pot was a typical literary theme. The treatment in such works was without vitality, conventional, intended to be humorous. The stories contained little truth and were written from the outside. Writers played on variations of such themes as that of the stage Irishman who was manufactured by some nineteenth-century Irish novelists for English consumption. In a vulgar and insulting manner, such fiction sentimentalized Jewish characters. It was a literature of the Cohens and the Kellys, of Abie's Irish Roses, Uncle Remus, a literature of the upper classes and of good old Star-Spangled Banner patronage."

What had followed more recently was the realistic revolt against the traditional short story, a revolt that "in part took the form of turning upside down the familiar views, notions, ideals, and themes that had been dominant in our fiction during the early years of this century," and also "threw overboard the plot conception of the short story and the happy ending, the traditional patterns of the English Victorian novel." As part of the revolt, writers "began articulating the experience of groups in America, of phases in American life that had hitherto received false and patronizing treatment, or no attention at all. Immigrant groups, the working class, the poorer elements in general began to receive some degree of realistic representation in American fiction" (xli–xlii). Farrell judged that the revolution so described was "to a certain degree, victorious." Great changes had been made in both form and content, creating a new short-fiction tradition that ran counter to the "plot story" perfected by the likes of O. Henry and Bret Harte. As examples, Farrell cited stories by Sherwood Anderson ("I'm a Fool" and "I Want to Know Why"), Theodore Dreiser ("The Lost Phoebe"), Ring Lardner ("The Golden Honeymoon" and "Some Like Them Cold"), and Ernest Hemingway ("Hills Like White Elephants").

And yet, Farrell continued, harmful effects of the "earlier acceptance" of the plot story, with its glorification of structure, had persisted into the 1930s—on the stage, in Hollywood film-making, and, crucially for the genre, in short-story criticism. Rather than doing the work of appreciating and evaluating short fiction, Farrell argued, critics were still falling back on the formal question: "Is this specific work a short story?" Citing a number of definitions of the genre, he then asked, "Which of these definitions is best suited to the stories of Chekhov?—in my opinion the greatest short-story writer who ever lived. Or which one is most applicable to the stories in Joyce's *Dubliners*? To *Winesburg, Ohio*?" Rejecting the formulaic criterion that a short story should create a "*single* or a *unified* impression," Farrell cited Chekhov's "A Woman's Kingdom," as "literally, a cross section of many phases of life [in Tzarist Russia]. One gets from it impressions of class relationships, of characters, of moods. What, then, of the singleness of impression? In fact, Chekhov's stories are an excellent refutation of all these definitions. His stories are, in my opinion, like doors of understanding and awareness opening outward into an entire world" (xlviii).

Farrell concluded this "Preface" by discussing the most conspicuous example of his era's blind faith in content: the demand in left-wing magazines such as *The Anvil* for didactic, so-called proletarian fiction featuring "a purely conceptualized, hypothetical, and non-existent worker [as] the hero. The stories produced in this movement were bad, lifeless, wooden.

In place of the happy ending of *The Saturday Evening Post* variety, they had an 'uplifting' conclusion based on a sudden conversion to the sole correct faith in progress and the future of humanity." Thus, Farrell attacked distortions of content in the name of form in the mechanical "plot story" of popular magazines and college writing courses, and distortions of form in the name of content in "local color" and "proletarian" stories about minorities and the working class. There is little to choose, he declared, between fiction produced and endorsed by political standards or by short-fiction handbooks: "The former hypostasizes, narrows, and freezes content; the latter achieves a similar effect with form" (l–li).

Just as Farrell's earliest writing about short fiction emphasized the lack of critical realism about American life, his own novels and stories were attempts to provide the first sustained critique of the Irish-American subculture, and by extension, of much else in urban American lives in his time. In this endeavor, no writer was more important as a model to Farrell than Anton Chekhov, whom he had first read seriously in 1927 while beginning work on his own fiction. In his 1942 essay on Chekhov, Farrell clarified the connection between them. He described Chekhov's characters as "idle dreamers who live sunk in the commonplace; men and women who cannot react to cruelty, who cannot be free, who cannot lift themselves above the terrible plain of stagnation—people in whom human dignity is dissolving." Farrell emphasized two characteristics of Chekhov's work, both previously noted by Maxim Gorky, which were central to Farrell's own aims. The first was Gorky's assessment that "banality always found in him a discerning and merciless judge," to which Farrell added, "Chekhov raised the portrayal of banality to the level of world literature." The second was Gorky's statement of Chekhov's essential message: "You live badly, my friends. It is shameful to live like that." Farrell went on to assert that "the translation of [Chekhov's] stories into English has constituted one of the greatest single literary influences at work in the short story of America, England, and Ireland." His example, Farrell continued, has "encourag[ed] the short-story writers of these nations to revolt against the conventional plot story and to seek in simple and realistic terms to make of the story a form that more seriously reflects life. With the aid of Chekhov's inspiration, some of our own short-story writers have learned to tell us that there is too much dreariness, too much cruelty, too much banality in our own lives. Chekhov has not only influenced the form of the short story, but he has also influenced its content."[4]

* * *

There have been in American literary history three windows of heightened tolerance for narratives of ethnic and working-class characters. In the 1890s, the golden age of urban journalism fostered interest in "slum stories" and explorations of "How the Other Half Lives" (sociologist Jacob Riis's title). Reporters covered zealously the collision of burgeoning immigration and the severe national depression of 1893–97, and many turned their journalism into ethnic fiction of urban local color and social critique. In the 1930s, economics was again the catalyst for literary production, as the Great Depression spurred an American socialist/communist movement that in turn encouraged the rise of "proletarian" writers, many from immigrant and ethnic backgrounds, who began telling their stories and finding their audience in this political context. In the 1980s, a third window of tolerance opened for ethnic and working-class narratives (not always the same thing, of course), this time through the academy. By then, the proliferation of American paperback publishing houses and institutions of higher learning had combined to make literary study and the shaping of course syllabi big business. Ethnic narrative began to be noticed again through support for the concept of "multiculturalism," and working-class narrative was newly sanctioned through praise of what came to be known as "minimalism."

Each of these periods has implications for James T. Farrell's career as a writer. He was inspired by the journalists-turned-fiction-writers of the turn of the century (Dreiser, Norris, Crane, George Ade, and for his own Chicago Irish, Finley Peter Dunne). He came of age with the proletarian writers of the 1930s (with Mike Gold, Edward Dahlberg, Langston Hughes, Jack Conroy, and others). In that decade, however, Farrell employed his critical energies warning artists against the contaminating influence of politics on literature, and excoriating those critics who were judging books ideologically. His efforts here were later to damage his own artistic reputation.

In 1936, Farrell published *A Note on Literary Criticism,* his book-length analysis of the relationship between literature and Marxist cultural criticism.[5] There, with detailed discussion of sources as varied as the Japanese *Tale of Genji,* Spinoza, Thomas Aquinas, Dickens, Proust, Dostoevski, and Joyce, he defended the integrity of art against the corruption of political propaganda, which he saw as an urgent threat from the intellectual left. In this campaign, Farrell's was an early and very strong voice, and it made him several enemies who established an unjust and unfounded literary party-line about his work. *Studs Lonigan* was characterized as creditable but limited fiction, an instance of the dated naturalism of Theodore Dreiser, and Farrell's subsequent books were often dismissed as obsessive and clumsy reworkings of the same materials. As luck would have it, some of these critics went on to become respected shapers of literary reputation in the 1940s and 1950s. They included Malcolm Cowley, Granville Hicks, Alfred Kazin, and other New York-based critics who came to embrace a high modernist/New Critical aesthetic. (Daniel Aaron has said that after World War II Farrell was "run over by the Henry James machine.")[6] That Farrell should be thought of as a crude, repetitive, and unselfconscious writer is especially galling given the realities of his highly deliberate development as an artist and intellectual.

Certainly, no one who gives his other books a chance will credit this blanket rejection of a lifework, and yet, it is in part the early critical denigration of Farrell as an artless, one-book writer that has kept from his fiction the attention that should have been his due by now, particularly in the context of the third window of tolerance for ethnic and working-class narratives. In the 1980s and beyond, advocates of both multiculturalism and minimalism have continued to ignore Farrell, mostly because they've believed their elders and haven't bothered to read past *Studs Lonigan*. Many haven't even read *Studs*.

There are other causes as well. Multiculturalism has come to be identified with the literature of higher-profile, more recently or still disadvantaged minority groups: African Americans, Hispanics, Asian Americans, and American Indians. By such political criteria, the older, now more successful, European ethnic groups, including the Irish, have tended to be ignored. But certainly Farrell belongs in any ethnically grounded canon. The U.S. census of 1890 counted more Americans of Irish birth than any other before or since, and the Chicago neighborhood life between 1910 and 1940 that is a major focus of Farrell's fiction had still a dominant ethnic dimension. Thus, Farrell has much to tell us about Irish-American and other experiences of doubleness.

Furthermore, he also contributes in important ways to the chronicle of working-class American life. Many essays that praise contemporary "minimalist" chroniclers of that life—such as Ann Beattie, Barry Hannah, Frederick Busch, Bobbie Ann Mason, and Raymond Carver—share a pattern that helps by negative example to locate Farrell's special contribution.[7] Often reviewers find two ways to sanction narratives of ordinary, limited lives such as occur, for example, in Carver's stories. First, such narratives are praised if they are written tastefully, with a sort of cold restraint that is interpreted as craftsmanship. The words "austerity" and "dispassion" are casually invoked, and sometimes even the "scrupulous meanness" of Joyce's *Dubliners* is cited, though with little sense of the possible indicting irony of "meanness." Second, these stories are praised if they contain bits of odd, dark, even grotesque behavior. Reviewers pick up on details that they find mysterious, sinister, and often comic, and they react with laughter that comes more from assumed superiority than complicity. I believe that both criteria often mask condescension toward the lives being chronicled, certainly on the part of the critics, as the term "minimalism" itself suggests, and sometimes on the part of the writers. Stylistic felicity makes the medicine go down more easily; it helps the reader to read (and maybe the writer to write) about ordinary and limited characters. Grotesque quirks of behavior serve to distance the reader and the writer from a character, thus providing relief from the discomfort of possible identification.[8] In contrast, a great strength of Farrell's fiction is his avoidance of both of the palliatives, stylistic and thematic, that pervade much minimalist fiction. From the beginning, he created truly austere, plain-style narratives of ordinary lives unmarked by exaggerated and thus mitigating grotesquerie. In this regard, his short fiction is particularly strong.

* * *

As with his novels, Farrell wrote short fiction as a realist committed to plausibly creating the consciousness—the thoughts, feelings, reactions to events and experience—of characters in a great variety of social and economic situations. Most live in American cities between the turn of the century and World War II. Often the city is Chicago and often the people are identifiably Irish. Two types of stories are dominant, and both of them are pioneering for American literature: portraits of the artist as an urban Irish American, and portraits of working-class urban Americans whose lives are thwarted by limited self-awareness. The autobiographical figure of "Danny O'Neill" appears, named or unnamed, in more than fifty stories, according to leading Farrell critic Edgar M. Branch, who also points out that this important group "add[s] significantly to Farrell's picture of youth and age, boyish aspiration and adult acceptance, ardent love and tired middle-aged infidelity, the social life of the high-school set and young married couples, family life and the tension between the generations." Branch goes on to chart the impressive range of Farrell's short fiction:

Similarly, Farrell's tales inspect the Catholic Church and the clergy, education up through the university, unions and laboring men (especially express-company workers and gas-station attendants), the politics of the ward heeler and the radical, Bohemian and literary circles, organized urban violence (sexual aggression, racial strife, criminal racketeering) and organized sports (boxing, baseball, basketball, football, tennis), and the everyday life and death of city people of numerous nationalities (Irish, Greek, Polish, Lithuanian) and of many sorts (the bum, the struggling immigrant, the white-collar serf, the chain-store magnate, to name some). Working outward from many Chicago neighborhoods—not confined to what is loosely called Farrell's "South Side"—the stories eventually reach to New York, Paris, and Europe at large.[9]

Selected from the 158 stories in Farrell's first ten collections, the twenty-five stories gathered in this book represent the full range of his characters and themes. In keeping with the emphases of Prairie State Books, all are set in Chicago, the fertile heartland of this writer's imagination. The stories are arranged chronologically according to the publication dates of the books in which they appeared, with one exception—the last two are reversed. The earliest story here is "Mary O'Reilley," completed in 1928, and the latest is "Norman Allen," begun in 1947 and finished in 1957. However, the 1948 story "Kilroy Was Here," with its description of the development of a working-class writer, is a natural coda for any gathering of Farrell's fiction.[10]

In June 1932, Farrell had written his sister Mary: "I shall probably bring out a book of stories, called 'These Chicagoans,' which I plan to cut up into series, kids, high school kids, collegians, young people non-collegians, older generations, divided into groups, perhaps, priests and professors, mothers and fathers, etc, and it will be anything but a series of pleasant comments on my own dear Chicago."[11] It was, however, as *Calico Shoes and Other Stories* that this book appeared in September 1934. This was the young writer's fourth published book, following the novels *Young Lonigan* (1932), *Gas-House McGinty* (1933), and *The Young Manhood of Studs Lonigan* (January 1934). This new Prairie State anthology of *Chicago Stories* opens with Farrell's epigraphs and the first five stories of *Calico Shoes* in their original order, so as to recreate the careful sequence by means of which Farrell staged one fresh assault after another against the trite, slick-magazine fiction that he found so contemptible.[12] We need look no further than these stories to see how clear Farrell was from the beginning about his goals as a writer of short fiction, and how extensive were the means and materials already available to him.

In "Helen, I Love You," two boys around twelve, placed carefully "in the 5700 block on Indiana Avenue" on Chicago's South Side, test their toughness by exchanging insults. Neither really wants to fight, so they push each other to the limit of words—the convincing dialogue carries the story—and then turn away. In contrast to this external verbal battle, we are privy to an interior struggle in which the language of feeling is tested in the consciousness of the protagonist, Dan (Farrell's alter ego, Danny O'Neill, though his last name isn't given), who explores his first infatuation with a girl by repeating to himself "Helen, I love you!" Dan daydreams about impressing Helen by beating up the other boy, after which "everything would be all so swell, just like it was at the end of the stories he sometimes read in *The Saturday Evening Post*." No such scene occurs, and Dan walks home alone in the gathering dusk, frightened by the wind and his own "strange feelings." Thus, the first story in Farrell's first collection is a casual incident on a Chicago street, carried by and measuring the distance between realistic dialogue and reverie, and pointedly referencing the formulaic short fiction against which this is his first blow.

The second story, "The Scarecrow," powerfully describes the heartless mistreatment of a fourteen-year-old Chicago girl. Addressed only as "the Scarecrow," this girl is malnourished, unattractive, and of seriously limited intelligence. Her mother, deserted by her husband, works as a night-shift ticket taker for the Illinois Central Railroad. Often ridiculed and beaten at home, the girl wanders the neighborhood in a daze, staying out until morning or sleeping around with anyone who pretends to want her company. Set on Hallowe'en, the story ends with a party at which the girl gets drunk, takes off her dress to show how badly she has been beaten, and is abandoned by the departing revelers. There is a starkness and restraint in "The Scarecrow," an effect of Swiftian savage indignation. In discussing his early fiction, Farrell has said that his aim was objectivity, "letting life speak," and that he was "strongly determined not to produce received sentiments." In these efforts, he saw "The Scarecrow" as "a leap into originality."[13]

The third story, "Looking 'Em Over," opens out to reveal the rich variety of South-Side neighborhood life. Not that the protagonist appreciates what he sees. Don Bryan is the Danny O'Neill of "Helen, I Love You" in arrested development; he's a dim young man in his early twenties, who idles away a summer Sunday afternoon watching girls on the South-Side streets and the Seventy-fourth Street beach. Here Farrell measures the disjunction between Don's daydreams of sexual and economic conquest and the reality of his inarticulate conversational exchanges, which consist mostly of wolf whistles, song lyrics, and monosyllabic lusting grunts. This is a study in the banality of an unimaginative voyeurism that transforms the "hot glory" of summer in the city into monotonous dross.

The fourth story expands to wider, social issues and also to a stylistic innovation for Farrell. "The Buddies" utilizes a third-person omniscient narrative to chronicle the rise and fall of an informal organization of teamsters. Two innocent, enthusiastic young drivers for Continental Express, Jack and Smitty, start up a social group that runs raffles, picnics, and a baseball team, and pays sick benefits of twenty dollars a week. "The Buddies" is successful enough to attract the attention of the "official" union, a corrupt organization that pads the wallets of its officers and operates by intimidation. Union "sluggers" beat up Jack and Smitty and their group is disbanded. Given Farrell's own working-class background (his father was a teamster) and the burgeoning labor movement during the Depression (the story was written in 1931), this critique of abuses by organized labor shows a striking—but not unexpected—objectivity.

In the fifth story in this first collection, "A Front-page Story," Farrell returns to Danny O'Neill, now working his way at the University of Chicago as "the campus reporter" for a city daily newspaper. Danny gets word of a possible scoop—the sudden death by heart failure on graduation day of a senior from Iowa, Ruth Summer. Trapped in the role of "reporter," Danny is otherwise unnamed, but he remains both imaginative and sensitive, and therein lies the tension in this gem of a story. He interviews Ruth's family and friends, and in a series of "mental pictures" he visualizes the "whole university career" of "this unostentatious, unsung, practically unknown small town girl": her lonely freshman week, her round of grinding, diligent work as an education major, her standing unasked in a pink frock at campus dances. And, "he could see her, again," hearing from her doctor that her heart was so weak "that any undue excitement or violent exercise would induce her death." The reporter "admire[s] her persistence and courage" in continuing on as a full-time student and part-time waitress. After all her work, however, Ruth is notified just before graduation "that she lacked one grade point, and that her average, therefore, did not qualify her for a degree." She buys her cap and gown, sits for her graduation picture, and attends the senior breakfast; "then on the day of graduation, she had gone out to the sand dunes in the rain, and had attempted to run and swim."

At the funeral home, the campus reporter poses as a friend and over-hears the judgment of Ruth's cousin: "It was literal suicide." Concurring, the reporter has the materials for the "front-page story" that he then phones in to his paper, employing a principle of literary realism to instruct the rewrite man: "And listen! Give her a break. It'll be the first one she ever had. Try and keep out too much of the sob stuff. If you make it too gooey, the story will be spoiled." Far from pleased with himself, the reporter has a disturbing sense of Ruth's various identities in death. To university offi-cials, she is "an embarrassment." To himself, the campus reporter, she is "a scoop, a means of preserving his job." To the Chicago paper, she is "a front-page story, exciting the staff for the space of a few moments while the story was written and turned in." To editors of other dailies, she will be "a source of annoyance, something they had missed." This 1934 story ends with a revelation of startling contemporaneity—the reporter's disturbing sense of his complicity in a process by which distorted meanings are im-posed and "become" the person they describe: "And while she had become or was becoming all these various meanings, she lay in that oppressive undertaking parlor, blue and bloated in a sleeveless pink taffeta party frock, and all the fruitless dignity and courage of her life was betrayed, even after her death." This insight also supports Farrell's own criticism of short fiction that forces experience into molds of Marxist/proletarian content or maga-zine/formulaic structure.

To summarize, these first five stories, all set on the streets of Chicago in the 1920s, feature a sensitive boy waking to the power of words at Fifty-seventh and Indiana, a disabled adolescent girl who is callously victimized, a dull young man in his twenties on whom the potential of the city is lost, two naively hopeful teamsters thwarted by organized labor, and two stu-dents at the University of Chicago, one whose limited life is cut short, and the other whose "report" bears witness to a tragedy that otherwise would never have been noticed. There are few such characters and situations in previous American fiction. With this group of stories, Farrell was well on his way.

* * *

In keeping with his contempt for the formulaic, Farrell created stories in a wide range of modes, from the briefest sketches to elaborated long sto-ries and novellas. "Johnny's Old Man" is a deft four-page rendering of the suffering of a child terrorized by his brutal, bullying father. On the other end of the scale, "Boyhood" is a leisurely, thirty-page evocation of one South-Side Chicago autumn as refracted through the mind of young Danny O'Neill, a shy seventh-grader who retreats to the park and his imagination, with daydreams of pitcher Rube Waddell and boxer Benny Leonard. The tentative beginning of a friendship with the one neighborhood boy who is even poorer and more isolated than Danny himself is the epiphany of this fine depiction of early adolescence. And in "The Hyland Family," Farrell creates an extended group portrait of a stodgy, self-satisfied middle-class family, for whom we come to feel sympathy, thanks to the fully rounded presentation of their quite ordinary hopes, disappointments, and tragedies. The result is an Irish-American "Death of Ivan Ilych."

Though finished stories in their own right, "Studs" (1929) and "Jim O'Neill" (1932) also contain the seeds of Farrell's first two, complementary fictional cycles, the Studs Lonigan trilogy, which traces the decline and death of its hapless young protagonist, and the O'Neill-O'Flaherty pentalogy, in which Danny O'Neill emerges into the light of potential self-control and understanding through art.

A series of concentric circles moving outward suggests major concerns in the stories collected here from a thirty-year body of work. Farrell was critical of the prevalent distorted idealizing of children in fiction, and he wrote many stories featuring a city child's realistic perspective on himself, his family, and his neighborhood.[14] These include "Helen, I Love You," "Lib," "Boyhood," and "Johnny's Old Man." Extension into the lives of adolescents occurs in "The Scarecrow" and "Looking 'Em Over," where the emphasis is on crippling limitation (as in "Studs" and the Lonigan trilogy), and in "The Oratory Contest," which depicts the promise of release through intelligence and schooling (as in the O'Neill-O'Flaherty novels). Farrell knew as well as any writer that intellectual success in a working-class milieu is not usually unalloyed, and he registers a seldom examined part of that cost in electing to present "The Oratory Contest" through the consciousness of the boy's father. The result is a piercing treatment of the gulf that often opens between working-class parents and their better-educated children. The rich legacy of Chekhov is here—in Farrell's plain-style restraint in the telling, his realistic presentation of pain that can be understood but not alleviated, and his mutually reinforcing combination of clarity and compassion. The next giant step onto the campus of the University of Chicago in the late 1920s, just across Washington Park but a world away from the Farrell/Lonigan/O'Neill neighborhood, is the setting for several other stories: "A Front-page Story," "All Things Are Nothing To Me," "The Professor," and the first half of "Norman Allen."

In addition, the alternative worlds of various adult Chicagoans in the 1920s and 1930s are vividly evoked in "Mary O'Reilley" (a spinster's quiet death of the heart), "Jim O'Neill" (a bone-tired working man trapped in poverty), "The Professor" (a university writing teacher, world-weary but still effective), "Precinct Captain" (the political machine in action), "The Hyland Family" (one fateful Sunday for a conventional, middle-class widower and his children), and "The Wake of Patsy McLaughlin" (communal experiencing of worklife and death at an express company). Farrell also created many precedent-setting pictures of the Catholic clergy as real people: for example, nuns in "The Bride of Christ" and priests in "Reverend Father Gilhooley."

As his critical writings predict, a major accomplishment in these stories is Farrell's creation of voices for the inarticulate, especially the victimized and overlooked. Walt Whitman's aesthetic pledge in "Native Moments" comes to mind: "O you shunn'd persons, I at least do not shun you, / I come forthwith in your midst, I will be your poet, / I will be more to you than to any of the rest." Among the shunned in Farrell's stories are the abused adolescent girl known as "the Scarecrow," the quietly despairing college senior of "A Front-page Story," a raving homeless man in "Street Scene," and the children of poverty who become "Young Convicts."

Related here as well, and also predicted by Farrell's critical writings, are several hard looks at urban race relations in the wake of the great African-American diaspora from the rural South to Chicago between the two World Wars. These stories describe the harrowing effects of prejudice and discrimination in both communities: black youths beaten for swimming at the wrong beach in "For White Men Only," and a white boy who meets a sudden, horrible death during the 1919 race riots in "The Fastest Runner on Sixty-first Street." Moreover, in "Norman Allen," though hardly mentioned, race is a subtle, causal undertow in the tragic deterioration to madness of a promising black philosopher. Here, Farrell's powerful rendering of an asylum for the chronically insane is in the vein of his mentor Chekhov's fictional report from "Ward Six."

The forty-year-old Danny O'Neill returns to his old South-Side neighborhood in "Kilroy Was Here," and walks the streets with an aspiring African-American writer, a Richard Wright of the next generation.[15] The story is central and summarizing in its articulation of the motives and progress of an ethnic, working-class writer who has made his way to a wider world through art, but without loss of sympathy for those left behind. To the younger writer's frustrated dismissal of his former schoolmates as heedless and uncaring, Danny replies: "There's something more important than their not caring. They don't know. That's the point about the boys I grew up with—they didn't know." Danny's recall of his childhood community is lucid and balanced: "Behind that porch, inside the door of that flat, so much of his life had been lived, and all that life with its agonies and fears and worries had gone into making him what he now was. Once he used to think of the agonies of those days. Now he realized that inside that flat on the second floor he had dreamed, and his ambition had flourished." To the young man's assertion that "You licked this neighborhood," the older writer replies: "It wasn't the neighborhood that I licked; it was some of the fears in myself."

In its linking of artistic generations, this story embodies the hope of creating fiction that can shed light back into the community abandoned, thereby completing a circle; the hope of "forging" something like an "uncreated conscience," in the words of Stephen Dedalus, that precocious and callow twenty-year-old Dubliner. And for his place and his time, indeed, for any place and time, James T. Farrell has given us fiction that is worthy of the comparison. Farrell's stories are scrupulous without being mean-spirited. They are shot through with forceful, unembellished ironies. They contain solidly memorable characters and believable language—from South-Side streets and saloons to rectories, apartment kitchens, and university classrooms. They provide penetrating insight into the minds of both intelligent people struggling toward understanding and others who are crippled by circumstance and distorted perception. These stories are as arrestingly candid as the works of itinerant portrait painters in eighteenth-century America. Given the evidence of his essays and letters, we know that, unlike the innocent-eyed colonial artists, Farrell's austere immediacy was consciously crafted. Yet the effect is similar. Rather than calling attention to themselves as art, Farrell's stories force the reader to look beyond the page, directly to the people the stories are about. The result is powerful fiction going straight to the heart.

In point of fact, Farrell's first stories and *Studs Lonigan: A Trilogy* launched a remarkable body of work, one of the great, sustained accomplishments of twentieth-century American realism. Filling to date over fifty volumes (several remain in manuscript), this corpus includes four large fictional cycles, interconnected and progressive explorations of their characters' varying responses to American urban environments: the Lonigan and O'Neill sequences, the Bernard Carr trilogy, and the *Universe of Time* series, of which ten volumes were published before Farrell's death in 1979. As early as August 1934 he wrote to a friend that his aim would be "to describe, represent, analyze and portray connected social areas of Chicago that I have lived in, and that I have more or less assimilated. In these terms, then, the various books and stories are all panels of one work, expanding, and branching out to include more characters, and to catch something of the social processes as they come into the lives of these characters."[16] The fifteen collections of stories that he saw through the press may be the least known of these panels, but they are a considerable part of James T. Farrell's literary achievement.

Notes

1. "Introduction," *Childhood Is Not Forever* (Garden City, N.Y.: Doubleday, 1969), vii.

2. Farrell's collections of short fiction, including reprints and British editions, are listed in the accompanying bibliography.

3. "Preface," *The Short Stories of James T. Farrell* (New York: Vanguard Press, 1937), xxxi–xxxii. Subsequent references will be cited parenthetically.

4. "On the Letters of Anton Chekhov," in *The League of Frightened Philistines and Other Papers* (New York: Vanguard Press, 1945), 61. Another early guiding critique is Farrell's speech on "The Short Story," delivered in April 1935 in New York at the First American Writers' Congress of the communist-dominated League of American Writers. Here he discussed several stories that depicted lives "that hitherto had been unexpressed or unsatisfactorily expressed in American writing," including "My Dead Brother Comes to America," Alexander Godin's story of an immigrant crossing from the Ukraine; "So Help Me," Nelson Algren's story of a young Jewish hobo; "The Pension," Lewis Mamet's story of the suicide of an exploited factory worker; "Kneel to the Rising Sun," Erskine Caldwell's story of black and white sharecroppers whose division keeps them powerless against a sadistic landlord; and "Home from the Ways of White Folks," Langston Hughes's story of the lynching of a young black musician caught talking to a white woman while visiting his Missouri hometown. The speech was published in *The League of Frightened Philistines,* 136–48.

5. *A Note on Literary Criticism* (1936; rpt., New York: Columbia University Press, 1992).

6. "James T. Farrell (1904–1979)," *The New Republic,* 6 Oct. 1979, 38.

7. Kim Herzinger's working definition of "minimalism" runs in part as follows: "Minimalist fiction is a) formally spare, terse, trim; b) tonally cool, detached, noncommittal; 'flat,' affectless, recalcitrant, deadpan, laconic; c) oblique and elliptical; d) relatively plotless; e) concerned with surface detail, particularly with recognizable brand names. . . . [its] 'subject matter' is a) ordinary, mundane; b)

domestic, local; c) regional; d) generational; e) blue-collar/working-class or white/ yuppie" ("Minimalism as a Postmodernism: Some Introductory Notes," *New Orleans Review* 16:3 [1989]: 73).

8. Some examples of the distancing *frisson* of oddness in Carver stories are the baker's crazy, harassing phone calls in "A Small, Good Thing," the man frozen to his couch in "Preservation," the peacock as house pet in "Feathers," and the fetishistic lure of the apartment next door in "Neighbors." See Raymond Carver, "Neighbors," in *Will You Please Be Quiet, Please?* (1976; New York: Vintage Books, 1992), 9–16. The other three stories are in *Cathedral* (1983; New York: Vintage Books, 1984): "Feathers" (3–26), "Preservation" (35–46), and "A Small, Good Thing" (59–90).

9. Edgar M. Branch, *James T. Farrell* (New York: Twayne Publishers, 1971), 129.

10. Farrell worked over his stories frequently, sometimes for years, and he kept a careful record of the labor. Those dates of composition are included at the end of each story in this collection. See Edgar M. Branch, *A Bibliography of James T. Farrell's Writings, 1921–1957* (Philadelphia: University of Pennsylvania Press, 1959), passim.

11. Letter to Mary Farrell, 11 June 1932, James T. Farrell Archives, University of Pennsylvania. My thanks to Edgar M. Branch for showing me this letter.

12. For a writer who has renounced didacticism, gratuitous allusiveness, and overall "literariness" in the body of his fiction, epigraphs remain one of the few means of creating a larger and directing context. In Farrell's novels and stories they are always important. The *Calico Shoes* epigraphs reprinted here from Robert Louis Stevenson and Henry James are pointedly ironic, but the third epigraph, a passage from Spinoza, is a pledge to the reader that the stories to follow will examine seriously, even relentlessly, the specific origins and springs of certain behavior. Farrell went on to select a long quotation from Émile Zola's "Préface (to) Thérèse Raquin" (1873) as a new epigraph to the 1937 Vanguard compilation of his first three volumes of stories. A further gloss of Farrell's developing aesthetic, the Zola passage begins: "But now that everything is torn down, and swords and capes rendered useless, it is time to base our works on truth. . . . There should no longer be any school, no more formulas . . . there is only life itself, an immense field where each may study and create as he likes." Zola further declares, "We must cast aside fables of every sort, and delve into the living drama of the two-fold life of character and its environment, bereft of every nursery tale, historical trapping, and the usual conventional stupidities. The decayed scaffoldings of the drama of yesterday will fall of their own accord. We must clear the ground. The well-known recipes for the tying and untying of an intrigue have served their time; now we must seek a simple and broad picture of men and things."

13. Quoted in Branch, *James T. Farrell,* 133.

14. In his 1935 speech on "The Short Story," Farrell noted "similarities" in "writing where there is a condition of master and slave, oppressor and oppressed.

Thus there is a similarity between the Uncle Remus stories of the Negro and the stage Irishmen in such nineteenth-century Irish novels as those by Charles Lever and by Samuel Lover. Similarities even extend further. Thus, the writing about children by adults is also of the same nature. Booth Tarkington's *Penrod,* for instance, is put into the same kind of mold, and it is a combination of certain conventions necessary for the intercourse between children and certain types of parents, on one hand, and, on the other hand, of a wish fulfillment or an adult fantasy about childhood" (*League of Frightened Philistines,* 137–38).

15. The connection with Richard Wright is appropriate, for Farrell knew him well. They first met at the 1935 American Writers' Congress in New York. Wright had come East from Chicago, where his family was living on the South Side at 3743 Indiana Avenue, ten blocks north of Farrell's childhood home on the same street and twenty blocks north of the Studs Lonigan neighborhood. Wright was twenty-six, four years younger than Farrell, and had published a few poems and stories in little magazines. He also spoke at the conference—on "The Isolation of the Negro Writer." Michel Fabre has said that Wright "was enthralled to hear James T. Farrell speak on the revolutionary story," particularly Farrell's "true defense of art against propaganda and political tyranny." As Wright was just then becoming interested in short fiction, "Farrell's vigorous observations could not help but influence him, especially because he had his own reservations about the political demands of the Party. This was the beginning of a literary friendship that benefitted Wright enormously" (*The Unfinished Quest of Richard Wright,* 2d ed. [Urbana: University of Illinois Press, 1993], 118–19).

16. Letter to Jack Kunitz, 7 Aug. 1934, James T. Farrell Archives, University of Pennsylvania.

Works by James T. Farrell

SHORT FICTION COLLECTIONS

Calico Shoes and Other Stories. New York: Vanguard Press, 1934 [as *Seventeen and Other Stories* (London: Panther, 1959)].

Guillotine Party and Other Stories. New York: Vanguard Press, 1935.

Can All This Grandeur Perish? and Other Stories. New York: Vanguard Press, 1937.

The Short Stories of James T. Farrell. New York: Vanguard Press, 1937 [as *Fellow Countrymen: Collected Stories* (London: Constable, 1937)]. Reprints the preceding three volumes.

$1,000 a Week and Other Stories. New York: Vanguard Press, 1942.

Fifteen Selected Stories. Avon Modern Short Story Monthly, No. 10. New York: Avon Book Co., 1943. Reprints stories from several volumes.

To Whom It May Concern and Other Stories. New York: Vanguard Press, 1944.

Twelve Great Stories. Avon Modern Short Story Monthly, No. 21. New York: Avon Book Co., 1945. Reprints stories from several volumes.

When Boyhood Dreams Come True. New York: Vanguard Press, 1946.

More Fellow Countrymen. London: Routledge, 1946. Reprints stories from several volumes.

The Life Adventurous and Other Stories. New York: Vanguard Press, 1947.

Yesterday's Love and Eleven Other Stories. New York: Avon Book Co., 1948. Reprints stories from several volumes.

A Misunderstanding. New York: House of Books, 1949. Small press printing of a single story.

An American Dream Girl. New York: Vanguard Press, 1950.

French Girls Are Vicious and Other Stories. New York: Vanguard Press, 1955; London: Panther, 1958.

An Omnibus of Short Stories. New York: Vanguard Press, 1957. Reprints *$1,000 a Week and Other Stories; To Whom It May Concern and Other Stories; The Life Adventurous and Other Stories.*

A Dangerous Woman and Other Stories. New York: New American Library, 1957; London: Panther, 1959.

Saturday Night and Other Stories. London: Panther, 1958. Reprints stories from several volumes.

The Girls at the Sphinx. London: Panther, 1959. Reprints stories from several volumes.

Looking 'Em Over. London: Panther, 1960. Reprints stories from several volumes.

Side Street and Other Stories. New York: Paperback Library, 1961.

Sound of a City. New York: Paperback Library, 1962.

Childhood Is Not Forever and Other Stories. New York: Doubleday, 1969.

Judith and Other Stories. New York: Doubleday, 1973.

Olive and Mary Anne. New York: Stonehill Publishing Co., 1977.

Eight Short Short Stories & Sketches. Ed. Marshall Brooks. Newton, Mass.: Arts End Books, 1981.

NOVELS AND NOVELLAS

Studs Lonigan: A Trilogy. 1935; rpt., Urbana: University of Illinois Press, 1993. [Comprised of *Young Lonigan: A Boyhood in Chicago Streets* (New York: Vanguard Press, 1932), *The Young Manhood of Studs Lonigan* (New York: Vanguard Press, 1934), and *Judgment Day* (New York: Vanguard Press, 1935)].

Gas-House McGinty. New York: Vanguard Press, 1933; London: United Anglo-American Book Company, 1948; rev. ed., New York: Avon, 1950.

O'Neill-O'Flaherty pentalogy:

A World I Never Made. New York: Vanguard Press, 1936; London: Constable, 1938.

No Star Is Lost. New York: Vanguard Press, 1938; London: Constable, 1939.

Father and Son. New York: Vanguard Press, 1940 [as *A Father and His Son* (London: Routledge, 1943)].

My Days of Anger. New York: Vanguard Press, 1943; London: Routledge, 1945.

The Face of Time. New York: Vanguard Press, 1953; London: Spearman and Calder, 1954.

Tommy Gallagher's Crusade. New York: Vanguard Press, 1939.

Ellen Rogers. New York: Vanguard Press, 1941; London: Routledge, 1942.

Bernard Carr trilogy:

  Bernard Clare. New York: Vanguard Press, 1946 [as *Bernard Clayre* (London: Routledge, 1948); as *Bernard Carr* (New York: New American Library, 1952)].

  The Road Between. New York: Vanguard Press, and London: Routledge, 1949.

  Yet Other Waters. New York: Vanguard Press, 1952; London: Panther, 1960.

This Man and This Woman. New York: Vanguard Press, 1951.

Boarding House Blues. New York: Paperback Library, 1961; London: Panther, 1962.

Universe of Time sequence:

  The Silence of History. New York: Doubleday, 1963; London: W. H. Allen, 1964.

  What Time Collects. New York: Doubleday, 1964; London: W. H. Allen, 1965.

  When Time Was Born. New York: The Smith-Horizon Press, 1966.

  Lonely for the Future. New York: Doubleday, 1966; London: W. H. Allen, 1966.

  New Year's Eve/1929. New York: The Smith-Horizon Press, 1967.

  A Brand New Life. New York: Doubleday, 1968.

  Judith. Athens, Ohio: Duane Schneider Press, 1969.

  Invisible Swords. New York: Doubleday, 1971.

  The Dunne Family. New York: Doubleday, 1976.

  The Death of Nora Ryan. New York: Doubleday, 1978.

  Sam Holman. Buffalo: Prometheus Books, 1983.

LITERARY CRITICISM AND OTHER PUBLICATIONS

A Note on Literary Criticism. New York: Vanguard Press, 1936; London: Constable, 1937.

The League of Frightened Philistines and Other Papers. New York: Vanguard Press, 1945; London: Routledge, 1947.

The Fate of Writing in America. New York: New Directions, 1946; London: Grey Walls Press, 1947.

Literature and Morality. New York: Vanguard Press, 1947.

[Jonathan Titulescu Fogarty, Esq., pseud.] *The Name Is Fogarty: Private Papers on Public Matters.* New York: Vanguard Press, 1950.

[with Jeannette Covert Nolan and Horace Gregory] *Poet of the People: An Evaluation of James Whitcomb Riley.* Bloomington: Indiana University Press, 1951.

Reflections at Fifty and Other Essays. New York: Vanguard Press, 1954; London: Spearman, 1956.

My Baseball Diary: A Famed Author Recalls the Wonderful World of Baseball, Yesterday and Today. New York: A. S. Barnes, 1957; rpt., Carbondale: Southern Illinois University Press, 1998.

It Has Come to Pass. New York: Herzl Press, 1958.
[ed.] *Prejudices,* by H. L. Mencken. New York: Knopf, 1958.
[ed.] *A Dreiser Reader.* New York: Dell, 1962.
Selected Essays. New York: McGraw Hill, 1964.
The Collected Poems of James T. Farrell. New York: Fleet, 1965.
Literary Essays, 1954–74. Port Washington, N.Y.: Kennikat Press, 1976.
On Irish Themes. Ed. Dennis Flynn. Philadelphia: University of Pennsylvania
    Press, 1982.
Hearing Out James T. Farrell: Selected Lectures. New York: The Smith, 1985.

Secondary Sources

Our understanding of the writings of James T. Farrell springs from the work of
Edgar M. Branch, whose essays, books, and bibliographies have created Farrell
criticism and made further work possible. See his *James T. Farrell* (New York:
Twayne Publishers, 1971), and *A Bibliography of James T. Farrell's Writings, 1921–
1957* (Philadelphia: University of Pennsylvania Press, 1959). Branch has published
bibliographical supplements as follows: "A Supplement to the Bibliography of
James T. Farrell's Writings," *American Book Collector* 11 (Summer 1961): 42–48;
"Bibliography of James T. Farrell: A Supplement," *American Book Collector* 17
(May 1967): 9–19; "Bibliography of James T. Farrell: January 1967–August 1970,"
American Book Collector 21 (Mar.–Apr. 1971): 13–18; "Bibliography of James T.
Farrell, September 1970–February 1975," *American Book Collector* 26:3 (Jan.–Feb.
1976): 17–22; "Bibliography of James T. Farrell's Writings: Supplement Five, 1975–
1981," *Bulletin of Bibliography* 39:4 (Dec. 1982): 201–6.

Corroborating Branch, other critics have placed Farrell firmly in the context of
American realism. See Horace Gregory, "James T. Farrell: Beyond the Provinces of
Art," *New World Writing: Fifth Mentor Selection* (New York: New American Library,
1954), 52–64; Blanche Gelfant, *The American City Novel* (Norman: University of
Oklahoma Press, 1954), 175–227; Charles C. Walcutt, *American Literary Naturalism:
A Divided Stream* (Minneapolis: University of Minnesota Press, 1956), 240–57; and
Seven Novelists in the American Naturalist Tradition (Minneapolis: University of
Minnesota Press, 1974), 245–89; Nelson M. Blake, *Novelists' America: Fiction as
History, 1910–1940* (Syracuse: Syracuse University Press, 1969), 195–225; Richard
Mitchell, "*Studs Lonigan:* Research in Morality," *Centennial Review* 6 (Spring 1962):
202–14; Barbara Foley, *Telling the Truth: The Theory and Practice of Documentary
Fiction* (Ithaca: Cornell University Press, 1986), and *Radical Representations: Poli-
tics and Form in U.S. Proletarian Fiction, 1929–1941* (Durham: Duke University
Press, 1993).

William V. Shannon began the consideration of Farrell's ethnic dimension with
a section in *The American Irish: A Political and Social Portrait* (New York: Mac-
millan, 1966), 249–58. On Farrell and Irish America, see also Charles Fanning, *The*

Irish Voice in America: Irish-American Fiction from the 1760s to the 1980s (Lexington: University Press of Kentucky, 1990), 257–91; Fanning, "Death and Revery in Farrell's O'Neill-O'Flaherty Novels," *MELUS* 13:1 and 13:2 (Spring–Summer 1986): 97–114; and Fanning and Ellen Skerrett, "James T. Farrell and Washington Park," *Chicago History* 7 (Summer 1979): 80–91.

Other useful criticism of many aspects of Farrell's work includes: Jack Salzman and Dennis Flynn, eds., "Essays on James T. Farrell," special issue of *Twentieth Century Literature* 22:1 (Feb. 1976); Leonard Kriegel, "Homage to Mr. Farrell," *Nation* 223 (16 Oct. 1976): 373–75; Celeste Loughman, "'Old Now, and Good to Her': J. T. Farrell's Last Novels," *Eire-Ireland* 20:3 (Fall 1985): 43–55; Shaun O'Connell, "His Kind: James T. Farrell's Last Word on the Irish," *Recorder* 1:1 (Winter 1985): 41–50; Bette Howland, "James T. Farrell's Studs Lonigan," *Literary Review* 27 (Fall 1983): 22–25; Blanche Gelfant, "*Studs Lonigan* and Popular Art," *Raritan* 8 (Spring 1989): 111–20; Donald Pizer, "James T. Farrell and the 1930s," in Ralph F. Bogardus and Fred Hobson, eds., *Literature at the Barricades: The American Writer in the 1930s* (University: University of Alabama Press, 1982), 69–81; Marcus Klein, *Foreigners: The Making of American Literature, 1900–1940* (Chicago: University of Chicago Press, 1981), 206–15; Lewis F. Fried, *Makers of the City* (Amherst: University of Massachusetts Press, 1990), 119–58; Arnold L. Goldsmith, *The Modern American Urban Novel* (Detroit: Wayne State University Press, 1991), 39–58; Charles Fanning, ed., "Irish-American Literature," a special issue of *MELUS* 18:1 (Spring 1993), which contains essays on "Farrell and Richard Wright" by Robert Butler (pp. 103–11) and "Farrell and Dostoevsky" by Dennis Flynn (pp. 113–25), as well as a recently discovered 1931 essay by Farrell on "The Dance Marathons," edited by Ellen Skerrett (pp. 127–43).

Explorations of Farrell's relevance as a social critic include: Ann Douglas, "Studs Lonigan and the Failure of History in Mass Society: A Study in Claustrophobia," *American Quarterly* 26 (Winter 1977): 487–505; Alan M. Wald, *James T. Farrell: The Revolutionary Socialist Years* (New York: New York University Press, 1978); and *The New York Intellectuals* (Chapel Hill: University of North Carolina Press, 1987), 83–85, 249–63; Douglas Wixson, *Worker-Writer in America: Jack Conroy and the Tradition of Midwestern Literary Radicalism, 1898–1990* (Urbana: University of Illinois Press, 1994).

Robert James Butler has established both the philosophical underpinnings and the subtle architectonics of Farrell's fiction in these essays: "Christian and Pragmatic Visions of Time in the Lonigan Trilogy," *Thought* 55 (Dec. 1980): 461–75; "The Christian Roots of Farrell's O'Neill and Carr Novels," *Renascence* 34 (1982): 81–97; "Parks, Parties, and Pragmatism: Time and Setting in James T. Farrell's Major Novels," *Essays in Literature* 10 (Fall 1983): 241–54; "Scenic Structure in Farrell's *Studs Lonigan*," *Essays in Literature* 14 (Spring 1987): 93–103.

Dennis Flynn has begun to open the rich Farrell Archive at the University of Pennsylvania, a voluminous collection of letters, diaries, and manuscripts that constitutes one of the great personal records available to us of the social and intellectual history of America in the earlier twentieth century. See James T. Farrell, *On Irish Themes* (Philadelphia: University of Pennsylvania Press, 1982), edited by Dennis Flynn. Flynn's work-in-progress is an edition of Farrell's selected letters and diary notes that will open up the possibilities of the collection for other scholars to follow.

Much remains to be done to elucidate the full range and accomplishment of James T. Farrell as a writer. His work and influence in short fiction needs to be further explored. His last, unfinished sequence, *A Universe of Time,* has only just begun to be considered critically. In his later fiction he often left Chicago and the Irish to continue his explorations of time, death, and the possibilities in modern life for self-knowledge, growth, and creativity. Recent evidence of renewed interest in Farrell studies includes the completion since 1978 of at least twenty doctoral dissertations in which Farrell is a major figure.

Farrell's first posthumously published work, *Sam Holman* (Buffalo, N.Y.: Prometheus Books, 1983), is a novel of New York intellectual life in the 1930s, and there are other valuable works in manuscript form that have yet to be made generally available. A newly published story is "Cigarette Card Baseball Pictures," in *Crab Orchard Review* 1:2 (Spring–Summer 1996): 3–12.

Chicago Stories

Helen, I Love You

I

"You got a goofy look," Dick Buckford said.

"Yeh," Dan said.

The two boys stood in front of one of the small gray-stone houses in the 5700 block on Indiana Avenue, glaring at each other.

Dan didn't know what to say. He glanced aside at the hopeless, rainy autumn day. His eyes roved over the damp street, the withered grass and mud by the sidewalk across the street, the three-story apartment buildings, and at the sky which dumped down top-heavily behind the buildings.

"Yeah, you're goofy! You're goofy!" Dick sneered.

"Then so are you," Dan countered.

"Am I?" Dick challenged.

"Yes!" Dan answered with determination.

"Am I goofy?"

"If you say I am, then you're a goof, too!"

Dan hoped nothing would happen. He knew how, if he lost a fight when he was still new in the neighborhood, everybody would start taking picks on him, bullying him, making a dope out of him, and kidding him all the time because he had been licked. He hoped that he wouldn't be forced into a fight with Dick, who was about ten pounds heavier than he was. But he pretended that he was fighting Dick, beating hell out of him. He pretended that he slugged Dick in the face, and saw the blood spurt from his big nose. He slugged Dick, until Dick was bloody and winded and said quits, and a crowd of guys and girls watching the fight cheered and said that Dan was certainly a fine fighter, and then he pretended that Helen Scanlan came up to him and told him she was so glad.

But he'd already had his chance with her. She had seemed to like him, but he'd been too damn bashful. Once, he could have held her hand and kissed her, and they could have gone over to the park, and kissed some more, if he only hadn't been so bashful. She had even said that she liked him.

They were standing right in front of the parlor window of the Scanlan house. He thought again of himself slamming Dick around, with Helen in the window watching him. Red-haired Helen Scanlan, he loved her. He said to himself:

Helen, I love you!

"Why don't you pull in your ears? Huh?" said Dick.

"Aw, freeze your teeth and give your tongue a sleigh-ride," Dan said.

He wished Dick would go away, because he wanted to walk around alone, and maybe go over to the park, where it would be all quiet except for the wind, and where the leaves would be wet and yellow, and it would be easy to think of Helen. He could walk around, and think and be a little happy-sad, and think about Helen. And here was Dick before him, and Dick was supposed to be one of the best scrappers in the neighborhood, and he seemed to want to pick a fight, and right here, too, outside of Helen's window. And maybe Dick would win, with Helen there to watch it all.

Dan wanted Dick to go away. He told himself that he loved Helen. He told himself that he was awfully in love with curly, red-haired Helen. He remembered last summer, when he had peddled bills for half a dollar, putting them in mail boxes all over the neighborhood. The day after, they had gone riding on the tail-gate of hump-backed George's grocery wagon, and it had been fun, himself and Helen sitting there on the back of the wagon, holding hands as they bounced through the alleys, and while they waited for George to deliver his orders. And he had spent all his money on her. He told himself that he loved her.

He remembered how, after riding on the wagon, he had gone home, and they had bawled him out because he had worn the soles on his shoes out delivering the bills, and then had gone and spent the money so foolishly, with nothing to show for it. There had been a big scrap, and he had answered them back, and got so sore that he had bawled like a cry-baby. Afterwards, he'd sat in the parlor, crying and cursing, because he was sore. He'd had such a swell time that afternoon, too. And the family just hadn't understood it at all. And then Helen had come around, because all the kids in the neighborhood used to come around to his front steps at night to play and talk. Somebody had called to tell him she was there. He hadn't known what he was doing, and he'd answered that he didn't care if she was there or not.

After that Helen hadn't paid any attention to him.

He told himself:

Helen, I love you!

II

"If I was as goofy as you, I'd do something about it," Dick said.

"Yeh. Well, I ain't got nothing on you."

"No? Well, look at it, your stockings are falling down. You can't even keep your stockings up," said Dick.

"Well, you're sniffin' and don't even know enough to blow your nose."

"Don't talk to me like that!" Dick said.

"Well, don't talk to me like that, either!"

"I ain't afraid of you!" Dick said.

"And I ain't afraid of you, either!" said Dan.

"Wanna fight?" asked Dick.

"If you do, I do!" said Dan.

"Well, start something," said Dick.

"You start something," said Dan.

"But maybe you won't, because you're yellow," said Dick.

"No, I ain't, neither. I ain't afraid of you."

Dick smiled sarcastically at Dan.

"I don't know whether to kiss you or kill you," he said with exaggerated sweetness.

"Yeh, you heard Red Kelly make that crack, and you're just copying it from him. You ain't funny," Dan said.

"That's all you know about it! Well, I made it up and Red heard me say it. That's where he got it. How you like that?"

"Tie your bull in somebody else's alley," Dan said.

Dick tried to out-stare Dan. Dan frowned back at him.

"And today in school, when Sister Cyrilla called on you, you didn't even know enough how to divide fractions. You're goofy," Dick said.

"Well, if I'm goofy, I don't know what you ain't," Dan said.

Dan again pretended that they were fighting, and that he was kicking the hell out of Dick with Helen watching. And he remembered how last summer when he had gotten those hats advertising Cracker Jack, he had given one to her. He had felt good that day, because she had worn the hat he gave her. And every night they had all played tin-tin, or run-sheep-run, or chase-one-chase-all, or eeny-meeny-miny-mo. He had just moved around then, and he had thought that it was such a good neighborhood, and now, if Dick went picking a fight with him and beat him, well, he just wouldn't be able to show his face any more and would just about have to sneak down alleys and everything.

But if he beat Dick up and Helen saw him, he would be her hero, and he would be one of the leaders of their gang, and then maybe she would like him again, and twice as much, and everything would be all so swell, just like it was at the end of the stories he sometimes read in *The Saturday Evening Post*.

Last summer, too, he had read *Penrod*, and he had thought of Helen because she was like Marjorie Jones in the book, only more so, and prettier, and nicer, and she had nicer hair, because the book said Marjorie Jones's hair was black, and Helen's was red, and red hair was nicer than black hair.

"One thing I wouldn't be called is yellow," Dick sneered.

"I ain't yellow," Dan said.

"I wouldn't be yellow," Dick said.

"And I wouldn't be a sniffer, and not have enough sense to blow my nose," said Dan.

"Who's a sniffer?" demanded Dick.

"Well, why don't you blow your nose?"

"Why doncha not be so goofy?" demanded Dick.

"I ain't no goofier than you."

"If I was as goofy as you, I'd quit living," Dick said.

"Yeh, and if I was like you, I'd drown myself."

"You better do it then, because you're goofier than anybody I know," Dick said.

"Yeh?"

"Yeh!"

"Yeh!"

"And let me tell you, I ain't afraid of nobody like you," Dick said.

"I ain't, neither. Just start something, and see!"

"I would, only I don't wanna get my hands dirty, picking on a goof. If you wasn't afraid of me, you wouldn't stand there, letting me say you're goofy."

"Well, I'm here saying you're just as goofy."

"I couldn't be like you."

"And I couldn't be as dumb as you," Dan said.

"You're so goofy, I wouldn't be seen with you."

"Don't, then!" said Dan.

"I ain't! I was here first!"

"I live on this street."

"I lived in this neighborhood longer than you," said Dick.

"I live on this street, and you can beat it if you don't like it."

"You're so goofy you belong in the Kankakee nut house. Your whole family's goofy. My old man says I shouldn't have nothing to do with you because of all the goofiness in your family."

"Well, my old man and my uncle don't think nothing of your old man," Dan said.

"Well, don't let my old man hear them sayin' it, because if he does, he's liable to bat their snoots off," said Dick.

"Let him try! My old man ain't afraid of nothing!"

"Yeh? Don't never think so. My old man could take your old man on blindfolded."

"Yeh? My old man could trim your old man with his little finger, and it's cut off," said Dan.

"Say, if my old man's hands were tied behind his back, and he said 'Boo,' your old man would take to his heels lickety-split down the streets, afraid."

"Let him start something and see, then!"

"If he ever does, I'd feel sorry for your old man," said Dick.

"You don't need to be."

"My old man's strong, and he says I take after him, and when I grow up, I'll be like him, a lineman climbing telephone poles for the telephone company," said Dick.

"Yeh?" said Dan.

"Yeh!" said Dick.

"Yeh?" said Dan.

"Baloney," said Dick.

"Bouswah," said Dan.

"B.S.," said Dick.

They sneered toughly at one another.

"That for you!" Dick said, snapping his fingers in Dan's face.

"That for you!" Dan said, screwing up his lips and twitching his nose.

"If this is the street you live on, I won't hang around it no more, because it smells just as bad as you do," said Dick.

"That's because you're on it."

"I'm going, because I don't want nobody to know that I'm even acquainted with anyone as goofy as you."

"Good riddance to bad rubbage," said Dan.

"If you weren't such a clown, I'd break you with my little finger!" said Dick.

"And I'd blow you over with my breath!" said Dan.

III

Dan watched Dick walk away, without looking back. He sat on the iron fence around the grass plot, feeling good because he had proven to himself that he wasn't afraid of Dick. He said to himself:

Helen, I love you!

He sat.

He sat through slow, oblivious minutes. He arose and decided to take a walk. Wishing that he could see Helen, he strolled down to Fifty-eighth Street, and bought five cents' worth of candy. He returned and sat on the iron fence in front of her house, and for about twenty-five minutes he nibbled at his candy, hoping that she would come along, wondering where she was, wishing he could give her some of his candy. He told himself:

Helen, I love you!

He thought of how he had held her hand that day on the grocery wagon. He imagined her watching him while he cleaned the stuffings out of Dick Buckford.

The day was sad. He wished that it had some sun. The day wouldn't be sad, though, if she came along and talked to him.

He walked over to Washington Park. It was lonely, and he didn't see anybody in the park. The wind kept beating against the trees and bushes, and sometimes, when he listened closely, it seemed to him like an unhappy person, crying. He walked on and on, wetting his feet, but he didn't care. He stopped to stand by the lagoon. There were small waves on it, and it looked dark, and black, and mean. He said to himself:

Helen, I love you!

He continued gazing at the lagoon. Then, he strolled on.

Yes, if Dick had started something, he would have cleaned the guts out of him. Dick would have rushed him, and he would have biffed Dick, giving him a pretty shiner. Dick would have rushed him again, and he would have biffed Dick a second time, and Dick would have had a bloody nose. He would have stood back and led with a left to the solar plexus, and Dick would have doubled up, and he would have smashed Dick with a right, and Dick would have fallen down with another black eye. Dick would have yelled quits, and Helen, who would have been watching it all, would have yelled for him, and maybe she would have said:

Dan, I want to be your girl!

He walked. He looked all around him at the park stretching away in wet, darkened, dying grass, with shadows falling down over it. The light was going out of the sky, and he said good-bye to Mr. Day. He felt all alone, and thought how nice it would be if he only had someone to talk to. Maybe Helen. Maybe himself and Helen walking in the wet grass. Maybe some man would try to kidnap her. The man would run away with her under his arm crying for help. And he would pick up a rock and fling at the guy, and it would smack the guy in the skull, and he would drop down unconscious, but Helen wouldn't be hurt. And he would rush up, hit the guy with another rock so that he would be out colder than if he had been hit by Ruby Bob Fitzsimmons in his prime. Police would come, and he would have his picture in the papers, and he would be a real hero, and Helen would say to him:

Dan, I love you, and I'll always love you.

He walked. It was almost dark, and the wind sounds seemed worse than the voices of ghosts. He wished he wasn't so all alone. He had strange feelings. He wondered what he ought to do, and it seemed like there were people behind every tree. The park was too lonely to be in, and he decided that he'd better go home. And it was getting to be supper time.

The wind was awfully sad. There wasn't any moon or stars in the sky yet. He didn't know what he was afraid of, but he was awfully afraid.

And it would have been so nice, and so different, if he was only with Helen. She would be afraid, too, and he would be protecting her.

He started back toward home, thinking what he would have done to Dick if Dick had really started a fight. Yes, sir, he would have made Dick sorry.

Helen, I love you!

[1930]

The Scarecrow

There, little girl, don't cry!
They have broken your heart, I know;
And the rainbow gleams
Of your youthful dreams
Are things of the long ago;
But Heaven holds all for which you sigh—
There, little girl, don't cry!

—James Whitcomb Riley

I

"Either you be home when I get here tonight, or . . . never darken my door as long as you live! This time *it's final!*"

"But mother . . . it's . . . Hallowe'en."

"When I say final . . . I mean *final!*"

The Scarecrow was scrawny, and with her thin features and bony, angular body, she resembled her mother.

"You've been a disgrace long enough. It's all right to have a good time, but it's positively the limit when a fourteen-year-old girl like you makes a cheap whore out of herself for every little tramp and high-school bum that comes along. Young lady, while you live under my roof and eat my hardearned bread, you'll not carry on like a harlot. Here I am, an old woman, slaving for you. It's not fair, and I'm not going on with it. What are you? . . . What are you? A slut! *Slut!* God knows I tried to be a good mother to you. But what does it get me? What have you done in gratitude? It's no use. Goodness just ain't in you. You've got your father's blood. You're like him. I tried with all my power to make a good girl out of you, but it's no use. I'm through!"

The mother fell dramatically into a chair. The daughter, after gawking after her mother, moved toward the door and tripped over her own feet.

"Gee!" she exclaimed, sitting on the floor.

"Ox! Cancha even walk straight! Cow!"

The daughter arose and stared vacantly at her mother. Timidly, she took a chair.

"I don't know what they can see in you. You're ugly, and a bag of bones. You got his ugly cheekbones, and his consumptive pallor and chest. No figure. You're nothing but a homely, bow-legged little beast. But then, I suppose pretty girls don't have to make whores out of themselves for every little bum that comes along the street."

The Scarecrow gawked at her mother.

"Well, *madam,* are you coming home tonight, or are you sleeping with some little cur? And, *madam,* shall I have your bawth ready? And perhaps you'd like to bring your little *gentleman* home and use my bed!"

The girl sat on the edge of the chair. The mother arose, and violently crossed the floor.

"Answer me! Answer me!" the mother screamed, continuing, "you're no daughter of mine. You take after that bastard father of yours. I wish to Christ he had taken you along when he cleared out. I didn't want him, and I don't want his dirty little bitch of a daughter. You're not my flesh and blood, you filthy little whore!"

The mother dropped to her knees in the center of the room and lowered her head. The daughter continued to sit in speechless fear.

"Oh, God! Oh, God! God, why must I bear this cross!"

The mother sat on the floor, and her raggedy hair splattered down her angular back. The Scarecrow's face broke into a weak slow-motion smile. Lifting her head, the mother perceived the smile on her daughter's face. She leaped at the girl.

"Go ahead now, cry! Cry, you dirty whore!" The mother's pathetic face contorted with pain and ecstasy as she beat the girl, who cowered from the chair onto the floor. "Cry! Cry! Cry! Cry! Cry, you slut! God knows you broke my poor mother's heart without shedding tears. Goddamn you, cry!"

Breathless, the mother ceased beating her daughter.

"You didn't cry, though . . . oh, no . . . you didn't cry that night I caught you with a little grammar-school bum in my bed. You didn't, neither, when you went into the boys' toilet at the Edmonds school. Well, cry now, you pig!"

The mother slumped back into a Morris chair. The girl sniffled on the floor, and, red-eyed, gazed out at the awfully sad day.

"You got his face, and his dirty eyes. You look like him and I hate you!" the mother screamed, leaping at, and again striking, the girl.

The Scarecrow arose to flee. The mother caught her and roughly flung her into a corner. She took a slice of rubber hosing from the sideboard, and battered the girl to her knees.

"That for your bastard father! . . . And that! . . . And that!"

Exhausted from the effort, the mother turned and sat down. Through tear-glazed eyes she watched her daughter trembling like one shivering with the cold. She buried her head and moaned:

"George! George! I've suffered loneliness! I've been lonely, George! Please come back to this aching heart! Please! I'll forgive and forget everything. I'll work, I'll work the skin off my hands for you . . . God, oh, please, God, send my husband back to me, my husband, my sweetheart, my lover! . . . God, oh, God, must I go on wearing myself out, carrying the heavy cross of a poor, helpless, lonely old woman! God, please send him back to me before it's too late. God, have you given any woman a cross as heavy as mine! God, if I was only dead! God!"

The mother gradually subsided and retired to her bedroom. A few sobs were heard, and then quiet wreathed the house. The daughter, still on the floor, broke the silence with hysterical laughter. Her bruised back throbbed like an over-stimulated pulse. She went to her cot. Her tears slowly dried. Half-asleep, she dreamed that she was the beautiful wife of a handsome millionaire, and he gave her beautiful clothes, beautiful yachts, beautiful airplanes, beautiful beach pyjamas, beautiful automobiles, beautiful everythings. She dreamed that she was a beautiful queen in a beautiful palace, wearing a beautiful dress of beautiful purple velvet, with a beautiful train, and that she was arising from a beautiful throne, surrounded by beautiful servants, and she stood in all her beautiful majesty, sentencing her mother to horrible tortures, because she was a mean old witch and a cruel thing. She dreamed that she was Cleopatra, dancing the dance of the seven veils, while all her marcelled generals, as handsome as Wayne, watched her with love for her in their beautiful eyes.

The Scarecrow was still asleep, her beaten, ugly little body thrilling with dreams, when the mother, who was a ticket-taker in an Illinois Central Suburban station, departed for work. Before the mother slammed the door, she shouted back a final unheard warning.

It was dark and windy outside when the Scarecrow awakened. Sitting up on her cot, she rubbed sleepy eyes, and thought about how nice it would be if she could sleep all night with Wayne. Last night, Kenneth had had such cold feet. She laughed over the way she had fooled her mother. Her mother had come home sick last night, and had gone straight to bed without looking to see if she was home. And she had snuck in the house and gone to her cot at about seven in the morning, and her old thing of a mother had not known the difference. The old fool! Ha! Ha!

When Wayne rang the doorbell, the Scarecrow answered in her greasy kimono. She told him he could wait for her in the parlor, but he answered that he'd like to sit and watch her dress. She said that gentlemen didn't watch ladies dress for the ball in their boudoir. He followed her. He laughed when she dropped her kimono and faced the mirror in her soiled underclothing. She giggled. He told her that she was plug-ugly. He became excited, and kissed her all over and said crazy-nice things to her, using the nicest grammar. Afterward, he waited in the parlor, urging her to hurry. She combed her stringy hair, layered her face with cheap cosmetics, and fussed around putting on and taking off her ten-dollar black dress until she was finally satisfied that she looked like a society lady.

They were late and Wayne took a taxicab. He felt like a man-of-the-world. Even though she was ugly and not all there in the top story, she was another notch in his belt, and he could tell the boys at Tower Tech about it during lunch hours next week.

II

The party was being held at Ray's. Ray was a good guy. He made dough selling wholesale groceries. He was thick with Bill's old man, and like a kindly uncle to Bill. Whenever Bill and the gang wanted to throw a party, they called him up and told him. He usually said O.K. He was well stocked with food and liquor, and didn't care what they did, as long as they didn't break up the furniture and cleared out before he arrived home with his lady friend.

Bill opened the door for them, and, staggering before Wayne, hurried their entrance, bragging of the liquor they had all drunk. Wayne hastily deposited his wraps in a closet, and appeared in the parlor. Above the clamor of the greetings, Bill insisted that they had all poured plenty down the old swivel, and that Wayne had to do some quick and fancy drinking if he wanted to catch up with them.

"I'm old Kid Lightning," Wayne said.

"Well, you got lots of territory to cover," Bill said.

The girls laughed at the humor, and gave Wayne the eye, observing his handsome face and blond hair.

"Lookat that! Ain't she a sight for the sisters who teach her Christian Doctrine!" George said to Wayne, pointing at Lois, who lay, as if soddenly unconscious, on a couch, a cigarette dying in her hand, wisps of bobbed light hair falling over her flapper's face. They laughed boisterously, and her face twitched.

"Hello, Scarecrow!" Bill said, as the Scarecrow minced into the room imitating movie actresses she had seen in pictures.

"Hello, Nickel Nose!" George said in greeting.

The girls smiled at her, distantly. George grabbed her arm and led her to the center of the room.

"Ladies and Gents!" he called, gesturing profusely.

Bill asked where the ladies were because he, for one, could not see any. Joe asked did George think he was funny or what, calling the Scarecrow a lady. They were amused.

"Think of your mother!" George said in an exaggerated voice; they laughed; the Scarecrow picked her nose.

"Well, Bill, I certainly like your nerve!" little Marge said, babyishly elevating her pug nose in a gesture of mock indignation. She continued that there were ladies present, but that she could not see anything that would serve as a model even for an imitation of a gentleman.

"Aw, Hot Monkey Vomit!" Bill snapped, causing little Marge to throw a shocked look at him.

"Ladies and Bums!" George megaphoned through his hands, while the Scarecrow stood with a silly grin on her face, pleased to be the center of attention. "Ladies and No-dough Bums!"

Joe asked George why he didn't marry the girl, and George retorted that it would be foolish because the wench doled out the marriageable goods gratis.

"Ladies and Bums, I have here . . ."

"Doesn't he look like Harold Teen?" the Scarecrow tittered in interruption.

George blushed and sputtered incoherently as they gave him the razzberry. He held the Scarecrow's upper arm tightly, squeezing until she winced.

"Ladies and Dopes! Allow me to introduce you to a real, unadulterated celebrity. . . . I have here with us tonight none other than Miss Nickel Nose, the best known virgin in all the grammar schools of Chicago."

"Razzberries," Wayne said.

"Put him out of misery," Bill said.

"See if tickling the boy's funny-bone will make him amusing," Mary Jane said, blasé.

The Scarecrow gawked at them. Jack, a bath towel flung over his left arm, entered with a tray of filled wine glasses.

"Garçon," little Marge said in her best high-school French accent.

"Now you found your speed, being a bartender," the Scarecrow said, hoping they would laugh at her remark.

"Listen, Nickel Nose!" Jack hissed.

They scrambled for the wine, spilling some on the carpet. George proposed a toast to God's Guts. Lois, coming to, grabbed the last glass from the tray, leaped onto the divan, and told George that he should be more scientific and say God's alimentary canal. Little Marge expressed shock that Lois, a Catholic high-school girl, should speak like that. Lois proposed her substitute toast. Marge persisted in being shocked.

"Hey, wench, put a padlock on your buccal cavity!" Bill said.

"Well, of all the nerve!" little Marge said.

Mary Jane and Frances said they were totally disgusting and unregenerate. They sipped to the toast.

The Scarecrow planked herself down beside Wayne, considering her action to have been done in the queenly manner. She whispered to him that he had nice hair.

"Save it," he told her coldly.

Little Marge made room on her chair, and called Wayne to come and sit by her so that she could tell him a secret. George said that every time Marge got a yen for a guy, she had secrets to tell him. She told George that he was disgusting and insulting. Wayne sat by Marge. Lois immediately jumped on Wayne's lap and commenced to finger his tie.

"He's my man," Marge protested feebly, squashed under their combined weight.

"Hello, Handsome!" Lois said.

Wayne blushed. Marge protested until they both arose and gravitated to a corner. Marge frowned after them. The Scarecrow, viewing this by-play, seemed on the verge of tears. She asked for a drink. Jack told her that she was not a cripple. She hastened to the kitchen. She poured a glass of wine and sat down at the kitchen table. Crying, she drank a toast to herself, and thought of some tall, handsome, awfully rich millionaire's son who would come and marry her and make her his beautiful happy wife with all kinds of beautiful things and beautiful clothes of her own. Then, wouldn't these mean old girls at the party turn every color and green wishing they were her. She drank a toast to the handsome, awfully rich millionaire's son who was going to appear like in the story of *Cinderella* and marry her.

She arose, telling herself that a lady must always look her best. She went to the bathroom and smeared powder on her face and dabbed her lips with carmined rouge. She returned to the parlor while George told a joke about how fleas got in a preacher's soup. The fellows guffawed; Mary Jane protested that it was a vile joke.

"We tell much better ones than that down at Tower Tech," George bragged.

The Scarecrow laughed stupidly, and announced that she knew a joke that had nothing to do with you-know. She told it. Two men were lost and starving in the desert. The poor men were really awful hungry, because they had been traveling in the desert for days and days without anything to eat, and they were really almost dead from being hungry. They finally were beginning to get awful afraid that they would die of starving on account of their having had nothing to eat for all these days and weeks that they were traveling in the desert, and they didn't think that they could go even one more step unless they got something to eat. Just then, one of the men saw a dead horse that had been dead a long time, because he could see maggots all over the dead horse, crawling over it like ants. One of the men asked the other if he wanted to eat part of the horse, but his friend didn't want to, so the other man ate the whole horse. They walked along and soon the man who ate the horse vomited. The other man jumped up and down because he was so happy, and he said:

"Good, I knew I'd get a hot meal."

"Ugh!" Lois exclaimed.

"Somebody please chloroform the woman," Marge said.

"No, fumigate her," Mary Jane said.

"Say, I told you that joke, Scarecrow," George said.

"Well, I wouldn't brag about it," Lois said.

"See, wench, they all know you're vacant in the attic," Bill told the Scarecrow.

There was a round of smutty jokes, and Bill got a big laugh by saying that the dirtiest joke he had ever known of was the Scarecrow.

"Say, that reminds me," George interrupted.

"What?" asked Bill.

"The granary," George answered.

They rushed to the kitchen. Food and beer was taken from the ice-box. Several of them grabbed for items at the same time and some of the food was slopped onto the floor. The Scarecrow stood isolated by the radiator, gnawing at a cold chicken leg. Marge warned her to be careful or she would break her teeth off. The Scarecrow answered that she wouldn't do that. Clucking in disgust, Mary Jane said that she acted just like a dog with a bone.

"I'll bet her mater kicked her out again," George said, tapping Bill's shoulder.

"Hey, Scarecrow!" Bill hollered.

She looked at him with a grease-smudged face.

"Did the mater toss you out again into the crool, cold world?" Bill asked.

She cried.

"Yep, I told you so," Bill said.

"It ain't the first time," George said.

"Hell, no!" Bill said.

"Hey, Wayne, are you taking the Scarecrow home tonight?" George called, while she resumed her gnawing at the chicken leg.

Marge and Lois, hearing the remark, looked contemptuously at the Scarecrow.

"What you mean?" Wayne asked, irritated.

"Ain't you her boy-friend of the moment?" Jack said.

"I managed that business with her before I came," Wayne smirked.

"Jesus, fellows, look at her. She's flowing again," George said.

"I hate my mother!" the Scarecrow sobbed.

"Well, that's no reason for not wiping your nose," Bill said.

"Scarecrow, it looks to me like it's mutual. And anyway, whether the mater likes you or not, she certainly doesn't waste any time feeding you. Boy, I never saw a wench stow away the grub like you do. Better be careful or you'll be getting fat," George said.

"Yes, Scarecrow, you don't want to go and get sick from over-eating," Jack said.

"Hell with her troubles. Let's have a drink," Wayne said, talking with a mouth full of ham sandwich.

Jack prepared a round of drinks. George took a glass, mounted the table, and held his glass aloft.

"To the Scarecrow, may she find a bed . . . ump, a home!"

"Hell, she's just as used to alleys, garbage cans, and hallways for that. What the hell!" Jack said, gulping a drink, spilling some on his coat.

"You boys are horrid!" Mary Jane said, laying her glass on the sink.

Mary Jane walked over to the Scarecrow and told her not to cry. She listened to the Scarecrow's story sympathetically, and nodded an insincere agreement when the Scarecrow said that she couldn't see why her mean old mother should go beating her up for liking boys when she couldn't help liking them.

"But what's it like?" Mary Jane interrupted.

"Huh? What?"

"You know. I mean when fellows and girls violate the sixth commandment?"

"Some boys, like Kenneth, have cold feet," the Scarecrow said, after giggling.

Mary Jane said that she always wondered how it was when you were just such a naturally frigid person that your icy blood froze your heart.

The doorbell rang. The party answered the ring ensemble. It was Caroline and Mike. Caroline was a tall, handsome girl of sixteen, who looked to be at least twenty. She had milky skin, expressive blue eyes, and a wealth of lovely chestnut hair. Wearing a long, black satin panelled dress which emphasized her hips, she was alluring. While the fellows were stupid in their attempt to greet her wittily, and the girls were formal, Marge flung her arms around her classmate, and they kissed.

"Carrie, dear, you look just ducky," Marge exclaimed.

George repeated Marge's words, and embraced Caroline. They were amused. Jack and Bill scrambled to procure her a drink. Her wraps removed, she vamped into the parlor, swinging her hips effectively. She accepted the glass Jack offered her, and drank it in one gulp.

"We learn to take our drinks at St. Paul's," she said in a stagey amateur-theatrical voice.

During a round of dancing, the Scarecrow sat alone in a corner of the floor. Lois, with a coated smile and sweetness of voice, asked Caroline how she attracted all the men. Caroline arched her eyebrows.

"You maybe don't know how," the Scarecrow said to Lois, giggling.

"I hate you, you dirty old . . . Nickel Nose," Lois said.

Caroline and Wayne danced through three successive jazz pieces. Then Marge cut in on her. Caroline majestically retired to the kitchen, and consumed a full jar of stuffed olives. The Scarecrow followed her, and sat down at the opposite end of the kitchen table. In tears, she told her story. Caroline listened until Lois, with a challengingly possessive manner, appeared on Wayne's arm. Caroline eyed Wayne and offered him a sip of a drink she had just poured herself. The Scarecrow said to Wayne that he was her partner at the party and that he had not danced with her once.

"Why don't you eat while you have the chance, and not bother? You'll find someone to sleep with you tonight," Lois said spitefully.

Caroline purposefully broke her beads, and asked Wayne to fix them. She walked back to the front with Wayne, bumping Lois with her hip in passing.

"I always thought that that big can of hers was good for something!" Lois said, watching them go down the hall.

Caroline and Wayne talked in the parlor, oblivious of the others. The Scarecrow came in lost-eyed, and sat beside them. Caroline turned to her and said that the seat she had taken belonged to someone else. The Scarecrow meekly arose and took a place in a corner of the floor.

"Well, all I say is that when Ray comes home, he'll get a nice surprise," Bill said.

"He'll be bringing his latest damsel home to this mess. And you know, when he brings a damsel home, he keeps her for breakfast, dinner, and supper," George said, emphasizing his last words.

"No man ever knows how to treat a woman right," Marge said apropos of no previous remark.

"Sure he does. Whip 'em! Treat 'em rough!" Wayne said, inclining his head toward her.

"Say, big boy!" Caroline challenged.

"I didn't mean you, darling. You're different, a queen. You're a beautiful empress of a glorious empire of Love and Dreams that no mere mortal can attain. You're an angel with orbs like stars, and skin as beautiful as the milky ways, and to compare you, an ineffable creature, with any of the profane, mundane beauties of this mundane terrestrial spinning globe is a sacrilege. Why, a miserable homo sap like myself is not worthy to kiss the hem of your garment, or the sole of your dainty slippers," Wayne said in his most polished and sophisticated high-school fraternity manner.

"Hey, Wayne, there's a word for all that," Jack said.

Oh, I wish I were a ring, upon my Lulu's hand,

George sang.

"What have you been feeding the man?" Caroline asked.

"Why he tol' me all those things tonight when . . ." the Scarecrow tittered.

"She's your speed, Wayne," Caroline haughtily said, pointing derisively at the Scarecrow and leaving him.

Wayne was laughed at. He sulked to the kitchen for a drink. Several fellows crowded upon Caroline.

"See her! Ain't she a comely wench!" Mike said, pointing at Caroline, and toppling about with a half-filled glass in his hand.

Mary Jane inclined an elevated nose in Mike's direction.

"Yes, she's a comely wench. And I brought her here, see! I'm the guy that brought her to this party. I am. Hey, wench ! Hey, Caroline ! . . . Didn't you make Wayne yet?"

"Mike, you're perfectly despicable. You're too unspeakable for words, and if you utter another sound, I'll never speak to you again," Caroline said.

"O.K., wench!" Mike said, with a salute.

Jack, followed by Wayne, appeared with a new tray of drinks. The Scarecrow took one and drank it down. It warmed her insides, and made her laugh. She forgot that Wayne had ignored her, and that her mother had beaten and cursed her. She sat on the floor in an exhilarating state of animal comfort. She giggled. She twisted her right foot, watching it with keen curiosity. A look of surprise lit her face, and she giggled again. She stared dazedly about the room. Suddenly, she was awful sad. She arose with tears flowing, looked at Wayne with dumb, meek admiration, and sang in droning drunkenness:

My man, I love him so!
My man, I love him so!
My man, I love him so!

"Put a nickel on the drum," George said.

"She's maudlin," Caroline said.

"Go ahead, Wayne, be a man, and satisfy the wench," said Mike.

The Scarecrow, imitating her mother, swooned onto the floor, and sat heaped like a scared, lost child.

"Another shower bath," Mike said.

"Christ, doesn't she ever stop flowing?" George said.

"I ain't got no home," she sobbed.

"Hey, Scarecrow, I got an idea," George said.

"Spill it before it expires of Siberian loneliness," Jack said.

"Pipe down there, wise guy! . . . Hey, Scarecrow, you'll be safe in the park now; it's too cold for the squirrels," George said.

"I'll bet she's already slept there," Mike said.

She looked sheep-eyed from person to person, her face splotched from tears. Her thin hair tumbled down her back.

"I ain't got no place to go. If I go home, my mother will beat me 'n' call me bad names. She beat me today with a rubber hose she keeps for beating me 'n' she made my back all sore and red, and put lumps on it. I ain't got no home, and ou, it's cold out tonight," she sobbed.

"You got pounded full of lumps, huh, Scarecrow?" George said.

"George, you don't need to be vicious," Caroline said.

"God's guts, she's used to it," George said.

George gave her a drink, and she gulped it.

"What'll I do? It's so cold out. *Ou!*"

"What I want to know is where did the Scarecrow get that hair?" Jack said.

"Yeh, it is awful. It falls down her back just like the rain," George said; they laughed.

"I got black-'n'-blue marks all over my back," the Scarecrow sobbed.

"Let's see 'em," Mike said.

She arose and quickly pulled off her dress. She stepped out of it on the floor, and stood before them in her soiled underwear. She gulped down another drink, and they examined the welts on her back. She raised her legs, one by one, to reveal the welts on the inside of her thighs. She showed them a bruise between the pathetic little knobs of her breasts. The fellows revealed curiosity.

"Well, where are you going tonight?" Caroline asked her.

She accepted another drink, and swayed about the room, kicking her dress into a corner.

"Can't you go back to Kenneth's?" Wayne asked.

"Last night I didn't like him so much because his feet were so cold and I couldn't make them warm. Oh, they were almost like ice," she said; they laughed.

"Who's Kenneth?" Caroline asked.

"Oh, a boy-friend. His family are all nomads. They're never home. The pater is a beer-runner, and the mater and sister, they're nomads and are never home. Kenneth and his brother generally have an eight-room apartment to themselves, and the brother is always too busy with his own damsels to bother about Kenneth's," Bill said.

"Well, Scarecrow, are you going back to Ken's?" asked George.

"His feet are so cold in bed," she replied, looking plaintively at Wayne.

"Well, where are you going?" asked Marge.

She stood in their midst, sheepish.

"My God, what a frau!" Caroline exclaimed.

"She's so dumb, she's been in the seventh grade for three years now," George said.

"I wonder if I could bring her home with me?" Caroline said to Marge.

"I tried that once. You'll never get her out. She'll just squat on you, and she'll be making eyes at the janitor and peddlers. And then her old witch of a mother will come around and throw a scene. I took her home out of kindness of heart, and that's what happened to me," Marge said.

Bill suddenly remarked that it was getting time for them to be blowing before Ray came home with his ladyfriend. The Scarecrow was neglected in a flurry of straightening up, furniture moving, and bed-making. She staggered about getting in everyone's way. When they left, she threw her coat on over her underwear, forgetting her dress, and tagged out after them. They stood before the building, half seriously, and half humorously, discussing her plight.

"I'd go to Kenneth's, only he has such cold feet."

The group gradually thinned down. Caroline and Mike, the last to leave, departed in a Yellow Cab. They looked back through the cab window and saw her, unsteady of foot, shivering in front of the building.

[1930]

Looking 'Em Over

I

Don scrutinized the mirror, and saw the reflection of Don Bryan, looking just about as well as Don Bryan could look. He was an angular young man in the very early twenties, with a vertical face, slightly pocked and marred by pimples, and ratty greenish eyes. His light hair, gradually darkening from the frequent administration of hair oils, was brillianteened and meticulously split in the center. He guessed that his appearance was O.K. If he had more of the appearance of an athlete, with burly, football shoulders, a darkling aspect of eyes and brown, naturally curly hair, he would have been more pleased with himself. But he did the best that he could with a bony and skinny frame, and thanks to budget plan collegiate clothing—purchased at the store of Sankey, Hatfield, and Cohen—polo shirts, nobby ties, and patent-leather pumps, he was prepared to cut some figure. He stepped backward to achieve a more complete survey of himself; then he came forward to observe his face close up and to determine whether or not he had put too much powder on his cheeks. He passed satisfactory judgment upon himself, having worked wonders with limited possibilities.

Giving a final scrupulous part to his hair, he left his bedroom, and in the parlor, his mother examined him approvingly.

"Yessir! Um, the girl will be proud of her tall, handsome cake-eater to-day," his father said, distracted from his *Sunday Questioner.*

"I ain't got any girl. I'm just going to walk down to the beach and see the fellows," Don protested.

"Old stuff!" Mr. Bryan snorted.

"No kiddin'," Don said.

"Now, Donald, do be careful, because these girls nowadays, they just are looking for husbands. And I won't stand for none of these fast, ciga-rette-smoking immoral girls stealing my son from me," Mrs. Bryan said.

She disconcerted him with a kiss.

"I was young myself once, lad, I know. You're going to see your girl, and don't try to kid an old duck like myself," Mr. Bryan said good-naturedly.

"No kiddin', I ain't got a girl," Don said.

"That's splendid, Donald. You listen to your mother, and don't let any of these here fast-living, cabareting girls get their hands on you. You're too young."

Don did not appreciate his mother's sentiments. He stated, in a dis-gruntled voice, that he had no girl. Withal, he liked the old man intimat-ing that he had. It gave him a feeling of expansive and justified maleness.

"Now I told you, don't try and deceive an old duck like myself," the father said, chortling.

"No kiddin'. It's just that . . . well, that I'm a lone wolf."

Don departed, ruffled at the way his mother tried to baby him. But mothers were mothers, and he had learned plenty of times, through sad ex-perience, that he couldn't talk sensibly to his mother.

He strode through a section of lazy streets. The day was good, full of sun, and warm, with a slight hot wind blowing. He was glad for the free-dom of Sunday, and hoped that he would be able to make the most of it. He gave attention to the many automobiles lining the curbs, and those which shot through the streets. He spotted a pearl gray Stutz; bitchey road-ster, all right. A dark, flannelled Jewish young man, a roadster personality, drove it, and beside him sat a blonde girl who looked like hot stuff.

"Oh, daddy, buy me a bow wow!" he said half-aloud.

He commenced to sing in a dragging, heavy voice which falsely accentuated the words and tune.

Blue heaven and you and I
And sand kissing a moonlit sky;
A desert breeze whispering a lull-a-by.
Only stars above you
To say I love you.

He started supposing that his father owned a car. It would be the nuts. And suppose, too, that he was a bigshot instead of just a twenty-five-dollar-a-week clerk.

It was nice to walk, as long as he did not have to do much of it. But how much nicer wouldn't it be to loll in a keen sporty roadster, say a Marmon, or a Stutz like the one he'd just seen! Nowadays to get yourself a first-class girl, a fellow had to have a car. If he only had any kind of a one, a Ford, Chevey, even an Essex. And if he or his old man were only filthy with money!

Coming in his direction was a mincing girl. Something not to be sniffed at, and yessir, it could park its itull shoosy-woosies under his beddy any old time, he decided. Keen! H'lo, baby, let's you and me cooperate! H'lo, baby, for you I faw down! He eyed her as she approached. He could not complain about the figure as it grew toward him into the life-size tantalizing flesh of a young female with Irish eyes, dark brows, black hair, Irish face, and just the nicest little figure, and the cutest little bouncing . . . Slender, too, but just enough meat in the right places. And she was dressed just perfect, in a silver-gray, caped suit, with stockings and shoes to match. He wished she'd give him a tumble, or that he could snap out a wisecrack. All he was able to do to attract her attention was to express surprise and elation by whistles. She passed him cold as ice. He gaped after her, observing that she had the fetchingest little wriggle.

He proceeded, supposing that he had picked her up. He held snappy imaginary dialogues between her and himself, and all kinds of bright sayings came to his mind. He hoped that at the beach he could pick up something as sweet as she was. But generally, he was not the one who picked up the swell ones. Now and then, he made the grade with one of the tramps that the boys would dig out somewhere or other, but he'd never been speedy enough for a rich, virtuous girl who rated. He supposed himself having a romance with the girl who had just passed him. Perhaps she was the daughter of a Savings' Bank, with a car of her own, and plenty of crisp greenbacks. Romance, kisses

in the moonlight, dances in dimmed rooms to the graceful strains of senti-
mental waltzes, days on white-sanded beaches, parties at which he showed
her off to the fellows, boat trips, golf at the exclusive country clubs, weekends at that ritzy resort, Grand Beach and . . . Wouldn't that be jake, and
wouldn't that knock the boys for a row or two!

Don Bryan walked along, smoking a Lucky Strike, wishing that it were
a Pall Mall.

II

People flooded the beach at Seventy-fourth Street. It was a miserable beach, irregular, and with cramped space. The sandy portion had
been fenced off and made into a private beach by a parvenu club, and the
remainder was more rock than sand. The lake looked insensate, dirty.
Waves slapped the shore. But the people were in a laughing picnic mood.
There was much loud talking and high-pitched laughter. Beach games
were in progress, and one group was playing blue-my-blackberry. Many
collected to watch it, it was so screaming. A Jewish girl, with extended
buttocks, was down, and the lad guarding her made only feeble attempts
to tag those who came in to slap her. The spectators were splitting with
laughter, as one after another of the players shoved the guard over and
cracked her on the buttocks. The beach was colorful with the many hues
of bathing suits, sensuous with female flesh. There were no lockers, and
the sidewalk of Seventy-fourth Street broke off abruptly and the sand and
rocks sloped downward.

Don stood at the sidewalk edge and surveyed this scene, attempting to
stand in a loosely confident manner like a young man who was somebody,
who had gone places and done things, who rated. He spied a girl by the
wire fencing of the club premises, and he judged her a pip, admiring her
curving line of hips. She wore a tight, powdery blue suit, her legs were long
and thin, her breasts small and round, her body bronzed. He watched her,
wishing that he knew her, sagaciously proclaiming to himself that he would
not throw her out of bed. H'lo, baby! Whatcha say, kid! He hoped and
determined, but then perceived that she was accompanied. The fellow with
her familiarly slapped her in the rear. He wondered if that meant anything,
because generally a girl who permitted a fellow to slap her in that part was
not so very innocent. Often, he guessed, such girls would go the limit. He
watched, supposing that she ditched her friend, and picked him up. And
she would turn out to be the only daughter of a Beef Trust, a Corner on

the Wheat Market, or a City Hall racket. He imagined himself and her falling in love, a whirlwind, happy and frenzied courtship, preliminary to a wedding in the Holy Name Cathedral at high noon.

"Hello, Don!"

"Hello, Paul!"

"What you doing out here?"

"Oh, Paul, I'm just looking 'em over."

"Lookin' 'em over, huh?"

"Yeh, I'm lookin' 'em over."

"Plenty of nice stuff out here."

"And then some."

"I like that in brown, don't you, Don?"

"Me, too."

"I sa-ay there, Buster Brownie. Hum, I sa-ay."

"Yeh, I sa-ay there," Don parroted.

"Stuck up! I'll bet she's lace-curtain Irish."

"Yeh, ritzy now, and probably used to be nothing but pig-in-the-parlor Irish, that's what I'll venture," said Don.

"Well, there's a lot of good stuff out here," Paul said.

"Damn tootin'," said Don.

"Guess I'll mosey along and look 'em over myself. See you later."

Don remained in his strategic spot, smoking a cigarette. It occurred to him that the world was full of girls. He attempted to calculate the number of them that there might be in the world. There was little excuse for a fellow not getting all that he wanted. Hell, the dance halls were full of them, waiting to be picked up, and prepared to go to the limit. And he always argued that any of them will say yes if the right guy comes along and uses the right technique at the right time. He had been hearing plenty about girls from rich or well-to-do Catholic homes, girls you would think of only as decent girls, who were losing their cherries, one right after the other. He didn't get any of that luck. He generally had to take pushovers, or do like he did last night, pay for it.

He eyed a girl near him, who was wearing Chinese beach pyjamas. His mind drifted and he ecstatically thought of how it would be the nuts if all girls went swimming naked. He saw another, in a tan suit and shoes to match. Nice legs, narrow hips, pretty. A tuft of wind blew her dress up. No pants, cute little pink thighs. Just what he liked. I say, baby, h'lo! Why in hell didn't he have a ready line? Have to learn one. I sa-ay there, ba-bee! I sa-ay. . . . There's danger in your eyes, Cherie, I sa-ay, ain't we met before? . . . He wondered about approaching her. And there was another, Irish, too. Nothing like Irish girls. The dark-haired, dark-eyed ones were the prettiest in the world. And once they go, they go plenty far. Hot! She was wearing a white plaited skirt, and a golden-colored sweater in a broken pattern, and she was a proper handful. Gee, if only a rich broad would come along and give him a tumble. Another one, wearing sport shoes. But anyway, it was the fundamentals that counted, not the clothes. That was one he would have to remember and spring when some of the boys were around.

"Don! What you doing out here today?"

"Oh, Larry, I'm just lookin' 'em over."

"Well, there's no shortage of 'em."

"Enough out here today for all tastes."

"Now take that in red. She's what I call cosy," Larry said.

"You said it," Don agreed.

"Anyway, I think I'll scrootch around and look 'em over myself. So long, Don."

"Don't get strained eyes, Larry."

"There's plenty of reason to," Larry called back.

Don sang, low and in a mumble:

There's danger in your eyes, Cherie!
There's danger in your eyes, Cherie!

He could not remember the remaining lines; he lit a cigarette, and stood, posing.

III

Don leaned against the thrown-together red-hot stand munching at a hot-dog sandwich. A dab of mustard splashed on his thumb, and he cursed with annoyance as he wiped it off with a clean, neatly ironed handkerchief. He perceived the automobiles, tightly lined along both curbs. A blue, low-lined Buick fascinated him. The tan, winged Chrysler, three cars down from it, was a better choice. Beside the Chrysler there was a Cadillac that was the real ticket. He supposed that he owned it.

"Here's Don Bryan."

"Hello, Jack."

"Looking 'em over?"

"Yes, Jack, I'm looking 'em over," Don said weightily.

"Well, they're here to be seen. Now, look at tha-at! I like it!" Jack said.

Tha-at was a tall blonde girl, lecherous in blue-and-orange beach pyjamas. They stared at her, their eyes swelling lust.

"Whizzz!" Jack exclaimed.

"Wheeee!" Don exclaimed.

"Yoo-hoo," Jack called.

"What do yuh say, baby!" Don said.

Tha-at flung her head around, glared, elevated her aquiline nose, and shook herself along.

"Swell stuff, we are!" Jack called.

"We're swell stuff," Don shouted.

"Yeah, we're real swell!" Jack brayed.

Tha-at again about-faced, snapped her fingers disdainfully and mumbled; the only words they heard were "small change."

"Stuck up or not, she could blow her nose in my soup any time she wanted to," Jack said.

"I'll say this much for her; she's got something to feel stuck up about that plenty of broads ain't got," Don added.

They crossed the sidewalk to stand in front of a new Ford. The space to its left was vacant, and a Chrysler, driven by a tall, burning blonde in purple, was driven into it. She sat by the wheel, powdering her nose. Replacing the powder puff in her bag, she lit a cigarette with a nickel cigarette-lighter.

"She's got what I call meat," Jack said, surreptitiously back-glancing at her.

"And class," Don said.

"It's just meat!"

"She makes most of them out here today look like pikers," Don said.

A dark-haired girl in a black bathing suit strode boyishly by them. She was long, supple, and tanned; her thighs were narrow, and she was flat-chested.

"Oh! Oh!" exclaimed Don.

"She's jail bait," Jack said.

"Know her?"

"I know who she is. She goes to St. Paul's. All the boys around the beach here have a feel-day with her, and she doesn't mind it."

"Piggly-wiggly girl, huh?" Don said, his mind inflamed.

"Well, now, I think that Monk Sweeney made the grade with her over on the Jackson Park golf course one night. I wouldn't say for sure, but that's my suspicion."

"Ummmm!" Don meditatively exclaimed.

"She's not hard on the eyes, but she's jail bait."

"Well, you can see that there's something to be said in her favor."

"By the way, she was with some cake last night at the Neapolitan Room of the Westgate Hotel."

"How is that place these days?"

"Same as ever. Pretty hot orchestra. Good crowd. All the old bunch that used to be up at the Grove when it was the place to go, are usually up there now. Lots of guys who rate, and broads from sororities like Alpha go there."

"I was at Shannon's last night," Don said.

"Have they got any new girls?"

"I had one. She's swell."

"What she look like?"

"Big, but knows her movements. After all, it's not the looks, but the fundamentals that count. And she has them. She gives you your money's worth."

"But me, I'd prefer something like that in the Chrysler behind us."

"Wouldn't I!"

"And take a squint at what's coming along," said Jack.

"She turned off. Well, anyway, she was nice."

"Edge a little closer to the Chrysler. I think the broad in it is waiting to be picked up," Don said.

Dear heart, Romance is ended. . . .

The girl singing needed only a stick of gum to complete the picture she made. She was a bushy-headed brunette, with thick solid legs, and her blue dress was outlandishly bright.

"Hello Sophie!" Jack said.

"Hello baby, what do you say!" she sing-songed.

"Well, if I said what I think, I'd burn you up," Don said.

"Not me. I'm asbestos," she retorted.

Shaking her shoulders, she sang staccato.

We'll be so happy, we'll always sing,
If we remember one little thing,
A little kiss each morning, a little kiss each night,
Who cares if hard luck may be ahead?

"Going fishing?" asked Jack.

"Sa-ay, don't be a mud turtle," she said.

"That your swimming suit?" Jack asked, pointing at her dress.

"You wouldn't kid any one, would you?" she said, cynically.

"Me, I just asked was that your swimming suit?"

"He wants to know if you think it'll rain tonight," Don said.

"Say, don't be a mud turtle," she said.

She performed several Charleston steps, and sang:

Where is the song I had in my heart
That harmonizes with the pines?
Anybody can see what's troublin' me,
I'm cryin' for the Carolines.

She cut short her song, and winked.

"Ain't I seen you before?" Don said.

"Say, big boy, whatcha think I am?"

"Well, you know, there's girls and girls," Jack said.

"Say, what's your meaning?" she asked in a harsh voice.

Jack smiled fatuously at her.

"Take a sugar cookie and snookie cookie," Jack sing-songed.

"Take a great big papa," she sing-songed in reply.

"Listen, don't kid me now, ain't I seen you some place before?" Don said.

"Sa-ay, I seen your kind before hanging around with your tongues lopping out. Don't kid me, big boy! I know tings. I go aroun', see," she said, flustering Don.

"Well, I know I seen you before," Jack said, more possessed than Don.

"Don't you hang around at The Bourbon Palace?" Don said, still flustered.

"Sa-ay, where you get that way? Me hang around a joint like that! Wrong number. Ring again!"

"What do you do, lay down, instead of hang out?" Jack asked.

"Don't get fresh, see!"

"Anyway, baby, what do you say?" Jack asked.

She ogled suggestively.

"I don't catch your meanings," she said.

"Oh, I only mean, think you'll go fishing?" Jack said, superciliously.

"Come on now, don't be a mud turtle."

"But listen, where have I seen you before?" Don asked insistently.

"Say, Skinny, how about a new tune. You been singing that one pretty regular, haven't you?"

Don was hurt at being called Skinny, and decided that she was only a goddamn Polack anyway, and she looked worse than a beer truck.

"You go to colledge?" she asked Don.

"Sure. I'm president of the intra-fraternity council down at the U," Don answered.

"Y'are? Say, I got a boy fren down there in a frat named Jack Von Williams. Ain't that a name?"

"I think I know who he is," Jack said.

"He's a blond and good-looking, and does he dress!"

"Yeh, he's a classy dresser," Jack said.

"He's a funny guy. You know, he uses words a yard long. I never know what he's talking about half the time," she said.

Jack got a telephone number out of her, and they watched her plunge through the crowded beach, singing jazz songs.

"She's dumb," Don said.

"A Polack, but what the hell! Some night when I got nothing to do, I'll ring her up. She ought to be worth a night's investment," Jack said.

"I'd like that in the Chrysler for a night's investment," said Don.

"Might be hard, making the grade with her. She looks pretty high-hat," Jack said.

"Hello, kid, what do you say?" Jack said to Kenny.

"What are you fellows doing, looking 'em over?" Kenny said.

"Yeh, Kenny, we're looking 'em over," Don said.

"Any luck?"

"I just got lined up with a Polack, and I'll get myself fixed up with her some night when I got nothing more important to do," Jack said.

"South Chicago?" asked Kenny.

Jack nodded.

"Those broads out there are like rabbits," Kenny said.

"But they're ice. I had one who calmly picked blackheads off my forehead," Don said.

"There's something neat behind us," Jack said.

"Sa-ay, I like tha-at. That's perfection," Kenny said, seeing the girl in the Chrysler.

IV

"Jesus, he's made the grade," Jack said; he and Don watched Kenny, who sat beside the girl in the Chrysler and talked familiarly with her. When she laughed in animation, they stared with envy.

"Now how in the hell did he pull that stunt off so quick?" Don said.

"Say, look at the way that boy's jaw is working. You got to give him credit. Credit, I say! When he starts jawing he could sell real estate right out in the middle of the lake."

"Yeh!" Don exclaimed with mounting envy.

"When he starts pumping that line of his into a broad, she's as good as made. Once I was with him and he picked a broad up at a street carnival, and took her over to Jackson Park, and she just said to him 'Daddy, I never did this before, but I'm sure going to now!' And she did. When he cranks his jaw up, the story's ended," Jack said.

"He's lucky," Don said.

"Luck, hell, it's art. He's an artist in that line."

"He gets swell ones, too," Don said.

"Listen, I'll bet he ain't stringing that one along nohow! No, he's not stringing her!" Jack exclaimed.

"We should have tried something ourselves," Don said.

A girl in a two-piece bathing suit without brassiere walked by them.

"Oh, baby, you can make me so happy!" Don sing-songed.

"Neat!" Jack appraised.

"Keen!"

"I sa-ay!" Jack exclaimed while she re-passed them, daintily biting into a red-hot sandwich.

"I sa-ay!" Don said.

"Don't!" the girl snapped at him.

"How's the water?" Don asked.

"Cold," she answered.

"I know where it's warm," Jack leered.

"I know where it's like a refrigerator," she said, passing out of hearing.

"Well, it's plenty thick with them today, isn't it, boys," Eddie said, coming along with Dapper Dan O'Doul.

"Get a load of that in the Chrysler," Jack said.

"Kenny's making the grade with her," Don said.

"Plenty keen if you ask me," Eddie said.

"Bo-oy!" Dapper Dan said.

"Watch O'Doul's buttons," said Jack.

"Did you seen what I just seen?" Eddie said, referring to the sight he had viewed when a girl in a black dress bent over to retrieve a dropped handkerchief.

They blocked the sidewalk debating why seeing a thigh under a dress had more effect on a fellow than seeing the same girl in a scrimpy bathing suit would. Don forgot their conversation, and supposed about the rich girl he hoped some day to meet and marry.

V

The hot glory of the summer evening spilled over the corner of Sixty-seventh and Stony Island Avenue. Many people were out walking, and in automobiles. Don and his group clogged the sidewalk in front of the Walgreen drug store on the southeast corner, and Don continued supposing about rich girls.

"What are we going to do?" Jack asked.

"What?" asked Kenny, fresh from a drive with the girl in purple. She had invited him to come on next Wednesday night for a parlor date, and she'd added that no one would be home.

"How about a show?" Eddie asked.

"Too hot," Jack said.

"We might go up to The Bourbon Palace, and jig a little," said Eddie.

"It's too hot to shimmy with Polacks," Pat said.

"Shannon's?" asked Jack.

"Last night was enough for me," said Don.

"Reformed, Don?" asked Pat.

"Hell, you never get your money's worth in those joints," Eddie said.

"But what'll we do?"

"Yeah, what?"

"That's what I like to know."

They went to Shannon's brothel. Don stayed behind because he was too low in finances. He stood on the corner staring at passers-by. At eleven o'clock, he drank a chocolate malted milk, and purchased an evening's copy of the following day's *Chicago Questioner*. He wished that he didn't have to work in the morning.

"Well, son, you're home early," the father said when Don entered the flat.

"I got tired," he said, lackadaisically.

"She sent you home early. Ha! Ha!"

Don yawned. His father was a fool. He went upstairs, read his paper, and turned in, still supposing about a rich girl whom he would love and marry. It was a hot night and he tossed in his sleep.

The alarm clock knelled the end of Sunday's freedom, and he arose sleepily, hating the very idea of going down to that office. While shaving, he supposed.

[1930]

The Buddies

Jack and Smitty drove single wagons out of the South End barns for the Continental Express Company. They were clean-cut twenty-one-year-old kids. Nobody could say that they were company men, and they were frank, friendly, and hard-workers. They each had only a grammar-school education, and their hopes of getting ahead were day-dreams rather than ambitions. They wanted to end up as something better than teamsters, and occasionally they imagined and spoke of how they might make a killing on the baseball pools and get a stake so that they could make some kind of a start in life. They were healthy with plenty of animal spirits, and they liked their good times; but some day they figured that they would settle down, marry a decent girl, have kids and give the kids a better chance than they had, pay down installments on their own homes, and buy a Ford or second-hand Buick. They had quickly become well-rooted in the service of

Long John Continental, and they would most likely continue on his vehicles until they had passed their days of usefulness.

They generally ate their lunch at a little restaurant near the South End barns, which all the men called Nelly's Greasy Spoon. One day, while at the counter, they happened to get talking about an idea which interested them enough to take precedence over kidding with Nelly, ragging each other, or arguing about baseball. They got to feeling how swell it would be to get all the fellows from their stables organized into some sort of a club in which they could do things together outside of working hours, where they could get to know each other better, and where they could have some really good times. They figured that such a club could run regular dances and picnics, and athletic teams that might compete with teams from other stables and company garages. They thought that they might even get an inter-stable and garage baseball league going. It was a dandy idea, so good that they feared it could never be worked out. If it did, it would make for more friendliness and sociability among all the lads from their stable, and it would give them mutual interests. While the idea remained only as a hazy and hoped-for dream, they discussed it, and soon they had other wagonmen interested. It was expanded to include a sinking fund for sick benefits, and probably for death insurance also.

The plan spread contagiously, and a meeting was held and enthusiastically attended. A constitution was drawn up and officers elected. Smitty was elected president, Jack treasurer, and Old Billy McGee secretary. Billy was one of the old-timers, liked by every one in the Wagon Department from the superintendent, Patsy McLoughlin, on down, and his election was a very popular choice. There was a lengthy debate over naming the organization, but it was finally titled *The Buddies*. Smitty appointed an entertainment committee of three, and they immediately commenced outlining plans for a picnic. They prepared raffle tickets, and conducted the raffle on the square. Jim Bates, considered by most of the wagonmen as a goddamn company stool pigeon, won the ten-dollar gold piece. In less than a month after the initial meeting, four hundred men from the five hundred odd number working out of the South End stables had joined *The Buddies*, paying their first monthly dues of a dollar.

The picnic was held out at the Forest Preserve, and there were games, dancing, and odd races, with prizes for the winners. Several kegs of beer, supplied by Jerry Looney the bootlegger who had once driven a single wagon for the old Continental before the war, were on hand, and nobody complained of thirst. Many of the younger men brought girls, and they danced, or strolled off in the woods. Smitty had his girl there, and he took her off in the woods, and she was very willing in the soft grasses under a tree where it was very nice. A few lads got drunk, but there were no fights. And the oldtimers had a good time, sitting under the trees, retailing anecdotes of the old days and drinking beer.

The first picnic was so successful that they immediately planned a second one; and it also went off to their satisfaction. The men all felt that *The Buddies* was going good, and that there was no danger of its breaking up. They realized that they were getting along better together, and that it was making their work more interesting. They had mutual affairs to talk about, an organization which was theirs, planned for their mutual and collective benefit. They discussed plans for the winter, and Smitty and Jack labored, preparing a winter program. They also began practicing baseball, hoping that for the following summer they could put a good team on the diamond. And about fifty fellows all bragged that they would win the bowling tournament planned for the late autumn. They even talked of some day building their own club-house.

For three months, *The Buddies* functioned smoothly. Several drivers and helpers were laid up sick or injured, and they received sick benefits of twenty dollars a week. The meetings were well attended, and most of the men were anxious not to miss them. Dues were paid regularly, without the use of pressure and force that was necessary in the case of the regular wagonmen's union. It, on every pay day, stationed sluggers at each stable and garage, and dues were paid up immediately. Otherwise, men would have been pulled right off their trucks and wagons. *The Buddies* was quite different from the union. It belonged to the men. They knew that the union was not theirs. It was a racket for Joey Murtry, the ex-teameo, and a few of his gangster sluggers. And the men knew, also, that Joey was always going up to sit on the laps of Charley Leonard and the other bosses and assistant superintendents. They hated Joey because they knew that at one time he had been nothing but a common ordinary manure whaler like themselves, and that now he was putting on the dog, and getting high-hat. He wore loud and expensive clothes, flashed a diamond, lived like a king in a home out on Washington Boulevard, and drove about in a Lincoln on "union business." They knew that Joey would sell them out whenever there was an opportunity. They had to pay their union dues because they wanted their jobs, and they knew that if they squawked or tried to oust Joey from his control, they would be terrorized by Joey's hired sluggers. If they tried to get radical, they would be fired, and Joey would not go on the carpet for them, because he was working hand and fist with Long John Continental. And after all, their jobs did pay them better than they would have gotten working as teamsters and helpers for practically any other establishment in the city. The union dues were only two dollars a month, with perhaps an added dollar or two a month in special assessments for sick members, and deaths, because the union treasury was usually empty. Even with the union as crooked as it was, they could do much worse for some other company, although they had their many complaints and grumblings against Long John Continental.

But *The Buddies* was their own, different from the union. And the insurance plan of *The Buddies* paid a higher sick benefit than the company's insurance plan. The latter charged a sliding scale of rates, and paid out five hundred dollars at death, or at the end of twenty years. It also provided sick benefits if the accidents were not due to personal negligence.

One day in the fourth month of the existence of *The Buddies,* Old Billy McGee told Jack and Smitty that he had to resign because the organization was taking up too much of his time, and he was getting along in years. His excuse seemed lame, and they smelled something in the air. They talked it over, and decided that nobody could do anything to them, because they were running things honestly, and not forcing men out of the union or the insurance plan. They were within their rights, and the company couldn't fire them. But still, they knew that there was something queer, because Old Billy was a square-shooter, and his resignation was funny. Finally, they decided that Billy was old now, with a wife and three kids, and that he was getting cold feet because he wanted to feel absolutely safe on the job.

A few days later, they were both called up to the general office of the Wagon Department to see their assistant superintendent, Charley Leonard. Charley was a long-nosed, falsely jovial man, and most of his men called him a rat. They knew that behind his jokes, and his air of democracy, there was a plain face and soul of a snooper who did not mean any good for them. When Jack and Smitty approached his desk in the large office, he smiled pleasantly, and cracked a joke. He laughed so enthusiastically at his own joke that all the stenographers and girls working on loading tickets in the office turned to glance at him. In his oiliest manner, and with bowing regrets to the rigors of outright necessity, he told them that the wagonmen had their union, and that the company had a well-organized insurance plan, and that, therefore, *The Buddies* was totally unnecessary. He did not blame

them for having started such an organization, because they had done it
evidently without thinking, and he was not going to hold their efforts in
its behalf against them. But he would have to ask them to disband it immediately.

They had no choice. They walked away after Leonard had patted them
on the back. They went to the Wagon Call Department to see Heinie Mueller, one of the Wagon Dispatchers in that department. They always liked
to say hello to Heinie Mueller, because he was a funny Dutchman, and he
was white. They wished they were working under Heinie instead of their
own boss, Mike Mulrooney, the route inspector. But Mike was not as bad
as many of the other route inspectors, like Emmett Carr. Outside, they
cursed, and squawked. Their disappointment cut deep because *The Buddies* was their own creation, and they had been betrayed. When they told
the other men at the stables, there was more kicking. But they all knew that
these gestures would get them nowhere. If they tried to pull a strike, they
would simply be S.O.L., and they would see others on their wagons. *The
Buddies* was disbanded. Jack paid all its debts from the treasury funds, and
divided up the remaining funds equally among the members, totalling one
dollar for each of them. Privately, Charley Leonard was called a pretty lousy
sonofabitch. They still wondered why they could not keep their organization going. But that was hopeless.

Two weeks after *The Buddies* was disbanded, Jack and Smitty were
walking from the stables to the streetcar line. The rankling from their betrayal still persisted, and they walked along gloomy and silent. Joe Murtry
suddenly accosted them, and four husky fellows with padded shoulders
stepped out of an entrance way. Joe said:

"These two guys!"

Two of the sluggers cornered Smitty, and the other two took care of
Jack. Before he was able to defend himself, Smitty was punched in the eye
and the jaw. Jack was knocked down with three simultaneous belts in the
face. Smitty was knocked on top of Jack. They were jerked to their feet,
and knocked down again. Smitty's nose streamed with blood, and his face
began to swell and discolor. Jack was punched in the mouth, and the sharp
pain made him realize that one or two of his teeth had been broken. As he
bent his head down to spit out the broken pieces of teeth, he received a
terrific uppercut. Both of them lay on the curb, bleeding, punched into
helplessness. They were kicked in the ribs for good measure. Joey Murtry
leaned over their semi-prostrate forms, and told them that the next time

they had better think twice before starting any of their rackets to demoralize the union.

Thus ended *The Buddies*.

Jack and Smitty were both laid up for several days, and they lost that much pay. When they returned to the stables they told the men what had happened to them. There was a general and spontaneous rage. Many talked retaliation, and of starting a movement to take the union away from Murtry. But beneath this rage and talk, most of them were cowed, and rather glad that they had not been the victims.

A month later, a special union meeting was called for a vote on a proposed special assessment to be levied in order that Joey Murtry could buy a new Lincoln which was, he explained, absolutely needed for the conducting of "union business." He also delivered a long speech, full of salve, in which he defended his work, and told them that he was always at their service. He asked the men if they had any complaints against the manner in which he was rendering his stewardship. A few chauffeurs and drivers glanced around the hall, and saw Joey's sluggers. There were no complaints. The vote was taken. Most of the men at the South End stables had determined to vote against the assessment. Jack and Smitty had kept their mouths closed, and had not attended the meeting. They later learned that there were only five votes against the special assessment.

[1931]

A Front-page Story

The undertaking parlor seemed oppressively formal and impersonal, with its subdued lights, its dull green carpet, waxed flooring, scrupulously polished but stiffbacked chairs, weighty sofas, and potted green plants set upon marble-topped tables. And shadowed toward the rear of this room of artificial sublimity Ruth Summer was laid out in a sleeveless pink taffeta dress with a shoulder corsage. She had been a short dumpy girl with thin, stringy, blonde hair, and a commonplace oval face. Now, she was a blue and bloated corpse, and her fatty bloodless arms gave one the impression of semi-nudity. The dress had evidently been her best party frock, purchased after stinting sacrifices, and lovingly doted over. It had been saved and preserved for those parties and affairs which she had been only infrequently able to attend, and when she had worn it in life, it must have hung like a sack on her squat figure, the inappropriate type of dress that just such a monotonous and uninspired girl would wear. In death, it draped her like a last treachery.

The young campus reporter for *The Chicago Questioner* studied this twenty-one-year-old corpse, feeling like an impostor. Near him stood a small and repressed group which spoke in semi-articulate whispers. In its center was Ruth Summer's father, a tall, homespun man with unpressed clothes, lop-sided shoulders, and a genial but rutted visage. He had just arrived by train to send his daughter's body back home to Iowa for burial, and he was speaking with Ruth's tall, homely cousin, the woman at whose house Ruth had boarded. The cousin was explaining that if Ruth had only taken her into confidence, such foolhardiness might have been prevented. Three of Ruth's student friends, bucolic carbon copies of the dead girl's own personality, completed the group. As they listened to the conversation between the father and the cousin, their faces were intent and bewildered. The young campus reporter continued staring at the corpse, surreptitiously straining to hear and remember every word of the conversation. He recalled the statement which the tall, homely cousin had inadvertently made, prior to the father's arrival:

"It was literal suicide."

He approached the group, his presence causing an additional awkwardness among them. Replying to the question of one of the student friends, he re-explained that he had been in several classes with Ruth. The confused father drew a frayed newspaper clipping from his worn wallet and, without comment, handed it around. The young reporter read it last, and as he read slowly, he forced himself in the effort of remembering as much of it, verbatim, as he could. It recorded that Ruth Summer, honor student and valedictory orator at the town high school, was leaving to attend the University, and that all her many friends, admirers, and classmates predicted for her a brilliant academic career at this famous Temple of Truth. After having read the clipping twice, he returned it to the father, and shook his head with sad expressiveness. No one spoke. No one looked at anyone else. The young reporter, after shuffling his feet nervously and turning his face aside to blow his nose, stated that he would be going. The father thanked him for having remembered his daughter, and the tall cousin reiterated this expression of gratitude. The three student friends stared after him with puzzled suspicion. After a final glance at the dead girl, in her sleeveless frock, he departed.

Outside on the Midway he paused to jot down as much as he could remember from the clipping the father had shown him. He perceived that he was using, for his notes, the blank sides of an official release from the Department of Public Relations. He knew what the release contained: a eulogistic description of the commencement exercises, six and a half mimeo-graphed pages of sugared words reflecting praise upon the University. That he should be using this release for his notes was, like the dress, another accidental irony. Even after her death this simple, betrayed girl must be humiliated. He stuffed the papers back in his pocket, lit a cigarette, and, walking toward the line of Gothic University Towers, attempted to think of other subjects. The Midway, and the buildings in the distance of sever-al blocks, glowed and were mellow under a spreading June twilight, and the sky was calm. All about him were the heedless echoes of living people, children playing on the shaven grass in the center of the Midway, strolling pedestrians, a succession of whizzing automobiles, a jazz song audible from a radio within an opened window, an Illinois Central Suburban electric train, drawing into and out of the Midway station, an airplane rumbling overhead, causing people to pause and gape skyward with dreamy oblivi-ous eyes and opened mouths.

He crossed over to the north side of the Midway and passed the white-stoned million-dollar Gothic chapel in which, on the previous day, the grad-uation exercises had been conducted, and he briefly glanced upward at the high and serene white-stoned tower. He entered a long, low and ornate hall dedicated to the recreation and social life of the female students. It was here that Ruth Summer had worked for two years as a checkroom girl. And it was from a garrulous elderly woman in this building that he had indirectly re-ceived the tip on the story. He nodded and smiled at the blue-uniformed guard who stood inside the door at the edge of the broad lobby, a rubicund jolly-faced man decrepit with age. Casually, he sauntered to the bulletin board, and paused as if he were interested in the few tacked-on announce-ments and notices. Copies of the University annual lay on a table which stood near the checkroom on his left, half-concealed by a post. Since he had to procure one immediately and he did not have the ten dollars to purchase it, a copy would have to be stolen. Once before he had had to steal one in the same manner. He glanced about the lobby, as if he were seeking some girl. He walked to the table, quickly snatched a copy, and proceeded around be-hind the checkroom where there were telephone booths and a cloister. In one of the telephone booths he concealed the annual under his jacket, holding it in place with a stiffened left arm. Coming out of the telephone booth, he sat at the edge of the lobby for several moments, arose, and drifted toward the door, while the guard was answering questions.

A few paces down from the building he removed the annual and placed it under his left arm. He knew that it contained a photograph of Ruth Sum-mer, but he had no curiosity to look at the picture.

He walked with a slackened pace. This one was a front-page scoop, and he experienced none of that quickening sense of keenness, that thrilling feeling of a dog on the hunt, which he should have. He harbored no illusions that he was more than a part-time campus reporter, whose principal duty was that of supplying *The Chicago Questioner* with a steady succession of leg pictures of prominent and attractive campus girls. And he had no ambitions of becoming a newspaper man, particularly one employed by *The Chicago Questioner* and working under Kelly Malloy, the triple-chinned editor. Withal, his work had permitted him to return to classes this last quarter. He desired to retain it, and to do so, he could not permit such stories to pass. If he did, they would be picked up by someone else, and then he would have to explain to Kelly Malloy why he was missing them.

As it was, Kelly was continuing his job largely on sufferance. Bobby Wallace, the ex-baseball writer who was now the University's Director of Public Relations, was tight on news, and barely deigned to recognize the existence of the campus reporter. Rather, he sent news in official releases, and whenever he needed a reporter or photographer, he telephoned the City Desk. He had countered Bobby's tactics by turning in as many ridiculous stories about the University as he could, and most of them had been printed. But it still seemed to puzzle Kelly Malloy that Bobby should always be telephoning for reporters and photographers. This story would settle all grudges with The Department of Public Relations. It was a sole measure of compensation for not having ignored the story, in the hope that no one else would have dug it up.

He sat on the steps of the main library building, smoking, shrinking from the moment when he would go inside to the phone booth and call up the City Desk. In quick, epitomizing mental pictures, he had a sense of Ruth Summer's whole university career. He could visualize this unostentatious, unsung, practically unknown small town girl against various familiar campus backgrounds. He could see her during that now forgotten freshman week of four years ago, when she had matriculated. He could sense that lost and lonely feeling that must have been hers as she stood in slow-moving lines, waiting to interview her dean, waiting to register for courses, waiting to apply for work at The Bureau of Vocational Guidance, waiting to pay her fees. He could see her sitting in chapel during that important first week, when deans and administrators officially welcomed the class of 1929, with lip-service to TRUTH, with clichés describing benefits and privileges which the University so altruistically placed at the disposal of its students, with stale stereotypes expressing the formal ideals of the institution. And he could see her attentively listening and literal-mindedly accepting their words, determining that she would make the most of her opportunity. Likewise could he see her in classrooms with a loose-leaf notebook before her, diligently copying notes from lectures. And again in the library studying. She had majored in Education, and had planned to become a teacher, and he could see her poring over her assignments in one of her text-books, perhaps a text-book with some such title as *The Theory and Method of the Theory and Practice of Teaching High-School English.* He wondered how many hours she had stolen from sleep, from fun, from dreams, from her life, to devote to her courses in Education. How much of her short life had she given to such problems as the scientific method of grading high-school English papers, to drawing up reading lists for English courses in junior high schools, to the laborious listing of the titles of innocuous books which she herself had no time to read, to considerations of the quantity of fresh air to be permitted twenty-five students, to theoretical discussions of the value and efficacy of using the True and False method in conducting examinations. And again, he could see her on some rare evening of relaxation, when she would have been able to attend an International Club Dance—affairs generally considered freak shows by the prominent campus men and women—when she would have stood like a wall-flower, perhaps in her sleeveless pink taffeta dress, waiting for someone to ask her to dance, watching dance after dance without any invitation, or, if she were dancing, moving so woodenly and awkwardly that she became a trial to her partner. He could see her, again, emerging from the office of her doctor at the beginning of her junior year, pondering and brooding on the words she had just heard, knowing that she had such a very weak heart that she could not hope for a long life, and that any undue excitement or violent exercise would induce her death. He was forced, from this reflection, to admire her persistence and courage in continuing with full-time schedules and going on with her work as checkroom girl and waitress, despite the doctor's warning. He could see her, constantly tired, moving from classroom to library, to hasty meals, to work, and then home to her room for study until she dropped off into a sleep of physical exhaustion. He could see her, a plainly dressed girl, proceeding along a campus walk, moving by the lilac trees on a sunny spring day, just another grind driving herself toward her goal of an education and a degree, smothering impulse after impulse to dally and deviate from her purposes. He attempted to imagine how she must have felt on such occasions, when she would have passed some athlete or club girl who had sat near her in a class, and who passed her by outside without even a formal nod of recognition. He thought of this dead girl, and of her career, that had been so completely fruitless. All her work and study, the more than a thousand dollars which she had paid for tuition, the strain of her effort to obtain an education—all fruitless.

And yesterday, a cold and rainy day, she had gone out to the sand dunes with a newly found friend who had been ignorant of the condition of her heart. While the successful members of her class were in the million-dollar chapel, listening to oratory on the subject of TRUTH, EDUCATION, and CITIZENSHIP, and receiving their degrees, she was out on the sand dunes, her unattractive body clothed in a swimming suit. She had known what the consequences of her gesture would be.

"It was literal suicide."

She had known that if she ran about the dunes, and that if she risked plunging into the icy waters of Lake Michigan, she would not return alive. It had been with a final desperation, nursing a final disappointment, that she had gone on this expedition. Her friend had been first in the water. Ruth had run among the dunes, shouting. She had stood with folded arms, waving to her friend while the latter swam outward. Shouting and laughing, she had pitched down to the shore line. She had collapsed in shallow water, and a wave had washed over her and dragged her to the shore where she had lain, buffeted by the steady charge of waves until her friend, coming in unaware, had discovered her. She had been dead for over an hour when a doctor had examined the body, diagnosing heart failure as the cause of death.

The young campus reporter tossed aside a half-smoked cigarette butt, and stood up. Twilight had settled and it was almost completely dark. The Midway was wrapped in an atmosphere of loneliness, with its passing automobiles, its blinking traffic signals, and its sauntering pedestrians. He turned toward the door of the building. He had forgotten that it was closed, so he walked over to an open hall at the other end of the campus, to telephone.

The City Desk gave him a rewrite man. He stated the facts simply, one by one. She had come to the University with the reputation of being a brilliant student at her small town high school. She had worked her way through school as a waitress and checkroom girl. This June, she had expected to graduate. She had been too busy to have many friends, or much fun during her four years. A few days before graduation she had received a formal notice informing her that she would not be permitted to graduate because she lacked one grade point, and that her average, therefore, did not qualify her for a degree. She had told none of her friends of this development, and had proceeded with her graduation plans. She had paid for her cap and gown, and had sat with the graduating class for the official picture. She had attended the annual senior class breakfast, held one day before commencement exercises. Then on the day of graduation, she had gone out to the sand dunes in the rain, and had attempted to run and swim. For two years, she had been the victim of severe heart attacks, and was under the care of a doctor. She knew that her action would result in death. Now her father was in town, and in the morning she was being returned home in a coffin without the degree for which she had struggled.

The rewrite man asked how the facts had been gotten.

"By lying," the campus reporter answered.

"Come on, I'm busy. How did you get them?"

"I posed as a friend, and spoke with her cousin, her father, and some of her friends. And I saw her laid out in the undertaking parlor."

"Anything else?"

"Yes, she lived with her cousin, and the cousin stated that 'It was literal suicide.'"

"Sounds like it was. How about her picture?"

"It's in the latest annual. I got a copy, and I'm sending it down in a cab."

"Swell stuff, kid! That's good work. I'll have to remind Kelly about it tomorrow."

"And listen! Give her a break. It'll be the first one she ever had. Try and keep out too much of the sob stuff. If you make it too gooey, the story will be spoiled."

"Yeh, it's pretty sad. All right, and are you sure you got it all in now? Nothing else?"

"You got it."

"Well, listen while I repeat it for you."

After hanging up, the campus reporter telephoned for a taxi cab. Waiting for the cab he looked across the street at the gymnasium, which stood darkened and clothed in shadows. He gave the driver the annual, instructed him to get it down to the city desk of *The Chicago Questioner* as quickly as possible, and that he would be paid down there. He watched the cab shoot off. In the morning, his story and Ruth's picture would be on the front page, and the girl's body would be on the train, moving toward home. And the father, with the unpressed suit, the lop-sided shoulders, and the genial but rutted face, would be sitting by the train window, looking out, a bewildered man.

He walked eastward, reflecting on the final meanings of this girl's life. Bobby Wallace would read the story, and become furious. He would receive a telephone call from the office of the vice-president, and he would be called on the carpet to explain why such unfavorable news had gotten into the papers, and particularly at this time, following the commencement exercises, and all the favorable national publicity which the University had received following its recent surprising appointment of the new "boy president" from Yale. Bobby would have to say that he knew nothing about it. He would have to confess defeat. Then the dean of women would get him and demand an explanation. And even the chairman of the board of trustees, Morton G. Quick, the stockyards capitalist and power behind the University throne, would telephone Bobby and ask about the story. Bobby would telephone Kelly and brand the story as a lie, and the campus reporter as a liar. Kelly would chuckle to himself, his three chins moving, and answer ambiguously. Ruth Summer, who in life had merely been one undistinguished student out of about five thousand, a name on reports, a source of one hundred dollars tuition fees every quarter, a student employee with a name on payrolls, a student who must have a desk in various classrooms, and, finally, a member of the class of 1929 who had had to be formally notified that she lacked the prerequisites for graduation—in death, she would be an embarrassment to all the institution's officialdom. To the campus reporter, she was a scoop, a means of preserving his job, and the instrument of settling his grievances with The Department of Public Relations. To *The Chicago Questioner* she was a front-page story, exciting the staff for the space of a few moments while the story was written and turned in. To the editors of the other papers, she would be a source of annoyance, something they had missed, and her story in *The Questioner* would be turned over to their rewrite men to be hashed up for their own editions. To a nameless taxi-driver, she was a long and easy haul from the University all the way downtown, with no passenger to watch whether or not he took a long route to jack up his fare.

And while she had become or was becoming all these various meanings, she lay in that oppressive undertaking parlor, blue and bloated in a sleeveless pink taffeta party frock, and all the fruitless dignity and courage of her life was betrayed, even after her death.

[1934]

Mary O'Reilley

I

One morning Mary O'Reilley glanced a second time into her dresser mirror and discovered that she was an old woman. Her hair was completely gray. Her thin, plain, serene face was becoming the frame of a dried, weedy expression. Several wrinkles were making their inevitable announcements about the edges of her faintly drooping lips. Her bluish eyes were sad and tired.

Mary had never considered herself an old woman, not even the last ten years when she had been under a doctor's care because of her heart. Always she had drifted along on the level acceptance of middle age. Senescence, the clinging pathos of change, death, these thoughts had but rarely and briefly interrupted her peaceful days. Always she had lived with a hope. It was a wish nebulous and intangible. It seemed to tell her in a manner almost mystical that some day all the simple problems and irritations of her daily life would be washed out by a calm and absolute comfort and happiness. Deeper than the conscious acceptance of her religion was an intuition that the stains of fifty years would be cleansed, eliminated. But that morning, hope was gone. It had withered without her knowledge. She was an old woman who had been waiting through all of the years of middle age—for death. She had seen in the mirror's realism more than a mere wrinkled face; she had perceived the joy, the richness, the youngness, the pleasure of living, reflected as so many dead things.

Mary was unmarried. She lived with Joe, Martha, and their niece Gertrude. Joe and Martha were also unmarried. They had lived together in stiffly comfortable homes ever since the death of their parents. For two decades they had been at Fiftieth and Grand Boulevard, but the inrush of Negroes had driven them out to the southeast side of the city; and now, they owned a sprawling, red-bricked sample of American suburban architecture at Seventy-fourth and Crandon. Gertrude was the life and joy of their household. Uncle Joe had educated her, given her the refined advantages of a supposedly superior education at St. Paul's High School for girls, and at Chicago Normal College. Every summer, when she was not teaching, he sent her to the University of Chicago or else Wisconsin. She was charming. Everybody said so. Now she was a grown girl of marriageable age. Her youth was a pathetic announcement for the two old maids. However, life had gone on in the O'Reilley household unruffled, as placid as the conventional lake set in the center of the very conventional landscape oil painting that adorned the stiff and overfurnished parlor. They never quarreled. That was a privilege of intimacy which they did not share. Each was a personality sealed to the others, inter-acting on a basis of patterned word formulas which generalized commonplaces.

That morning, after vividly perceiving the ruins of her gray hair, Mary could not go down to the breakfast table and explain how she felt. She could not explain to Joe and Martha that she was empty inside, that her soul was a barren field over which were scattered the corpses of her few, emaciated dreams. She must keep the freight of her new sorrow locked within, while she spoke of the accustomed breakfast trivialities, the weather, bridge, friends, Annie and her children, Lizz O'Neill, the news in the *Chicago Tribune,* obvious facts connected with Joe's legal cases.

Joe and Martha were already seated. Gertrude was gone. Joe was a grayed and handsome man, whose mellowed appearance was but slightly time-touched; he exuded a sense of well-being. Martha was dried and sapped like Mary, but her features were pointed, acrid, bitter in contrast with the sweetness and calm which sometimes seemed like a serene glow on Mary's countenance.

Joe read the newspaper. Mary listened while Martha talked of Lizz O'Neill. Martha said she liked Lizz, and that Lizz had a good heart. But she was a little common. And she talked too much of her children. They were good and dutiful children; they supported and respected their mother, like they should. But they lacked class, they lacked the class of Tommy and Annie's children. None of them could touch Gertrude for brains. Johnny's Annie, however, was a little like Lizz, a little common. Joe read on. After Lizz had been definitely described as common, he made a few remarks. Then he said that he was going to bring home a young priest for dinner in a few days. It was Father Malloy, a regular fellow of a priest who rooted for the Chicago White Sox, smoked and had a sense of humor. Joe had a regular-fellow complex. Mary and Martha expressed delight. Joe was a god in the family, a patriarch; his wishes were always devoutly acceded to. If he brought people home for dinner, they were inherently fine.

After breakfast, Joe departed for his office. Mary sat by the parlor window. Martha decided to do some sewing for Gertrude.

It was autumn. A sunless sky was pressing heavily over the gray day. Mary's perceptions were misty. She sensed a soul, a spirit, a thing gloomy, wearied, and unseen, passing up and down the street in company with the monotonous wind, shrouding all objects with its mantling mood of brooding dejection—the red-brick apartment building across the street, pedestrians, occasional automobiles, the wind-split trees, the expired lawns, the cheerless sameness of the pavement, herself, everything.

She would have liked to sit by the window remembering things; but there was very little for her to remember. So much of her time had been spent in trivial gossip, in eventless breakfasts and unemphatic teas, in long hours of doing nothing but waiting. She had sat through countless hours, listening to Martha reaffirm that Lizz O'Neill was good-hearted but untidy, that Father Kildea was a saint and scholar blessed in a special manner by the Lord, that Mamie Moriarity was common. Such things were but slight props for memories.

She listened to the wind rattling the window pane. She reflected how it curiously symbolized her own existence. Sitting at a window, protected from storms and colds, watching people, hoping inarticulately—such was her life. Now it was lost, and she had only a few recollections, which she held like a slim bouquet of desired flowers that had withered. Everything she saw, all her thoughts, were like the unseen soul she seemed to sense traveling with the wind. The wind against the pane, too, was cruel, a cruelty felt to be slashing against her.

Martha asked if anything were wrong.

"Nothing. I just feel a little tired, and thought I'd sit by the window here. It's kind of sad today," she replied.

"Yes, but, darling, you ought to rest a little while. Rest is what you need with your heart."

"I will. I just thought that I'd sit here for a little while first."

"I'd take care of myself if I was you."

Mary did not seem to hear her sister.

"Martha, do you remember John Newton?" she suddenly asked.

"No. Why?" Martha responded.

"Oh, I just wondered. Joe brought him out to dinner once, when he was in law school. He seemed like a nice young man, and I wondered what had happened to him."

"I can't remember him. What did he look like?"

"I don't remember, except that he was a nice-looking young man, and he dressed well, and his grammar was as good as Joe's," Mary said.

Martha spoke of a number of people out of the past whom she did remember, only too vividly. She recalled that the Mahoney twins were fat slobs, and that Catherine Malloy had married a good-for-nothing drunkard, and that Joe Collins, who had always been such a roughneck, was now driving a truck, and becoming an old man.

Mary did not listen. She reflected on the oddness of her sudden recollection of John Newton. And yet it was not odd either. Subconsciously she had carried him along with her through the endless flatness of the years. Yet she retained only a vague if pleasing impression of him. His appearance, his features, seemed to evade her memory completely. All she could recall was that she liked him, and that he had been quiet; a very dignified quiet like Joe's. And she had often wished that Joe would bring him out again, or that she would meet him again somewhere. But John Newton had disappeared.

She had been going with Myles Rierdon at the time that Joe had brought John out. Myles was a successful lawyer and politician now, rich and well-known, with a wife and family. On Sundays, she and Myles used to take walks along Michigan Boulevard. When walking with him, her attention was always attracted to the shiny, transparent window panes of some of the houses, set back from well-tended lawns. They had seemed so much like Myles. She would walk along for blocks thinking that Myles' soul was like a clean, transparent pane of glass. It was a queer comparison, and yet it seemed accurate. After she had met John, she had sensed a difference in quality between him and Myles. Myles had shrunken in her estimation.

She could not recall ever regretting her refusal of Myles' proposal. Now, sitting by the window, she was stung with no lamentations. She would not have altered her life, and re-lived it as Mrs. Rierdon, if such powers were given her. Her memory of him carried with it the same repulsion that he had always caused in her. Confidently and with the insensitivity of a crass male, he had asked her to marry him, vainly unaware that she might decline his offer. There was something about Myles, his brashness, that had often caused her to wince. After Myles would kiss her, she would lie in a hot bed wondering if she were the Mary O'Reilley who had allowed that man to kiss her, to press his lips heavily upon hers. It had shamed her. Even now she reacted to that sense of shame. She watched a woman pushing a baby buggy past her window, and she experienced a soiled feeling; a lingering nausea from kisses which Myles Rierdon had now probably forgotten. Everybody had thought her a fool for not accepting him. No, she was not sorry, even though she was barren and unfulfilled, going to death without having known a woman's warmest feelings and experiences.

She sat looking out of the window.

"Oh, Mary, Lizz ought to be over today," Martha said, glancing up from her sewing.

"Yes," said Mary.

"She hasn't been to see us lately, and when she was down at Annie's the other night she said that she might be around today."

"That'll be nice. I have a dress I want to give her."

"Well, she needs it," Martha said aggressively.

"Yes, she's poor. The poor thing," said Mary.

"She's dirty and sloppy. She most certainly needs a new dress," Martha said.

"She's had a hard time."

"Yes, but there's no excuse for a woman being so sloppy. She could comb her hair and wash her face. Water is free, and a bar of soap only costs five cents."

Mary did not answer. Martha spoke on. She suddenly changed the subject to a party they had attended when they were young girls. There had been a young man there named O'Connell. Martha spoke of him confusedly. Poor Martha! Mary thought. She, too, was oppressed by the past.

Martha's tongue finally lapsed, and she proceeded with her sewing.

Mary wondered about John Newton. What had happened to him? Was he married? Was he unhappy, and approaching the end of a stream of wasting trivialities, coming into the hands of death? People went in and out of each other's lives with such strange abruptness. They disappeared—for eternity. There was a certain horror in this realization; and she changed her thoughts to the time she had contemplated entering the convent of the Poor Clares. When she was thirty, she had sensed life shrinking and shrivelling inside of her. Perceptions had commenced to sting her; the laughter of young people who walked summer nights arm in arm, innocent of future misery and the inroads of age; the spring madness of green leaves and trees; Annie and Tommy with their babies; youth; love. The world had seemed to press upon her with insistent fingers. She was stifled, nervous; her thoughts seemed like a succession of boils. She wanted escape, peace, a fortressed calm. At the Poor Clares convent, over at Fifty-third and Laflin, she had learned of the cloistered nuns, who were isolated from all contacts with the outside world. Living in complete solitude, they prayed and meditated, and passed an easeful life. There was neither struggle nor sorrow, but only devotion; so she had felt. When she had attended benediction there on Sunday afternoons, she had heard them sing through a partition. Their voices had seemed sweet and flowing with a spiritual peace. Once a Protestant friend had said that their voices were shrill; but she had never felt them so. She had spent long hours in wishful contemplation of joining them, of escaping from the hurting continuities of everyday existence into a quiet that seemed like an endless summer evening's swoon. But she had never entered the convent. She had lived on into the comfort of middle-age, losing the pain of those final, suppressed, youthful gasps. She had sunken into the final ditches of the human static and the commonplace.

II

In the afternoon Lizz O'Neill, and their sister-in-law, Annie, visited them. Lizz was fat and sloppy, a woman in her middle forties. Annie was thin with angular features. They sat in the parlor and talked and talked. Mary sat by the window, only half attentive, sunken in her own thoughts. Lizz said that her children were fine children. Annie told how Good and Fine her children were. Her Annie, and her Gertrude, and her Tommy, and her Martin, and her William. Lizz became equally as explicit about her brood. Then she switched her subject to the recently beatified eighteenth-century nun, The Sacred Rose of Jesus Christ. The talk spun along. They spoke of Mrs. Nolan's sloppy clothes, Mame's dead husband, the dreadful way in which A.P.A. schools, like the University of Chicago, turned out atheists, and of what Lizz O'Neill heard Mamie Moriarity say to Nellie McBride about Bridget Malloy at the wake of Sadie O'Brien.

Mary glanced out the window.

Lizz was speaking profusely, emphasizing her words with facial and manual gestures. . . . "And the airs of them. Humph! Her Peter is getting a new car, and they are moving out on Jeffery Avenue, and her Nellie is going out with a swell college guy. . . . Now, let me tell you, college guys are slick. Oh, but they're slick! And they don't take girls out for no good reason. You can't tell me that they do. . . . You can't be too careful nowadays about them slick college guys. A mother must watch her girls. Now my Margaret and my Catherine, they never go out with a young fellow, unless they have brought him home and introduced him to me. And if they're out after twelve o'clock, their brother Dennis is wild and wants to go and get them. Dennis is going to take care of his sisters. But as I was saying, the airs them Dempseys put on. Humph! . . ."

Annie took the floor from Lizz, almost by assault.

"You speak the truth, Lizz. A mother must keep her eyes primed on her girls. Now, I only let my Annie go out with the finest type of young men. Young men with—*class*. Now, there's that Roycroft boy. He's a student at Loyola, and he's studying law, and gettin' educated, and his family has—*class*."

Mary had heard all this maternal braggery before. At times, it had even interested her. Now it was devoid of meaning. It slid out of her consciousness without the least strain upon her attention. She watched a group of children moving down Crandon Avenue. There was an entangling pathos, an almost tragic beauty about them as they trooped by, their forms wistfully etched against the dull October day. She thought of the intangible beauties of childhood; and she wished that she had had children of her own; children of hers and . . . John Newton's. She dismissed the thought before it became either painful or shocking. She remembered being with Annie when hers were born, the pain and bloodiness of it! And these children she had just seen pass beneath her window, they were born in pain, to live like she had, or else like Lizz and Annie. She again thought, almost enviously, of the Poor Clares. It seemed beautiful to her; lives lived in such quiet noiselessness, lives of escape from . . .

"Mary, would you like to make the novena to The Sacred Rose of Jesus Christ? It starts next Toosday," Lizz said.

"Yes," Mary answered.

Lizz spoke of the Sacred Rose of Jesus Christ, seemingly bragging as if the latter's purity, virginity, and sanctity were her own. Then Mary served tea, and there was more conversation. At five-thirty they both had to rush home to prepare late supper for their families. After they were gone, Martha spoke of how common they both were. Mary was uninterested.

III

Days slipped along, and Mary's strength waned. She tired easily, and her interest in people, parties, and gatherings lagged. She seemed to have given up after that morning when the fact of approaching old age had been imprinted vividly upon her. Joe asked her to accompany him on a vacation to California, but she lacked the resistance for such a journey. She spent most of her time seated by the window, watching autumn coffin the street, her memory slipping through the flimsy satisfactions of her own past. School children always gauzed her spirit in melancholy. She was getting thin. She was suffering from frequent heart-pains. One day, she heard Gertrude remark, "Poor Aunt Mary!" There was no use pretending. She was near to the end.

Yet she was unterrified. Sometimes she even hoped for death. She was in bed most of the winter and did not leave the house until spring had come with its gaudy greenness.

Her first walk was in Jackson Park. The world was foreign, alien with its own happiness. She was but a weakened stranger, allowed merely to observe its parade. And the fresh young and gay impressions of the sticky leaves and trees pained her like a sad melodrama. Sometimes, her depression became like a naked sore. She wished intensely that she were young again, that love and a future were hers. Death was altered into something nightmarish. She even grew to hate youth. She prayed and she cursed, and, alone, she cried because she could no longer identify herself with the freshness that pervaded the park on her walks. She was a sick, old woman.

The summer passed for her, slowly, pantingly, miserably, with its suffocating hotness. Once again the world slid into decay. Mary was happier. Autumn was her season. Its melancholy was hers. She even liked its windy monotony. But after autumn was winter.

In November, she was sent to the hospital, a thin old woman. She had a private room with all possible conveniences and attentions. Joe secured the services of three renowned heart-specialists. The room was often filled with flowers. There she lay, waiting for death. But she enjoyed the quiet of the hospital. It seemed something like the mists of solitude which she imagined as the surrounding mood of the cloistered Poor Clare nuns. Sometimes she would even try to recreate memories where there were none. Sometimes she grew moody with longings for home, wishings for her parlor window, tea, conversation with Martha, Lizz, and Annie, for novenas to The Sacred Rose of Jesus Christ, church socials. Sometimes, she prayed. However, she more often lived in fogs and shapeless, melancholy moods. . . . And she had visitors. They came to see her and tell her that she looked well and would get better. Joe came, and Martha, and Annie and Tommy, and Lizz. She was usually happier alone.

December came; winter came, with ice blasts and holiday moods of simulated joy. Mary remembered other Christmas days. She was gloomy with the realization of an approaching Christmas in the hospital. It was to be her last. She grew more weak, living on borrowed time. She even began to hope that she would die before Christmas. The mists about her mind thickened. She received the last sacraments. The hope of dying before Christmas became almost an obsession. To lie in bed, looking back across a stretch of fifty-one years, remembering the doll her mother had given her on her eighth Christmas, the candy and dress her father gave her for her fourteenth birthday, the whole cluster of memories that had suddenly grown so significant with a lost beauty—she wanted to die.

At five o'clock on a morning of the week preceding Christmas, when a surly wind was crashing against the bleak bricks of the Mercy Hospital, her wish matured in an expiring darkness. As she lay awake, gasping for breath after a fatiguing, sleepless evening, the world was slowly crushed into silence. She sensed her faculties and powers ebbing; and blackness, soothing and restful, spread calmly over her room, engulfing all her perceptions in its tremendous, suffocating hush. It covered her, and her lips grew cold and tight with the imprint of a satisfied smile that she carried with her to the grave.

[1928]

Jim O'Neill

Lizz had closed the window, and when he awakened, the bedroom air was stale and musty. He lay awake, very tired, and glancing idly at the drawn shade around which there were cracks of daylight and the yellowing afternoon sun. He rubbed his right fist and wondered how long he would last. Then he swung himself up to sit on the side of the rumpled bed in the long drawers in which he had slept. From the vacant lot outside his window, he could hear the shouts and arguments of a boys' game of indoor ball. His son Bob was playing in it. Jim made a pass at the air with his right fist, and then rubbed the knuckles of that hand. Sure he was all right. He was over that stroke. Everything was all right. Sure. He remained seated, listening to noises from the ball playing outside.

With that recurrent feeling of pride, he pulled the chain turning on the electric light. For it was the first time in his life that he had lived in a flat of his own with electricity in it. And it was only two years now since he had moved into this building on Calumet Avenue. Well, the war had not been good for a number of men, but it had for him. Except for the war, he probably never would have been promoted to Wagon Dispatcher at the Continental Express Company. It was getting somewhere to be promoted to the supervision with a salary of one hundred and eighty-five a month, and now, with this new raise, he would be earning two hundred and twenty-five a month. That would mean many things for his family.

He touched his hand again. Not any too much feeling in it, and he grew worried. He clenched his fists, and gritted his teeth, determining not to worry. He had, goddamn them all, supported his family with his hands and his back for years, and now he was better off than he had ever been, he had come through, and nothing was going to take that away from him. He was in a position to give his kids a better start in the world than he had had. They wouldn't have to teach themselves how to read and write, after they had become grown men. And goddamn them all, they couldn't say that he wasn't an honest man.

He remembered that time, back in the days when his cousin, Joe O'Reilley, the lawyer, had been coming up in politics, and he and Joe had been together in the loop. They had accidentally met Bart Gallivan, the Democratic boss of Cook County.

"Bart, I want to introduce you to my cousin, Jim O'Neill."

"Pleased to meet you, Jim," Bart had said with that put-on friendliness of the politician, extending that glad hand of his.

"There's at least one man in the city of Chicago who won't shake hands with a crook."

And he had walked away. Well, he was proud to be an honest man, and to have turned down that political job which Joe had offered to get him at the City Hall.

And now he was all set. He squeezed and patted that hand, stimulating the circulation.

He drew on his trousers, and looked into the mirror, rubbing the whiskers on his long, rough, leathery face.

"Oh, Lizz, get me something to eat!" he called loudly.

There was no answer.

"Oh, Lizz!"

He walked through the narrow dark hallway and stood at the entrance to the small, square dining-room, seeing rags, paper, dirt and confusion, an opened loaf of bread on the table, butter and sugar attracting buzzing flies, dirt.

"Lizz!" he called surlily.

He walked through to the kitchen. Dirtier! That goddamn woman. Always praying at church. It was all right to go to church and pray, but a wife and a mother had some duties to her family, and order was heaven's first law, and cleanliness is next to godliness. He tightened his lips in inarticulate and impotent anger.

He re-entered the dining-room, and paused by the window, to watch Bob, his youngest son, who was at bat. The other boys all were shouting at him, and he seemed to be giving them back their talk in kind. A sassy kid, and Jim didn't like the sass in him. He watched, hoping that Bob would connect with the ball. Bob swung into a pitch, and the ball sizzled along the ground to the pitcher. Watching Bob get thrown out at first base, Jim was disappointed.

He turned from the window and went to the bathroom, the first bathroom he had ever had in his own home. He remembered the cottage at Forty-fifth and Wells, with the privy in the yard, and the smelling kerosene lamps, and the dirty five-room clapboarded cottage, and Lizz always slopping around the house in house slippers, with a dirty face, uncombed hair, and an unwashed calico rag around her chin. And Artie, his baby boy, a beautiful child with blond curls, the little face, the laugh and excitement as he was learning to walk, the questions he asked after first having learned to talk. The way he always chased and stumbled after his brothers and sisters, Bob, and Margaret, and Catherine, and Dennis, and Bill. Jim thought of that night in June when he had come home from work with a basket of fruit under his arm, and Artie had had a sore throat. The next morning the child had been worse. And all the kids had had sore throats. Diphtheria! They had telephoned for that damn Doctor Callaghan, and he hadn't come for over twenty-four hours. He remembered his baby boy, with blond curls, dying at its mother's breasts, for Lizz had not weaned it, because she believed that while she was still nursing one child she would not get caught with another. There was the sick child, dying in its mother's arms, at its mother's breasts, in a house full of kids sick with diphtheria.

The kids were all sent to the hospital, and Margaret, the oldest girl, who, like the boy Danny, lived with the aunt and grandmother, also went with them. Himself and Lizz burying the baby in a small white coffin, the beautiful boy turning black in the box from streptococcic poisoning. He had cried that day. Yes, he had cried, and asked was there a God? Remembering it, thinking of those rotted bones of his baby boy out in Calvary Cemetery now, he cried again, alone in his bathroom, the first real bathroom he had ever had in his home in his whole life. He cried.

Jim shaved, his right hand tiring as he ran the straight razor over his face. He went to the kitchen, and fried eggs and bacon, and heated the pot of coffee. He carried his food to the dining-room, shoved the cluttered objects on the table aside, and sat down to eat. He glanced out of the window and saw Bob make a two-base hit. He hoped that Lizz would return shortly. He determined that he would tell her a hell of a lot. He ought to give her a good smack in the teeth. Hell, she was such a goddamn fool, praying all day in the church, until the janitors had to ask her to leave so that they could close up. Why wasn't she cleaning her house, taking care of her children, making things at home pretty and orderly—why wasn't all that as much of a prayer as kneeling down in St. Patrick's church and praying by the hour. That goddamn woman!

She still wasn't back when he finished his meal. He did not remove the dishes from the table, and went out to the kitchen to make some ham and cheese sandwiches for his lunch. He placed them, along with a slice of Ward's cake and an apple, in a newspaper, and wrapped a neat bundle.

He determined that he would tell that goddamn woman what was what.

He waited impatiently in the parlor, looking with pride at the stuffy, ugly installment-plan furniture. Then he looked at his old horned victrola. He went over to it, and ran his hand along the curved horn, almost fondling it. He dug through his records, and put one on, sitting down to listen:

"Call me back through the years, pal of mine,
Let me gaze in your eyes . . ."

He re-played the record, thinking of black-haired Elizabeth, his beautiful young bride. His anger with her melted. After all, she and he had stuck it all through, stuck through all that poverty in the days when he was a teamster. And she had borne him eleven kids. She had suffered through all that, seeing one of her kids die, holding Artie to her breasts while he gasped his last feeble breaths. Yes, she was in church praying, because she was still stricken with grief over little Artie's death. Through these last three years she hadn't forgotten, hadn't forgotten how he and she, tears streaming down their faces, had walked out of Calvary Cemetery in the rain, the freshly dug earth smothered over their dead son. Mothers love their children, and they don't forget. Why should he get so sore? Hell, it still put a catch in his throat.

He slowly wound the victrola, and set the needle back at the start of the record, these practical details diverting his thoughts.

Let me gaze in your eyes . . .

He listened to the slow, whining words of the song, and remembered that they had come through it all, goddamn it, they had. He was not the man he had been, and that stroke, too, but he was going to go on pulling through, and his kids would never have to know the same kind of a life that he had known, the drinking, poverty, fighting, strikes, like that teamsters' strike back around 1904, when the company sluggers and thugs had tried to get him. He felt his right hand, the hand that had spoken straight from the shoulder in many a fight. He had pulled through, and goddamn it, he had been honest. He suddenly sat up erectly. He remembered that scrippers' strike during the war, when he had scabbed. Well, a man had his family, and it came first, and it was right after Artie had died. Where would he have been, if he hadn't scabbed.

Call me back through the years, pal of mine . . .

Yes, his kids were going to avoid all that.

He wanted Lizz to come back. He wanted to kiss her as he had used to kiss her when they were first married. He waited as long as he could, and she still was not home. He had to leave for work.

Calumet Avenue, with its lines of gray-, red-, and brown-stone apartment buildings of two and three stories, its many lawnless patches of dirt before the buildings, its few scabby trees, was still bright and sunny, and many children were playing along it. He saw Catherine, a black-haired girl with a dirty face and dirty dress, skipping rope with some girls. And Dennis, with a group gathered about a bicycle. He called to Catherine, and gave her three nickels, one for herself, and one for Bob and Dennis. He picked her up and asked her whose girl she was.

"Papa's!"

He passed on, and there was another catch in his throat. He thought of his son, Danny. When Margaret had been born, Danny had been sent to stay with his grandmother. He had been so poor then that they couldn't afford to feed another mouth, and the boy had remained with his grandmother to this day. Jim had gotten him a job for the summer vacation down in the Wagon Call Department at the Express Company, and he had brought all the goddamn dude manners he had learned from his uncles down there. He had told them all in the department that the boy lived with him, and then the kid had gone and made a liar of him by saying he lived with his grandmother. And he had bought box-seat tickets for the ball game every Sunday, and showed them off in the department. Jim knew goddamn well that he should take the boy back and . . . he didn't have the nerve to after all these years, and the boy acted as if he scarcely knew his father.

He thought again of Lizz when she was younger, small, shy, with straight black oily hair and dark eyes. He rubbed his right hand, and dragged that right leg that had been affected by the stroke. He felt tired, washed out. His work was easy, and all he had to do was sit up in the department, answer telephones, and keep wagon sheets. Still, he was slow at it, and at the end of every night he was tired. He fell asleep every morning, riding home from work on the elevated train. Well, he and Lizz had been able to pull through this far. They would not stop now.

Jim went to work. Work was much as usual, but he was slow in answering the phones, and keeping the sheets. And Billy McLaughlin, the old man's nephew who was a clerk on nights for the summer vacation, shouted at him to hurry. He called Billy a rat, and told him to shut his mouth. Billy did. But Jim was very angry. He worked on, and his right hand grew numb from writing. About eight o'clock he went out to the lavatory, dragging that right leg of his a trifle. He looked at himself in the mirror, but he didn't need the mirror to tell him that he was slipping. He rubbed his hand to get a good circulation in it. Not any too much feeling in it now.

He clenched his fists, assuring himself that he still retained the old fighting spirit. And a man could go along on that if he was the Jim O'Neill kind. By Christ, he would, he would battle through. Just give him ten more years to get all his kids through school, and give them a better start than he got.

He looked out the window, up at the summer sky that stood serene above the alley and the express building. He experienced a moment of intense clarity, and he saw what kind of a fight his kids would have, the same kind of a struggle that he'd gone through. He raised his arms.

God make the kids tough, make them hard as iron, scrapping O'Neills! Make them strong and tough and hard like steel! And God, Jesus Christ, give them guts! God, they'll be workingmen, and they'll have to fight like workingmen. Give them fight, God, and two big fists!

God, don't give them flesh, make them steel and iron and wood! Make their jaws cement! Make them tough, tough as nails!

God teach them to take it because they gotta! Their old man, God, couldn't stand the gaff, please make them better men than him! God, I know the game, and it's beat me. Please, don't let it beat them! Please, God, God make them sluggers, and make them slug, and take it, and slug again. And when they get slugged down, make them get up, please, God! God, give them stone, brass, anything, but not a heart! God, make them hard, cold, fierce, like white-hot hissing steel, with hams for fists, and brass for a heart.

God, please give the kids a chance! Please make them better men than their old man! Please!

Only ten more years, but nobody needed to tell Jim that he was slipping. A tall, half-wreck of a man, he returned to his chair in the department, dragging his right leg a trifle.

[1932]

Studs

AUTHOR'S NOTE   *This, one of my first stories, is the nucleus out of which the Studs Lonigan trilogy was conceived, imagined, and written. It should suggest the experience and background of these books, and my own relationship to their background. But for the accident of this story, and of the impressions recorded in it, I should probably never have written the Studs Lonigan series.*

After writing this story in the spring of 1929, before I had ever published any fiction, the impressions here recorded remained with me so vividly that I could not let them rest. It was then that both Young Lonigan *and* The Young Manhood of Studs Lonigan *were begun. Originally they were planned as one volume, to end with a scene similar to the one presented in this story. As I worked over them, they were changed, split into two volumes, and finally they grew into the trilogy as it has been published. However, to repeat, this story is the nucleus of the entire work, and so I include it here.   JTF [1935]*

It is raining outside; rain pouring like bullets from countless machine guns; rain spat-spattering on the wet earth and paving in endless silver crystals. Studs' grave out at Mount Olivet will be soaked and soppy, and fresh with the wet, clean odors of watered earth and flowers. And the members of Studs' family will be looking out of the windows of their apartment on the South Side, thinking of the cold, damp grave and the gloomy, muddy cemetery, and of their Studs lying at rest in peaceful acceptance of that wormy conclusion which is the common fate.

At Studs' wake last Monday evening everybody was mournful, sad that such a fine young fellow of twenty-six should go off so suddenly with double pneumonia; blown out of this world like a ripped leaf in a hurricane. They sighed and the women and girls cried, and everybody said that it was too bad. But they were consoled because he'd had the priest and had received Extreme Unction before he died, instead of going off like Sport Murphy who was killed in a saloon brawl. Poor Sport! He was a good fellow, and tough as hell. Poor Studs!

The undertaker (it was probably old man O'Reedy who used to be usher in the old parish church) laid Studs out handsomely. He was outfitted in a sombre black suit and a white silk tie. His hands were folded over his stomach, clasping a pair of black rosary beads. At his head, pressed against the satin bedding, was a spiritual bouquet, set in line with Studs' large nose. He looked handsome, and there were no lines of suffering on his planed face. But the spiritual bouquet (further assurance that his soul would arrive safely in Heaven) was a dirty trick. So was the administration of the last sacraments. For Studs will be miserable in Heaven, more miserable than he was on those Sunday nights when he would hang around the old poolroom at Fifty-eighth and the elevated station, waiting for something to happen. He will find the land of perpetual happiness and goodness dull and boresome, and he'll be resentful. There will be nothing to do in Heaven but to wait in timeless eternity. There will be no can houses, speakeasies, whores (unless they are reformed) and gambling joints; and neither will there be a shortage of plasterers. He will loaf up and down gold-paved streets where there is not even the suggestion of a poolroom, thinking of Paulie Haggerty, Sport Murphy, Arnold Sheehan and Hink Weber, who are possibly in Hell together because there was no priest around to play a dirty trick on them.

I thought of these things when I stood by the coffin, waiting for Tommy Doyle, Red Kelly, Les, and Joe to finish offering a few perfunctory prayers in memory of Studs. When they had showered some Hail Marys and Our Fathers on his already prayer-drenched soul, we went out into the dining room.

Years ago when I was a kid in the fifth grade in the old parish school, Studs was in the graduating class. He was one of the school leaders, a light-faced, blond kid who was able to fight like sixty and who never took any sass from Tommy Doyle, Red Kelly, or any of those fellows from the Fifty-eighth Street gang. He was quarterback on the school's football team, and liked by the girls.

My first concrete memory of him is of a rainy fall afternoon. Dick Buckford and I were fooling around in front of Helen Shires' house bumping against each other with our arms folded. We never thought of fighting but kept pushing and shoving and bumping each other. Studs, Red O'Connell, Tubby Connell, the Donoghues, and Jim Clayburn came along. Studs urged us into fighting, and I gave Dick a bloody nose. Studs congratulated me, and said that I could come along with them and play tag in Red O'Connell's basement, where there were several trick passageways.

After that day, I used to go around with Studs and his bunch. They regarded me as a sort of mascot, and they kept training me to fight other kids. But any older fellows who tried to pick on me would have a fight on their hands. Every now and then he would start boxing with me.

"Gee, you never get hurt, do you?" he would say.

I would grin in answer, bearing the punishment because of the pride and the glory.

"You must be goofy. You can't be hurt."

"Well, I don't get hurt like other kids."

"You're too good for Morris and those kids. You could trim them with your eyes closed. You're good," he would say, and then he would go on training me.

I arranged for a party on one of my birthdays, and invited Studs and the fellows from his bunch. Red O'Connell, a tall, lanky, cowardly kid, went with my brother, and the two of them convinced my folks that Studs was not a fit person for me to invite. I told Studs what had happened, and he took such an insult decently. But none of the fellows he went with would accept my invitation, and most of the girls also refused. On the day of the party, with my family's permission, I again invited Studs but he never came.

I have no other concrete recollections of Studs while he was in grammar school. He went to Loyola for one year, loafed about for a similar period; and then he became a plasterer for his father. He commenced going round the poolroom. The usual commonplace story resulted. What there was of the boy disappeared in slobbish dissipation. His pleasures became compressed within a hexagonal of whores, movies, pool, alky, poker, and craps. By the time I commenced going into the poolroom (my third year in high school) this process had been completed.

Studs' attitude toward me had also changed to one of contempt. I was a goofy young punk. Often he made cracks about me. Once, when I retaliated by sarcasm, he threatened to bust me, and awed by his former reputation I shut up. We said little to each other, although Studs occasionally condescended to borrow fifty or seventy-five cents from me, or to discuss Curley, the corner imbecile.

Studs' companions were more or less small-time amateur hoodlums. He had drifted away from the Donoghues and George Gogarty, who remained bourgeois young men with such interests as formal dances and shows. Perhaps Slug Mason was his closest friend; a tall, heavy-handed, good-natured, child-minded slugger, who knew the address and telephone number of almost every prostitute on the South Side. Hink Weber, who should have been in the ring and who later committed suicide in an insane asylum, Red Kelly, who was a typical wisecracking corner habitué, Tommy Doyle, a fattening, bull-dozing, half-good-natured moron, Stan Simonsky and Joe Thomas were his other companions.

I feel sure that Studs' family, particularly his sisters, were appalled by his actions. The two sisters, one of whom I loved in an adolescently romantic and completely unsuccessful manner, were the type of middle-class girls who go in for sororities and sensibilities. One Saturday evening, when Studs got drunk earlier than usual, his older sister (who the boys always said was keen) saw him staggering around under the Fifty-eighth Street elevated station. She was with a young man in an automobile, and they stopped. Studs talked loudly to her, and finally they left. Studs reeled after the car, cursing and shaking his fists. Fellows like Johnny O'Brien (who went to the U. of C. to become a fraternity man) talked sadly of how Studs could have been more discriminating in his choice of buddies and liquor; and this, too, must have reached the ears of his two sisters.

Physical decay slowly developed. Studs, always a square-planed, broad person, began getting soft and slightly fat. He played one or two years with the corner football team. He was still an efficient quarterback, but slow. When the team finally disbanded, he gave up athletics. He fought and brawled about until one New Year's Eve he talked out of turn to Jim Mc-Geoghan, who was a boxing champ down at Notre Dame. Jim flattened Studs' nose, and gave him a wicked black eye. Studs gave up fighting.

My associations with the corner gradually dwindled. I went to college, and became an atheist. This further convinced Studs that I wasn't right, and he occasionally remarked about my insanity. I grew up contemptuous of him and the others; and some of this feeling crept into my overt actions. I drifted into other groups and forgot the corner. Then I went to New York, and stories of legendary activities became fact on the corner. I had started a new religion, written poetry, and done countless similar monstrous things. When I returned, I did not see Studs for over a year. One evening, just before the Smith-Hoover election day, I met him as he came out of the I. C. station at Randolph Street with Pat Carrigan and Ike Dugan. I talked to Pat and Ike, but not to Studs.

"Aren't you gonna say hello to me?" he asked in friendly fashion, and he offered me his hand.

I was curious but friendly for several minutes. We talked of Al Smith's chances in an uninformed, unintelligent fashion and I injected one joke about free love. Studs laughed at it; and then they went on.

The next I heard of him, he was dead.

When I went out into the dining room, I found all the old gang there, jabbering in the smoke-thick, crowded room. But I did not have any desire or intention of giving the world for having seen them. They were almost all fat and respectable. Cloddishly, they talked of the tragedy of his death, and then went about remembering the good old days. I sat in the corner and listened.

The scene seemed tragi-comical to me. All these fellows had been the bad boys of my boyhood, and many of them I had admired as proper models. Now they were all of the same kidney. Jackie Cooney (who once stole fifteen bottles of grape juice in one haul from under the eyes of a Greek proprietor over at Sixty-fifth and Stony Island), Monk McCarthy (who lived in a basement on his pool winnings and peanuts for over a year), Al Mumford (the good-natured, dumbly well-intentioned corner scapegoat), Pat Carrigan, the roly-poly fat boy from Saint Stanislaus high school—all as alike as so many cans of tomato soup.

Jim Nolan, now bald-headed, a public accountant, engaged to be married, and student in philosophy at Saint Vincent's evening school, was in one corner with Monk.

"Gee, Monk, remember the time we went to Plantation and I got drunk and went down the alley over-turning garbage cans?" he recalled.

"Yeh, that was some party," Monk said.

"Those were the days," Jim said.

Tubby Connell, whom I recalled as a moody, introspective kid, singled out the social Johnny O'Brien and listened to the latter talk with George Gogarty about Illinois U.

Al Mumford walked about making cracks, finally observing to me, "Jim, get a fiddle and you'll look like Paderwooski."

Red Kelly sat enthroned with Les, Doyle, Simonsky, Bryan, Young Floss Campbell (waiting to be like these older fellows), talking oracularly.

"Yes, sir, it's too bad. A young fellow in the prime of life going like that. It's too bad," he said.

"Poor Studs!" Les said.

"I was out with him a week ago," Bryan said.

"He was all right then," Kelly said.

"Life is a funny thing," Doyle said.

"It's a good thing he had the priest," Kelly said.

"Yeh," Les said.

"Sa-ay, last Saturday I pushed the swellest little baby at Rosy's," Doyle said.

"Was she a blonde?" Kelly said.

"Yeh," Doyle said.

"She's cute. I jazzed her, too," Kelly said.

"Yeh, that night at Plantation was a wow," Jim Nolan said.

"We ought to pull off a drunk some night," Monk said.

"Let's," Nolan said.

"Say, Curley, are you in love?" Mumford asked Curley across the room.

"Now, Duffy," Curley said with imbecilic superiority.

"Remember the time Curley went to Burnham?" Carrigan asked.

Curley blushed.

"What happened, Curley?" Duffy asked.

"Nothing, Al," Curley said, confused.

"Go on, tell him, Curley! Tell him! Don't be bashful now! Don't be bashful! Tell him about the little broad!" Carrigan said.

"Now, Pat, you know me better than that," Curley said.

"Come on, Curley, tell me," Al said.

"Some little girl sat on Curley's knee, and he shoved her off and called her a lousy whore and left the place," Carrigan said.

"Why, Curley, I'm ashamed of you," Al said.

Curley blushed.

"I got to get up at six every morning. But I don't mind it. This not workin' is the bunk. You ain't got any clothes or anything when you ain't got the sheets. I know. No, sir, this loafin' is all crap. You wait around all day for something to happen," Jackie Cooney said to Tommy Rourke.

"Gee, it was tough on Studs," Johnny O'Brien said to George Gogarty.

Gogarty said it was tough, too. Then they talked of some student from Illinois U. Phil Rolfe came in. Phil was professional major-domo of the wake; he was going with Studs' kid sister. Phil used to be a smart Jewboy, misplaced when he did not get into the furrier business. Now he was sorry with everybody, and thanking them for being sorry. He and Kelly talked importantly of pall-bearers. Then he went out. Some fellow I didn't know started telling one of Red Kelly's brothers what time he got up to go to work. Mickey Flannagan, the corner drunk, came in and he, too, said he was working.

They kept on talking, and I thought more and more that they were a bunch of slobs. All the adventurous boy that was in them years ago had been killed. Slobs, getting fat and middle-aged, bragging of their stupid brawls, reciting the commonplaces of their days.

As I left, I saw Studs' kid sister. She was crying so pitifully that she was unable to recognize me. I didn't see how she could ever have been affectionate toward Studs. He was so outside of her understanding. I knew she never mentioned him to me the few times I took her out. But she cried pitifully.

As I left, I thought that Studs had looked handsome. He would have gotten a good break, too, if only they hadn't given him Extreme Unction. For life would have grown into fatter and fatter decay for him, just as it was starting to do with Kelly, Doyle, Cooney and McCarthy. He, too, was a slob; but he died without having to live countless slobbish years. If only they had not sent him to Heaven where there are no whores and poolrooms.

I walked home with Joe, who isn't like the others. We couldn't feel sorry over Studs. It didn't make any difference.

"Joe, he was a slob," I said.

Joe did not care to use the same language, but he did not disagree.

And now the rain keeps falling on Studs' new grave, and his family mournfully watches the leaden sky, and his old buddies are at work wishing that it was Saturday night, and that they were just getting into bed with a naked voluptuous blonde.

[1929]

Reverend Father Gilhooley

I

Albert Schaeffer, from the sixth grade, sounded the sanctuary bell, its echoes knelling through the hush of Saint Patrick's barn-like church. Heads lowered in pews, and closed fists beat against suddenly contrite breasts. Low, sweet organ tones flowed, and Miss Molly O'Callaghan sang.

Agnus Dei, qui tollit peccata mundi,
Agnus Dei . . .

Communicants slowly and solemnly marched to the altar rail, heads bent, lips forming prayers, hands palmed together in stiff prayerfulness. Father Gilhooley, the corpulent, ruddy-faced, bald, gray-fringed pastor, choked his Latin, mumbled. Miss O'Callaghan's voice lifted, evoking and spreading through the church a spirit of murmuring contrition, a deep and feelingful Catholic humility.

Oh, Lord, I am not worthy
That Thou shouldst come to me,
But speak the words of comfort
And my spirit healed shall be.

Father Gilhooley descended from the altar carrying the golden chalice. His Irish blood plunged with pride, pride in his ascent to the priesthood from his lowly Irish peasant origins, pride in his power to change flour and water into the Real Presence and to carry it comfortingly to penitents and sorely troubled sinners.

Oh, Lord, I am not worthy . . .

The cassocked acolyte shoved the silver communion plate under the fat chin of the first communicant. The priest extracted a wafer of unleavened bread with his consecrated fingers, crossed it in the air, and placed it on the out-thrust tongue, muttering simultaneously:

Corpus Domini nostri Jesu Christi custodiat animam tuam in
  vitam aeternam.

Twenty-year-old Peggy Collins knelt at the altar rail, her dark eyes closed, her pert round face lifted, her tongue stuck out. She waited, praying please to God and the Blessed Virgin to guide her and aid her and give her the grace and courage to see and to do what was right in the eyes of Heaven. The priest laid the host on her tongue and swept along.

Corpus Domini nostri Jesu Christi custodiat animam tuam in
  vitam aeternam.
Oh, Lord, I am not worthy . . .

II

"Gee, I'll have to hurry. I'm going to be late at the office," Peggy Collins said, entering the kitchen, home from the eight o'clock mass.

"Well, the food is here. You can make your own breakfast and not be expecting me to be waiting on you hand and foot," Mrs. Collins, a beefy and coarse-faced woman, said, frowning as she talked.

Peggy turned on the gas under the coffee pot.

"When you're my age, I hope you won't be expected to slave for ungrateful children."

"Oh, Mother, please, now! I've just come from receiving Holy Communion. Please let's not quarrel!"

"And little good it'll do you!"

"Why, Mother!" Peggy exclaimed, turning toward her mother with a pained expression.

"Don't talk to me, you that would disgrace me in the eyes of the parish, and before a holy man, a breathing saint of God like Father Gilhooley. Well, you mark my words. There's never the day's luck that will shine on you and yours. I only hope that the day will come when your children won't turn their backs on you the way mine have on me," the mother slobbered.

"Oh, Mother, let's not be silly!"

"So, it's silly I am! She with her airs and her primping and powdering and cooing and billing for a black devil of a Protestant. So, it's silly I am!"

Peggy poured coffee, buttered a slice of white bread, and sat down at the kitchen table.

"Marry a black devil out of Hell! A Protestant!" the mother exclaimed sarcastically, standing over Peggy with her hands on her hefty hips. "Setting yourself against the wishes of one of God's noble men. Disgracing your home and your hard-working father, and me, your mother, who bore you, and washed your diapers, and raised you."

"I'm not doing anything wrong, and you can't talk to me like that! I'm not a child or a baby any more," Peggy said, struggling to check a flow of tears.

"Why, the priest of God won't even marry you. He knows your ilk. Ah, the day will come! The day will come when you'll regret what you're doing to your poor mother. And when it does, I only hope that your heart does not ache as my poor heart aches, and that the curse of God will not be put on your soul."

Mrs. Collins followed Peggy to her bedroom and to the front door.

"Go, you whore, and never come back for all that I may care!"

Peggy slammed the door and went down the stairs sobbing.

III

"Mary, God has given us another spring day," Father Gilhooley floridly said as he expanded comfortably in a chair. His housekeeper set an ample breakfast on the table before him, and he said Grace before eating heartily.

As he slowly stirred his coffee, Mary ushered in a boy of about twelve who stood by the entrance, blushing and breathless with awe.

"What's the trouble, son?"

"Father . . . can . . . can you give me Holy Communion?" the boy asked.

"But you know, son, mass is at eight o'clock."

With several stuttering lapses, the boy exclaimed that he was making the nine first Fridays for a very special intention, and this morning the alarm clock had not worked, so he hadn't woke up until around eight-twenty. He'd run all the way to church, but had arrived after Holy Communion. He was terribly worried for fear that his Fridays be broken, and he looked pleadingly at the priest.

Father Gilhooley answered that there were no more hosts and he couldn't consecrate any because he had already said mass.

"Father, does a spiritual communion count?" the boy said with timid hope, fumbling with his cap as he spoke. "When I was running to church, all the way, I tried to think of God and holy things, and keep my mind on them and imagine that I was receiving Holy Communion."

Beaming broadly, the priest reassured the boy, instructing him to receive Holy Communion on the following morning. He called the lad to him, patted his head, and gave him a nickel.

"God bless you, son!" the priest said as the boy left.

Slowly drinking his coffee, a glow of gratification spread through the pastor. For had not this small incident been another demonstration of the power of God and the Church to enflame young hearts with piety? And he and his assistants and the good sisters teaching in the parish schools, they were all doing their work well in the Master's vineyard. The seeds of faith planted in that lad's heart would sprout forth a thousandfold in rich spiritual fruits lovely to the sight of God Almighty. His name was Colahan, and his father ran a drug store at Sixty-first and Vernon. A good family. Mr. Colahan was a good man and he had contributed fifty dollars to last Sunday's Easter Collection. And the lad was just the type that God would call to His holy alter. He was reminded, too, that he should instruct the sisters to talk on vocations to the graduating class until the end of the school term in June. And he would deliver a sermon on the subject one of these Sundays. Also, Father Doneggan and Father Marcel could go over to the classrooms. For one of his few disappointments at Saint Patrick's was that not one of its sons from the parish school had yet been ordained. He believed that the parish school should be sending two or three boys, at least, from each graduating class to Quigley Seminary to start studying for the priesthood. This was an aim that required cooperation and concentration.

After breakfast, he read his morning mail in his small office. Several letters from needy parishioners requesting funds were marked off for Father Doneggan's attention, and he would refer them to a Catholic charity organization. He opened a vituperative letter from an anti-Catholic, unsigned, and he cast it in his waste basket with the word *bigot*. He knew that he was a minister of God's true church, and that Christ Himself had built the church upon the rock of Peter, promising that the gates of Hell would not prevail against it. Such missives could not shake him. His face suddenly broke into a beaming smile as he picked up several letters containing delayed donations to the Easter Collection. But two were five-dollar checks from families which could have well afforded at least twenty-five. Another was from a politician giving fifty dollars when twice that amount would not have hurt him. His flock was made up of people who were good and generous, but some of them required to be more strongly impressed with a sense of their duty to contribute to the support of their pastor. And he would have to remember that when he spoke on the next regular collection. That reminded him that he ought soon again to be delivering that sermon of his: *Mother Church; Why She Is the Only True One.* It was one of his best sermons. And since he had three shelves of the works of Longfellow, Shakespeare, and the other great literary masters, he would have to be looking through them to find a few apt quotations for his sermons. No harm in making them more erudite.

His mail read, he seated himself in a deep and comfortable chair, and discovered, as usual, that the morning paper was full of dismaying items. Ah, the age was sinful and pagan. Prohibition and bootleggers and gangsters, and the younger generation running wild, promiscuous dances, assaults on women, people going blind and dying in the streets from moonshine . . . ah, yes, a sinful and pagan age. Still, he knew that the people of his flock were much better Catholics than those in many a parish. And why? He was not immodest, no, he was only recognizing a true fact when he thought that it was his own example before them, his teaching and guidance in sermons and the confessional. He knew, too, that he was a much more conscientious shepherd than Kiley from Saint Rose's church. And Kiley wouldn't be a Monsignor today if he hadn't shown off and put on airs. Well, no one could accuse Father Gilhooley of advancing himself by showing off and playing politics.

But that Collins girl? She still seemed determined to marry that Protestant scamp after all his dissuasion, after he had talked to her parents, explained to her, given counsel that not only was the fruit of his own long experience but also of the Church's ten thousand years of wisdom. And she, only a chit of a thing. Well, they had come from Kiley's parish. What else could he expect? And her whole family had given only five dollars to the Easter Collection. If Kiley paid less attention to the Cathedral on the north side, and more to his own people, and if her parents had raised the girl properly, instilling in her respect for authority and her elders, and a proper fear of the Almighty, she wouldn't be crossing him now to the endangerment of her immortal soul. Well, he had told her, and he would not permit the marriage. It was a bad business. Ah, a bad business!

He read his office for the day, and then walked to look out the window with a drifting glance. Below him was the large rectangular-shaped parish yard. It was to the right of the church building and ringed with an iron picket fence, a half block of land alive with spring greenness. Soon the building on this ground would be started. Soon men would be digging, preparing to lay the foundation for one of the most beautiful churches in the whole city of Chicago. With pride and gratification, he continued to stand by his window, his hands in his trouser pockets beneath his cassock, his dream bursting like a rocket in his mind. When he had come to this parish in 1900 there had been nothing, only a handful of the faithful, and he had celebrated his first mass on a winter Sunday morning in a vacant and chilly store on Sixty-first Street. This parish, it was the work of his own hand, and his own heart, and his own mind, and his own soul, and his own faith, the dedication of his life, which he had given to God. And he had been happy here in this vineyard of the Master. Now his greatest happiness and triumph lay ahead of him. He prayed God to permit him to witness it. But God would. God had preserved his health to this date. Ah, yes, he had built up the present parish and school, and now it was free of debt. Saint Patrick's was one of the few parishes in the city totally free of debt. Of that he was certain. And with the slowly accumulating sinking fund he had established for the new church, and the drive for funds that he was now almost ready to launch, he would build an edifying house of the Lord, a monument to stand in the Creator's honor long after, years and years after, he would have returned to the dust from whence he had come. This dream and this hope, it was his life, his life's blood, and the mere contemplation of it intoxicated him with a sweet elation and pleasure. It would be a church second to none, the envy of pastors throughout the diocese, a temple and a house of beauty and worship that would make the Cardinal Archbishop take notice of him. Perhaps then and on the merits of his work he would be made . . . Monsignor Gilhooley. He could visualize himself in this parish, in the new church which would draw rich and well-to-do people to the neighborhood. He could imagine himself in the rear of the church at late Sunday masses when the people would file out, inspired after the mass and by the beauty of the church, going home to happy dinners with the word and fear of God in their hearts, nodding and smiling to him as they left. Ah!

The thought of that chit of a Collins girl again broke upon him. She, only eighteen years old, and to keep coming back to him, wasting his time with her begging and pleading after he had given her his final word. That chit of a girl! Well, he would not sanction the marriage to a Protestant. But now he had lost, beyond recapturing, that splendid vision he had just experienced. He turned from the window.

IV

"Gee, Kid, you look fagged out. Why are you so sad?" Madge said to Peggy as they sat munching chicken-salad sandwiches and sipping malted milks for lunch in a crowded and noisy Loop ice cream parlor.

"I'm terribly worried, Madge."

"I hope it's not your darling Graham again."

"It's serious. Graham's a dear. I adore him. But it's the same awful trouble. It makes me feel just awful. I saw Father Gilhooley with my mother again last night, and he still refuses to let us get married. And my mother sides with him, too, and we had such a terrible fight this morning. I left the house with the jitters, and cried halfway downtown on the elevated train."

"You're taking it too seriously, Collins. I'd like to see anybody pull that kind of a trick on me! I'd just like to see them! Come on, Kid, snap out of it. Tell them you've got your own life to live, and if they don't like the way you live it, they can lump it."

"But Madge, dear, you know if you're not married in the church it's not marriage at all, and then it will be living in mortal sin. He won't sanction our marriage, and my mother keeps throwing fits. Gee, Kid, I'm going nearly crazy."

"You poor kid! Now don't cry."

"I can't help it. I love Graham. And he's so sweet and kind to me. If I had to give him up, I don't know what I'd do. I'd just go and throw myself in the lake, I guess, because then I wouldn't care about anything any more."

"Listen, Kiddo, don't pay any attention to them. Take my advice, dearie, and you and Graham just step down to the City Hall, and then let them jaw their ears off. God isn't a school teacher or a fierce old giant, and he isn't going to go punishing people just because they love each other and are honest about it. You and Graham just go away and get married. It isn't hocus pocus that some old fool says that counts and makes you married. It's what you and Graham feel inside your hearts."

"Madge, darling, you're not a Catholic, and you just don't understand."

"Well, if that's what it means to be a Catholic, I'm glad I'm not one."

"Madge, please, don't say that!"

Madge shrugged her shoulders in a gesture of resignation.

"Of course, Peg, it isn't my business, but honestly, I can't understand why you let an old fossil of a priest who doesn't know what it's all about go sticking his nose in your business the way you do."

"But if we're not married in the church, it'll be living in sin."

"Oh, don't be a fool, Peg!"

V

The pastor partook of a sufficient luncheon with Father Doneggan, the wiry, thin, energetic blond assistant pastor who was in his early thirties. After suggesting to his assistant that they should start a drive to turn the minds of boys and girls in the school to the subject of vocations, Father Gilhooley mentioned the Collins girl. Father Doneggan, speaking with careful reserve, suggested that the only course of action, he feared, was to marry the couple.

"Pat, I shall not!" Father Gilhooley said with stern stubbornness, meaning will for shall.

"Father, you know, naturally, that I agree with you in total on the question of mixed marriages. But in this case, the girl being as set and as determined as she is, I think that marriage is the lesser of the two evils involved."

"Pat, it's a bad business. What she needs is for her mother to give her a hiding that will drive some sense into that flighty little head of hers," the pastor said as a prelude to filling his mouth with steak until his cheeks bulged. Chewing, he added, "I shall not permit it!"

Father Doneggan knew the uselessness of reply. He recalled with silent and frustrated anger two fairly recent run-ins he had had with Father Gilhooley. He had tried to persuade him that instead of preaching sermons and asking for contributions repeatedly, they might raise money for the new church by holding bazaars that would also serve the added purpose of giving the parishioners a good time and welding them together socially. And Father Gilhooley had disapproved because the raffles held at bazaars constituted, in his mind, gambling, and he feared demoralizing the parish and setting a bad example for the young. Father Doneggan had tried, also, to convince the pastor that they should organize a parish young people's society and conduct clean dances in the parish auditorium. But the auditorium was on consecrated ground, so Father Gilhooley had refused.

Now Father Doneggan continued eating. Father Gilhooley was in authority. And the assistant was living in his own agony of doubts and temptations. He was beginning to see that the priesthood was the wrong place for him. The cancer of doubt, doubt even of the existence of the very God he served, was poisoning him almost to madness. He was drinking more and more and he would not always be able to hide it. Sooner or later he would face a showdown. He would even, possibly, have to face the choice of a future of hypocrisy or else the road of an unfrocked priest, marked and scarred and defamed on every side, and almost totally unfitted for any worldly occupation. And the issue raised by the Collins girl only strengthened his doubts, adding one more instance to the contradictions between the raw life of emotions and passions and sins and waywardness poured into his ears in the confessional, and the dogmatization of life in the formal philosophy of the Church. He looked almost enviously at Father Gilhooley, who was so corpulently contented, the fires of the flesh now dead embers, with gluttony and eating his only sin. Did the complacency on that blown ruddy face extend clean through to the man's soul? Was it sainthood or a barricade of fat around his spirit? Anyway, he had not the energy to try convincing his pastor. He was drained by his own internal struggles. His will was paralyzed. Quickly finishing his luncheon, he left on the pretext of working over next Sunday's sermon.

VI

At three-thirty, Father Gilhooley left the parish house for his afternoon stroll. Walking, he gazed at the fenced-in grounds where he would build his new church. In a few years now, when there would be a Eucharistic Congress in Chicago, his beautiful new house of worship would be an honor to God, a credit to himself, a tribute to the faith he served. It would be a mark of such beauty that thousands of visitors would come to behold its wonders. Visiting clergymen, bishops, perhaps even the Papal Delegate, would view it, and after that he would take a trip to the old country, and he might go, too, as a Monsignor. He stepped into his church and thought, as if in fresh discovery, that it was very rapidly becoming increasingly inadequate for the needs of the parish. His new church would make the neighborhood grow, attracting to it the best types of well-to-do Catholics. It would be a rich parish. And Monsignor Gilhooley, wouldn't he then outshine Kiley!

As he stood thus in the rear of his church, his dreams and his visions alive within him, he saw a small boy leave a pew, hastily genuflect without touching his knee to the flooring, bless himself at the holy water font with his left hand, and bound through the swinging doors. Father Gilhooley quickly followed and called the lad back.

"Good afternoon, Father," the boy timidly muttered, retracing his steps up the church stairs.

Answering the priest's questions, the boy said that he was William Markham in the sixth grade of the parish school. Father Gilhooley promptly recalled that the only contribution from a Markham to the Easter Collection had been two dollars.

"Did Sister ever teach you how to bless yourself?" the priest sternly asked.

"Yes, Father."

He ordered the boy to demonstrate. William slowly and correctly made the sign of the Cross. Father Gilhooley told him that he should always bless himself with his right hand, and when he genuflected in the presence of the Blessed Sacrament his knee should touch the floor.

The pastor stopped in at Strunsky's drug store for a cigar. The pinched druggist, aware that Father Gilhooley's displeasure could decrease his business, obsequiously nodded agreement to the priest's platitudes, and in parting they agreed on the weather. Several passing laborers and school boys tipped their hats and caps to him, and he acknowledged the greeting with a dignified nod. Women parishioners greeted him with smiles and salutations which could have been no more humble had he been one of the Twelve Apostles. He paused to discuss the weather with the attractive and smartly dressed Mrs. Freeman. Her husband, a manufacturer of tennis rackets, had contributed a hundred dollars to the Easter Collection. Patting her youngster's head, he told her what a fine healthy child she had. She said she hoped it would grow up to be as good a man and a priest as the one who had baptized him. Beaming over the compliment, Father Gilhooley said that he knew with the good home influences in which the child was being reared, he was certain the baby would develop and one day be a tribute both to its parents and to Saint Patrick's parish. She thanked him, and they parted. A black shawled, hunched little Irish woman with a shrivelled face almost bent her back in bowing to him. Superstitious admiration and reverence brought life, even freshness, into her small, suspicious eyes. She again humbly bowed, and mumbled a foreign phrase learned by rote,

"Ga lob Jasus Christe."

The homage paid to him as a man of God was warming, gratifying. This peasant woman, with her simple faith and humility, stirred in him memories of his own Irish mother. Ah, that she were alive to see her son today. He prided himself on his ascent from lowly origins, his race. Had not the Irish preserved the faith in the face of oppression? And did not the Church owe a great credit to those simple Irish mothers who had been the backbone of Catholicism in Ireland, the women out of whose wombs heroic and sainted priests had come? If only the young chits of girls these days would learn the great simple lessons of truth from their Irish mothers and grandmothers! Chits of girls like the Collins one, with her powder and her lipstick, and her thinking she loved a Protestant.

He called the woman grandmother, said that it was a fine day, and told her how well and how young she looked. Passing on, his good humor lushly expanded, and again he grew proud in the dignity of his office. He walked like a great man. Only again the recollection of that Collins girl threatening to cross him bobbed annoyingly in his mind, and his cheeks flushed from anger.

I'll permit none of it! he vowed to himself.

Strolling back with an afternoon paper under his arm, he met Father Georgiss, the pastor of Saint Sofia's, the Greek Catholic Church across from Saint Patrick's. Father Georgiss was a bearded, dark-browed man who always looked at Father Gilhooley with a roguish and enigmatic twinkle in his eyes. Scholarly, urbane, skeptical, even cosmopolitan alongside of the Roman Catholic priest, he usually managed to impress an uneasiness, even a sense of inferiority, upon Father Gilhooley. Father Georgiss' church was larger and more impressive than Saint Patrick's, but seeing him, Father Gilhooley insisted to himself that it wasn't beautiful. Too Oriental. Too sensuous. The two clergymen spoke to each other with excessive politeness, and Father Gilhooley assuaged his falling pride by casually remarking that very soon now he would let out the contracts and begin operations on his church. Father Georgiss congratulated him, but again there was that disconcerting look in his eyes. He accepted Father Gilhooley's invitation to drop over some evening for a chat. He said that he was busy these days pursuing his studies of Byzantine civilization. It was a great civilization, and it had saved Christianity for centuries from the Turks, and Father Gilhooley should read of it. Father Gilhooley said he would like to have Father Georgiss tell him of it, thinking silently that with all this Greek priest's reading of history he could not see the truth and the simple necessity of the dogma of Papal Infallibility. They parted politely, agreeing that God had given them splendid weather.

VII

Peggy sat on the steps before the box-like yellow apartment building on Prairie Avenue where the Collins family lived. She studiously looked into her purse mirror, and dabbed her face to mask the evidence that she had been crying. She hated her mother. That was an awful thought. But she didn't care! She didn't. She hated her! She did! And it was all so silly. This business of Catholics and Protestants. Graham's little finger was worth more than any number of Catholic boys she knew. And he was good and decent. Good to her. And she didn't care. She loved him. He had such nice eyes, and she dreamed about his eyes, and his lips, and she was always thinking she saw him on the street. She loved him. She wanted to love him with all of herself forever, and forever, and her mother and Father Gilhooley were so silly about it. They must have never been in love. Because she knew that she couldn't help herself, and she would love Graham even if her soul would burn for all eternity in Hell. And God! He couldn't be like Father Gilhooley and want her to give up Graham. And the way her mother had cut up at the supper table! So silly. Oh, she just wanted to be away from it all and to be alone with her Graham.

And she was going to see Father Gilhooley and tell him he would just have to marry them. And again tears came to her eyes. Because maybe it was too late now. Maybe religion had already been thrown between them like some terrible shadow, and gee, she was afraid that they could never be happy together. She couldn't give him up, and she didn't want to, and . . . she saw him swinging along the street, so tall, so handsome. She tried to dry her tears.

VIII

Father Gilhooley was contented, at peace with himself, at peace with the world, at peace with his God, after his hearty supper. When his sense of almost somnolent well-being was disturbed by Mary who told him that that Collins girl was back again, he frowned. He said, sternly, that he wouldn't see her, and followed his housekeeper into the small reception room where Peggy and Graham waited.

"Good evening, Father!" Peggy said meekly and with respect.

"Good evening, Father!" Graham said, restrained.

"Good evening, my girl! Good evening, sir! Be seated!" Father Gilhooley curtly said.

"Father . . ." Peggy began in a hesitant manner.

"I am a very busy man. I do not see, for the life of me, why you return here to waste my time after I have told you definitely and finally that I cannot permit such a marriage in my parish."

"But, Father, what can we do? We can't get married in another parish," Peggy said, despair creeping into her voice.

"I have already explained my reasons fully to both of you. I have nothing personally against this young man, ah, Mr. . . . . ah . . ."

"McIntosh," Peggy volunteered.

"Mr. McIntosh, my decision is not personal and directed against you. I am opposed to mixed marriages on principle and on reflection after long years of experience as a clergyman. I have learned that oil and water do not mix. And this applies to the marriage of persons of different religions. I have witnessed the irreparable evil and the ruination of souls that results from mixed marriages. This I have already explained to you young people. If I sanction this marriage, others will come, and you two will set a bad example for all the young people of my parish. I am not the kind of a person who waits to lock his stable door after the horse has been stolen."

"But, Father, suppose I had been insincere and pretended to be converted. Then you could not have objected to our marriage. Because I have chosen not to be a hypocrite you refuse to let us be married in your church," Graham said, controlling his voice, but the expression in his eyes was hard, as if they were knifing the priest.

"Sir, that is a matter for your own conscience. My action is impersonal, and I am thinking not simply of your temporal happiness, but of the soul of this girl which has been placed in my care, since I happen to be her pastor, and thus her spiritual guardian. And also, I am thinking of the souls

of many more young people like her in my parish. I am older than you two
people, and I am drawing on long experience, and the wisdom of my
church through long years and centuries of history when I speak. You two
are young, and you are letting yourselves be blinded by what you call love.
I am older than you, and I see more. I see the danger to this girl's immortal soul, and to the souls of any offspring you might have."

"But, Father, Graham, Mr. McIntosh, is perfectly willing to let our children be raised Catholic, and he will not interfere with my fulfilling my religious obligations," Peggy said, blushing.

"My dear girl, a house divided against itself will fall. A home cannot
be built unless there is sympathy and understanding erected on the religion of God. There cannot be sympathy unless both parties see eye to eye
on religion, because religion is the foundation stone of the Catholic home."

"But Father, we love each other!" Peggy exclaimed impulsively, almost
despairingly, and Graham glanced at her with raised eyebrows, pained.

"You young people take my advice. Forget this marriage, and stay away
from each other for six months. Then come back to see me and see if I am
not right. Mixed marriages are the principal cause of the pagan evil of di-
vorce which spreads through the world these days like a cancer, and in so
many cases it paves a sure road to Hell. I have given my decision, my dear
girl, because I am your pastor, responsible to Almighty God for your soul."

"But Father . . ." Peggy exclaimed, startled, ready to cry.

"Father, you can't stop us!" Graham said, his face white, set.

"There is nothing further for me to say. Good evening!" Father Gilhooley said, arising and leaving the room with a swish of his cassock.

IX

From a window he saw them pass slowly, arm in arm, under a lamp-
light, and move on, their figures growing vague in the spring dusk. His
blood rose. He frowned, reassuring himself that he was right, and acting
wisely for the best interests of both of them and in accordance with the
dictates and spirit of God and of God's True Church. And in his whole time
as a pastor at Saint Patrick's no one had ever crossed him as this chit of a
girl had.

I'll have none of it, he told himself in rising fury.

His anger cooled. You could take a horse to water, but you couldn't
make him drink. He had done his best to explain and guide the girl, and
under the circumstances he was forced to recognize that marriage was the

lesser evil. But he felt, sure as the summer followed the spring, certain as the night succeeded the day, that the girl was paving the road to her own perdition. He called Father Doneggan and instructed him to telephone the girl in the morning and arrange all the details. But he would not perform the marriage as the girl had requested when she had first come to him.

He returned to the window. They were gone somewhere with their love and their hugging and kissing. The spring night now quilted and shadowed the yard, and he could hear voices and street sounds through the opened window. He thought again of how gray towers would rise above this quiet and darkened grass, piercing the blue heavens of God on nights like this one. The gray towers of his magnificent church, with vaulted nave, marble pillars, a grand organ, a marble altar imported from Italy, stained glass windows, hand-carved woodwork, a marble pulpit from which he would deliver the first sermon to be preached in the new church, packed with faithful parishioners for the first mass. He could see how the edifice, in stone and steel and wood and marble, would stand in beauty and inspiration to goodness and the doing of God's holy Will amongst his flock . . . and it would make him Monsignor Gilhooley.

But that chit of a girl! Suddenly he enjoyed the realization that she was making for herself a fiery bed in the eternal flames of Hell. A slip of a girl crossing him who might someday even be . . . Bishop Gilhooley.

He turned from the window, the excitement of his dream ebbing in his mind. And for the first time in his long pastorhood he knew that he had been . . . defeated.

[1932]

All Things Are Nothing to Me

I

"Who was the jigg I seen you talking with?" Jim Doyle asked Cousin Joe.

"That must have been Lincoln. He was on the track team with me in high school. He's a crack sprinter, and we have a class together this quarter. He lives near here."

"He does, huh? The goddam nigger! He's living around here, huh?"

"Why shouldn't he?" Joe asked.

"Why should he!" Jim stormed, becoming so angry that he paused, inarticulate, his face bloating with his wrath. "What are you, a nigger lover? Did that A.P.A. University do that to you too?" Jim turned to his younger brother, Tommy, who joined them in the musty and dim parlor. "He's starting to love niggers now."

"I suppose that next he'll be taking out a black dame," Tommy said with heated sarcasm.

"I wouldn't put it past him," Jim said.

"I don't see why we should think that we're any better than they are because our skin is a different color," Joe said calmly.

"You wouldn't. That's what comes of reading all those books the atheistic college professors tell you to read," Jim said.

"And I suppose you like a nigger's stink. Well, I don't. I worked with them, and I know how they smell. If you like their smell, you're welcome to it. They're animals, just like dogs. They ain't human," Tommy said with confidence.

"A white man can have perspirational odors."

"Never mind using them big words. Can that highbrow stuff!" Jim shouted.

"For Christ sake, talk American!" Tommy sneered.

"Well, what's the matter with them?" Joe asked.

"I'll tell you. Look at your aunt out there in the kitchen now, cooking your supper. She's getting old, and this building is all she has in the world. What are the niggers doing to its value? They're trying to come into a good white man's neighborhood, spoiling and degrading property values. They're robbing your aunt of the value of her building, and it's her bread and butter. Just to love niggers I suppose you'd even see her in the poorhouse," Jim bawled.

"He's got no appreciation or gratitude after all she's done for him. She took him as an infant when his mother died, and raised him, and that's all the gratitude he shows," Tommy said.

"I always said he never should have gone to that damn school," Jim said proudly.

II

"Hello, Unc," Joe said, smiling as they sat down to supper, and Unc's creased, unshaven face tensed into a scowl, his glasses set down toward the center of his nose.

"Stop plaguin' him," said Aunt Maggie, a stout, bovine, sad-faced woman with gray hair.

"Just because you think you're smart and educated, you don't have to be acting superior to him. There's plenty of people in the world smarter than you are, and they didn't go to an atheistic university to get their education, either," Jim said.

"I was only saying hello to Unc, that's all," Joe said, and Unc ate, heedless of their talk.

"Unc and me saw a movie last night, *Broken Hearts,* and I tell you it's a shame what these modern girls and women are doing with their smoking and drinking and cutting up something shameful," Aunt Maggie said as she cut a slice of meat.

"And those bobbed-haired dolls over on the campus, they're not slow," Tommy said.

"Don't be picking up with any of that trash," Aunt Maggie said with a mouthful, looking at her nephew.

"Yeah, you! Nix on the running around with the dames. You're going over there to get an education," Tommy said.

"You know, you can't get an education and make the most of your time if you go chasing after those shameless she-devils, with their bobbed hair and their cigarettes, and hardly a stitch of clothing to hide themselves. You got to mind your studies," Aunt Maggie said.

"What do you think, Unc? Think that bald head of yours would make the flappers fall for you?"

"Shut up!" Unc whined, scowling.

"Now, Joe, I told you to stop plaguin' him!" Aunt Maggie said.

"Well, I just thought the girls might like Unc's whiskers."

"You think you're wise, don't you!" Tommy said.

"If I was wise, I wouldn't have to go to school," Joe said.

"All that University does is make him half-baked like the professors he's got," Tommy said.

"I hear that Mrs. Swanson down the street is sick, and that her daughter has bobbed hair, and is cutting up something fierce. Poor woman, I seen her on the street two weeks ago, and I told myself that now there was a woman who should be home and in bed. And today I met Mrs. O'Neill and she told me."

Unc spilled gravy on the white tablecloth.

"It'll soon be spring, and all the trees will be green. I guess I'll have to fix a nice garden in the back yard," Unc said.

"And mother will be able to take some nice drives on Sundays soon," Jim said.

"I hope not next Sunday. I was planning on usin' the car," Tommy said.

"You're always planning on using the car," Jim said angrily.

"Why shouldn't I when it's idle in the garage?" Tommy quickly and hotly retorted.

"That car is mother's. And any time she wants to go riding you can forget about using it as a taxi service for them hoodlum friends of yours," Jim said.

"Boys, please, now, don't be quarreling!" said Mrs. Doyle.

"Hey, for Christ sake!" Jim yelled as Joe collected the plates. "Hey, don't be pulling such stunts. Take a few at a time and never mind a load like that. We don't want you breaking those dishes. They're a wedding present of your aunt's."

"All right, Coz," Joe said from the kitchen as he set the soiled plates on the board by the sink.

He brought in coffee and cake.

"I suppose he'd like it better now if he was eating with a nigger," Tommy sneered.

"Sure and glory be! He isn't going with the black ones, is he? What will be the end of it with him going to that school! And wasn't his father, Mike, telling me only the other day that Joe O'Reilley, the lawyer, wouldn't let his nephew go there because they hate the Catholics. And didn't I know from the start that no good could come out of that school where they have abandoned the word of God," complained Aunt Maggie.

"He could have gone to Saint Vincent's night school like Tommy O'Reilley, and he would get just as good an education," Jim said.

"He wanted the frills," Aunt Maggie said.

"What's wrong with the Jesuit university?" Tommy belligerently asked Joe.

"It's too far out on the north side," Joe said.

"It would have been better than that A.P.A. dump across the park," Tommy said.

"That house of the devil," Aunt Maggie added.

"Aunt Margaret, sure 'tis a terrible place, I tell you. Why, they take every Catholic student who goes there and lock him up in one of the towers of the main library building and keep him there until he promises he'll become an atheist," Joe said.

"Nix, wise guy! Never mind making fun of your aunt," Jim said.

"Somebody ought to kick his pants," Tommy said.

"I'd like to see one of your half-baked professors stand up to a priest like Father Shannon, the missionary, and give the arguments they use, weaning inexperienced half-baked students like yourself away from the faith. Those professors wouldn't know whether they were coming or going when Father Shannon got through with them," Jim said boastfully, as if he could take credit for the priest's abilities.

"If Father Shannon went over there he'd be locked up in a tower, too, and held until he swore to become an atheist," Joe said, drawing looks of disgust from the whole table.

"Some people talks too much," Unc said laconically.

"Why don't you go and try to give some of your arguments to Father Gilhooley?" Tommy challenged.

"He'd ask me for a contribution to the next Coal Collection," Joe said.

"He's even disrespectful of priests. See! I told you what would happen to him when he went over to that dump on the Midway," Jim gloated.

"Indeed, 'tis a bad business!" Aunt Maggie sighed.

"Well, he'll learn some day when he gets older and has to face life," Tommy said, arising and dropping his unfolded napkin beside his plate.

Jim frowned as Mrs. Doyle arose and followed her son out of the room. He shouted a warning for her not to be giving him any money, and nervously wrung and fingered his napkin. He arose, dropped it, left the room. Looking at Unc's stolid and unilluminated face, Joe heard shouting and cursing. He shook his head and thought of Edgar Guest's poem on the home which he had once read somewhere.

"Hop in the bowl!" he heard Tommy yell before slamming the door as he went out.

"But he's my son," he heard his aunt saying in answer to long and loud recriminations from Jim.

"Well, he'll be drunk again," Jim said, raising his voice.

"God forbid! He said he only wanted to see a show, and that he'd be in early and up in the morning to look for a job."

Joe cleared the table and washed the dishes. Unc, complacently smoking his corn-cob pipe, dried them.

"The grass and the trees will be green again soon."

"Yes, Unc. The grass will be green, and there will be leaves on the trees. That's indisputable," Joe idly said as he hung the dishpan on a hook above the sink.

III

The house was quiet now, with Aunt Maggie and Unc gone to see another movie at the Prairie Theatre and Jim out to see his girl. And always when he was alone in the house, Joe felt queer, with a vague unhappiness trickling through him. He had the feeling of being in a tomb that had been turned into a museum. The lights were dim. The parlor was stuffy and musty, and hardly ever used since his uncle, Aunt Maggie's husband, had died. He had the feeling that nothing could be touched, nothing disturbed, that most of the chairs were not to be sat in, that the victrola could not be played. Music, life, these were held without the door. He sat striving conscientiously to study his Pol Sci notebook, carefully proceeding through the notes he had so diligently scribbled down from his readings and from the classroom discussions and lectures, struggling as he read to retain as much as possible in his memory. The winter quarter exams were only a week off, and he was anxious and uncertain, because he always worried before his examinations, no matter how hard he studied. He lacked confidence in himself. And he felt that he knew why. His home, his background. It was only after having started at the university that he had become aware of the poverty in his home life, his background, his people, a poverty not only of mind, but of spirit, even a poverty of the senses, so that they could scarcely even look at many things and enjoy them. And he, too, he had been afflicted with this poverty. He wanted to live more, he wanted to know more, he wanted to see and enjoy more of life, and this limitation of his background was like a hook pulling the confidence out of him. And now, when he was preparing for his examinations, he worried more than he should. For the University had unleashed in him a kind of hunger. Doors to unimagined possibilities in life had been opened to him on every side, and here he stood, surrounded by all these opened doors and lacking confidence to enter them, trying to substitute intense determination for this deficiency. He bent over his notebook, gritting himself to grind on in his study. And stray thoughts intruded. He became restive. He discovered again and again that he was losing track of what he read and letting his mind float through vagrant thoughts and fancies. And he would pull himself back to the book, not even aware of what had been the content of his thoughts and fancies. And then again his mind resisted concentration, and he dreamily tried to imagine himself after the exams, free, feeling that so much more accomplished in his university career had been put behind him. But to do that he had to study. And tonight, study was hard.

Suddenly he gave up the struggle, left his study table, and donning a cap and old sweater went out for a walk. The night was clear in Washington Park, and the early March winds were stiff and invigorating. In the distance the lagoon glittered as he walked toward it over the hard, choppy ground. Once outside the house, he lost that sense of gloomy constriction. He was no longer restless. He could walk slowly, think. And these days, what he needed to do more than anything else was to think. And he scarcely had the time for it. He had three classes, and had to study two hours a day for each of them. Then there was the work on term papers, field work in sociology, daily work-out with the squad out for the track teams, and the housework he had to do at home. He was turning into a machine, and just at the time when he had to think, and think hard.

Here he was, twenty-one now, and he was just discovering how he had been brought up and educated on lies. All these years, at home, in church, in grammar school and high school, they had built up his brain on a foundation of prejudices, of things that were not true. Now he was seeing, learning how they had turned him into a walking pack of lies. And how was he going to go on? Was he going to pretend that he still believed in all these lies, or wasn't he? Because if he wasn't, it meant a break, it meant that scenes like the one tonight were only the merest dress rehearsal. He had one foot still in the world of lies. He carried it with him wherever he went, in memories and nostalgias, in ties that bound him by invisible threads. He was sunken in it, in the world of Fifty-eighth Street, and no matter what he did he felt that he would always carry it with him, as a sense of pain, as a wound in his memory. And it was stupid and prejudiced, and he no longer felt as if he fitted into it. He did not want to be insincere, a liar. And how could he retain his sincerity and live in it? He wanted to be honest, and honesty was impossible in a life builded upon lies. And they all believed in lies, would live for them, even perhaps sacrifice their lives for them. His aunt, and his father, and his cousins, and his brothers, and friends, they all lived benignly in these lies and stupidities. And he had to, or else he would wound and hurt them, fight with them. They would not let him attain his freedom. He had to pay a price for it, and the price was they. And now that his eyes were opened, what would he do?

He had never expected that such problems would face him when he had started in at the University. He had gone there thinking that he would acquire the knowledge that would make him a success in life, the same way that Joe O'Reilley, the lawyer, and Barney McCormick, the politician, were successes. And now, after five quarters in college, he was all at sea. Every truth in life seemed to have been ripped out of him, as teeth are pulled. The world was all wrong, and he felt that he should help to make it right, and not continue agreeing that it was all right, plucking profit out of wrongs and lies.

He felt, too, as if reading more books and studying was not going to help him unless he made up his mind. No book could really help him very much now. Will power alone could. For what he must do was to make up his mind. He must cast these lies out of him, cut them out as if with a knife. And he realized now that that meant that he would be forever estranged from the world of Fifty-eighth Street, and that never again could he be in rapport with its people, and its people were his people. He was saddened, and he stood still, thinking, idly listening to the wind as it shaved nearby bushes like a razor. His bonds were broken, or would be, once he announced his changed convictions without any equivocation. They would all look at him as a traitor, a stool pigeon. They would think that he had lost his mind. And because he liked them, yes, loved them, it would hurt him. And he would be alone, without moorings. Everything that he believed, held as truth, all that he had been brought up in . . . was gone. And again he heard the wind as if it were a melancholy song.

It was not just that they, his people, could not accept him. He could no longer really accept them. Worlds had been placed between them both. At best, he would go on, and his love would turn to pity for them. The very fact that he was going to college made them suspect him, as his cousins had shown at the supper table. And he had thought, too, that when a young man had tried seriously to work his way through school and win an education for himself, that the world would applaud and praise and help him, and that, at least, his closest relatives would give him all the encouragement and assistance they could. In the abstract, they all favored the idea. They assumed that it was the way to become a success. In the concrete, in his case, he was met with distrust, envy, suspicion. They nagged him. They seemed to try and hinder him at every turn. Every day, almost, it seemed that they strove to discourage him by telling him that he was wasting his time, and that he would be a failure.

It was jealousy, envy, spite. And it was fear. And hatred, the hatred begotten from narrowness, bigotry, ignorance. They hated knowledge. It was something mysterious and dangerous. Knowledge in politics would disturb the politicians with their hands in the grab bag. And the politicians were leaders, models, heroes, in the Irish milieu that had been his. Even his cousins, Jim and Tommy, fancied themselves to be politicians. Like two weeks ago, when Tommy had seen people looking at the vacant apartment over them and talking with these people he had said that he was in the political game. He was a politician because he wore a badge on election days and handed out cards asking people to vote Democratic. And Jim acted as a kind of assistant precinct captain and had a minor political job. So they, too, were politicians, and they had their fingers in the political grab bag. And they knew all that was to be known about politics. Knowledge in politics disturbed their petty little grabs, and their egos. It destroyed faith in the Church, and the Church was the heart of their world, and so many of the hopes that they saw frustrated in this life—these would be fulfilled in the Heaven of which the priests preached. Now he could see clearly why the Church had carried on such a relentless warfare against science, why priests attacked the University. And also, next summer, he would have to read through that book of White's.

He had talked with Schwartz about these problems, Schwartz who had read so much more than he, who had attained his freedom so much earlier. And Schwartz had told him about a book, *The Ego and His Own*, by Max Stirner. Schwartz had quoted one of the statements made in the book, and Joe had been so impressed by it that he had copied it down and memorized it. Now, thinking of the Church, of politics, he quoted it to himself:

If an age is imbued with an error, some always derive advantage from that error, while the rest have to suffer from it.

And these last quarters at the University he was learning how his own age was so imbued with errors, and how some profited from them, and how so many who did not profit from them wanted to. They were even suffering from the very errors out of which they wanted to snatch a profit. Like Jim and Tommy, and their being in the political game. And that was what he had planned to do, enter politics after he passed his bar examinations. Now if he did, he knew that it meant failure, or profiting out of errors, injustices, dishonesties. It would make him a crook and a liar. It would make Jim a crook. Jim was naturally good and honest and hard working, and he worked hardest to become part of a whole system of graft. And he was stupid, and in his own stupidity he wanted to keep others that way. Joe again asked himself, was that his ideal?

And still, he wondered why did they hate knowing things so? It brought to his mind an incident that had recently happened at home. Tommy had asked him a question about the Civil War. He had been reading about it in a history book, and he had handed the volume to Tommy, showing him the answer to the question, contained in two pages. Tommy had flung the book on the floor, sneered, and hadn't even spoken to Joe for several days. Such reactions made him want to give up and let them go their own way. At first he had tried to explain to them, to help them, to tell them the things he was learning so that they could learn, too. He had wanted to correct their errors, cut down the margins of their ignorance, break down their prejudices, such as the ones they held against Negroes and Jews. He had tried to tell them that the poor were not always poor because of laziness, that men out of work often could not find jobs, and even with the example of Tommy before them who would not work, they had condemned the shiftlessness of others and contended that there was some kind of a job for anybody who wanted to work. The same way, he had, after his field trips in sociology to Italian districts, tried to tell them that the foreigners were the same as any other people and wanted just to live as others did, and be happy. And it had only precipitated another of those stupid and hot-tempered quarrels. Knowing so little, they acted as if they knew everything. Nothing, it seemed, could be done to dent such self-conscious ignorance.

He stopped by the wrinkling lagoon where an aisle of moonlight reflected over the surface to the wooded island. He thought of how the last time his father had been up, he had looked so very old. His father was the same, though. He had worked for forty years in a railroad office. And during the Wilson administration, he had gotten a raise. So Wilson was the touchstone to all knowledge with him. But at the table his father's hand had shaken noticeably, and now the memory of it saddened Joe. It meant that perhaps soon his father would be dead. And what had the poor man gotten out of life? In a clear-cut focus Joe sensed and visioned his father's life for these last many years. His wife dying at Joe's birth. The family split up. The father living in a succession of rooming houses, ruining his stomach in cheap restaurants, lonely with his family separated. And soon now the father would be pensioned off to die. His hopes were centered in Joe. In him, he saw the triumph, the success, the happiness, that he had never sucked out of living. A beaten, frustrated old man now, waiting for his son to make amends for him. All he had ever seemed to have gotten out of life were those occasional drunks he went on. And even when drunk, the old man seemed sad and usually ended up in a crying jag. Joe shook his head. Because he saw clearly what it would mean for him to hurt his father. And hurt him he must, or capitulate. And could he surrender himself as a sacrifice for such things, the contentment of a few people, the broken dreams of an old man? Even if they were his people, his father? It was so damned unfair, too. And needless, if they could only be intelligent. If! His Aunt Maggie, too, she looked for him to do big things. And she, poor woman, had had her troubles. Her husband, a good man, had been a heavy drinker. And now Tommy, drinking, not ever working. And they would be so hurt. It would leave them bewildered, with a wound cutting them to the core of their consciousness. They would feel betrayed as he now felt betrayed. And the whole situation made him see so clearly how life was not something soft, something harmonious, something that was without contradictions. It was hard, stern, and demanded sternness.

He walked on. He knew that he could no longer aspire as they wanted him to, believe as they expected that he would. He could no longer retain his faith in their God, their church, their ideals of success and goodness. He had tried to, these last days. And now he was at the end of his resistance. To continue as he had meant compromising himself, and going on meant turning his whole life into lies and hypocrisy. And at home, their suspicions were not unjustified. They sensed it, all right, just as they had shown tonight at the supper table. And soon, if he told them of his loss of faith, he could imagine the scenes, the scorn they would pour on him. And at times it seemed also that they wanted to drive him to it, so that they could indulge themselves in self-righteousness and self-justification at his expense, so that they could stand superior to him. He shrugged his shoulders. It was all coming. He would have to tell them. He would have to show he had changed, and build his life on truer foundations. Because he was choking with hypocrisy. How could he go on like this much longer, pretending, going to church on Sundays, kneeling to a God in Whom he did not believe, pretending, faking, saying yes as if he agreed with so much of their self-assertive ignorance.

He had an impulse to pity himself. Here he was with no belief, no God, a world inside of himself twisted into a chaos. He often, these days, had the feeling that nothing mattered. Just like the statement he had heard Schwartz quoting from that Stirner book.

All things are nothing to me.

Again he stood by the dark waters of the lagoon with the wind sweeping them. A sense of mystery seemed to settle over them, pervade them. He was without words. He felt that beyond these waters there must be something. Beyond life, there must be something. This living as men did, all this suffering, all this defeat, and unhappiness, and self-inflicted pains and poverty, it could not be all that there was. If so, everything was useless. And if there was no God? And there was none. He could not believe in Him. He suddenly hurled a stone into the waters, and listened to the splash and watched the widening ripples in the moonlight. He hurled another stone, and turned his back to walk home.

He thought of how he would some day die, and there was no God. He was living in a world of death, and if he did not free himself from it he would die twice, many times. He would never have any honesty in his own life. And a pervasive pity seeped through him. He could not hate them, his people. He could only feel sorry for them. How could he hate his father, sitting at the dining-room table, his hands palsied, thin and sunken-cheeked, that ghostly dried-up look to his face? How could he hate his own past, even though it was part of a world that would kill anything that was honest within himself?

And he remembered how, as a boy, he had played in this park where he now walked. He had raced, wrestled, played football, chase-one-chase-all, run-sheep-run, looked at girls who reduced him to flustering shyness and speechlessness. Long and sunny days of boyhood idleness, and they now fell through the dark reaches of his brooding mind like sunlight filtering a feeble warmth on the cold stones of a cellar. Now he wished for them back, wished for their obliviousness to doubts, their acceptance of the stupidities he must now vomit out of himself, their faith. And it was just in those days that he had been betrayed. It was all through those years that false faiths had been implanted in him, that the threads knitting him to what he must now destroy, had been sewn. And yet, he wished, if only things were just simple again.

He heard footsteps behind him, and turned to see a stout familiar figure approaching.

"Hello, Mr. Coady."

The park policeman was older, slower now on his flat feet, than when Joe had been a boy.

"Out looking for them tonight?" Joe asked.

"Oh, hello! Hello, boy! How are ye, Joe?"

"Fine, Mr. Coady. How are you feeling these fine days?"

"Well, Joe, me feet, they ain't what they used to be."

"It's nice out tonight, Mr. Coady."

"Grand, Joe, grand, but still a little chilly for a man when he gets to be my age."

"I was taking a walk."

"Well, it's grand if ye don't catch a chill."

"Pretty soon it will be nice, all green. My uncle is getting ready to start his garden."

"Sure, and it will be spring in another month or so."

There was a moment of silence.

"And what are ye doing now, Joe?"

"Studying at the University."

"Fine. And study and apply yourself well, me boy, and make something of yourself, instead of becoming the same as the likes of them that's always about the boathouse in the summer looking for trouble. And I suppose it's the law you'll be going into."

"Yes."

"Well, work hard, boy, and apply yourself."

Joe turned toward home. No use thinking or brooding. And anyway, he had better be getting back to his studying. He suddenly crouched into a sprinting position and shot off, tearing fleetly away. He pulled up, crouched again, sprinted, exulting in unthinking muscular release, feeling his body as a well-developed instrument that would do his bidding, expending himself in a way that was release, was like a clean wind blowing through him. It made him feel better. He stopped, a trifle breathless, the joy of running and motion ebbing in him. He hastened out of the park. Back to his studies. And he had to keep his mind on them this time. Only . . . no, he had to keep his mind on them.

IV

As Joe walked up the steps of the building, he heard drunken shouting down at the corner, and saw some of the neighborhood hoodlums yelling with a female bum in their midst. And he heard Tommy's drunken voice rising. He went inside to study.

[1932]

For White Men Only

I

"Boy, I tell you, don' you go there," Booker Jones, a small and yellowish Negro, said.

"Booker, there is no white man alive who's gonna tell me where I is to go swimming, and where I isn't. If I wants to go swimming this lake here at Jackson Park, that's where I'm going swimming," Alfred, a tall and handsome broad-shouldered and coppery Negro, replied.

They were shirtless, wearing blue swimming suits and old trousers, and they walked eastward along Fifty-seventh Street.

"Oh, come on, Alfred, let's go to Thirty-ninth Street," Booker said with intended persuasiveness as they passed across Dorchester after they had ambled on for a block in silence.

"You go! Me, I'm going swimming over in Jackson Park, whether there's white men there or not," Alfred said, his face hardening, his voice determined.

"Alfred, you is always courtin' trouble, and just because you want to show off before that no-account mulatto gal . . ."

"What you say, nigger?"

"Well, no, I'm sorry, Alfred," Booker cringed. "But some day, you'll go courtin' trouble, and trouble is just gonna catch right on up with you, and it's gonna say, 'Well, Alfred, you been courtin' me, so here I is with my mind made up to give you plenty of me.'"

"Shut up, black boy!" Alfred said curtly.

Booker shook his head with disconsolate wonder. As they passed under the Illinois Central viaduct, Booker again suggested that they go down to the Thirty-ninth Street beach, and Alfred testily told him that Thirty-ninth Street wasn't a beach at all, just a measly, overcrowded pile of stones. The black man had no beach. But he was aiming to go swimming where he had some space without so many people all around him. He added that if the Negro was to go on being afraid of the white man, he was never going to get anywhere, and if the Negro wanted more space to swim in, he just had to go and take it. And he had told that to Melinda, and she had laughed at him, but she was not going to laugh at him again. Booker just shook his head sadly from side to side.

They entered Jackson Park where the grass and shrubbery and tree leaves shimmered and gleamed with sunlight. The walks were crowded with people, and along the drive, a succession of automobiles hummed by. Alfred walked along with unconcerned and even challenging pride. Booker glanced nervously about him, feeling that the white men were thrusting contemptuous looks at him. He looked up at Alfred, admiring his friend's courage, and he wished that he were unafraid like Alfred.

Turning by the lake, they passed along the sidewalk which paralleled the waters. Sandy beach ran down from the sidewalk to the shore line, and many were scattered along it in bathing suits. Down several blocks from them, they could see that the regular beach was crowded. More white people frowned at them, and both of them could sense hate and fear in these furtive, hasty glances. Alfred's lips curled into a surly expression.

Halfway along toward the regular beach Alfred jumped down into the sand, tagged by Booker. He gazed around him, nonchalant, and then removed his trousers. He stood in his bathing suit, tall and impressively strong, graceful. Booker jittered beside him, hesitating until Alfred, without turning his head, taunted him into haste. Booker removed his trousers, and stood skinny beside Alfred whose arms were folded and whose gaze was sphinx-like on the waters. They heard a gentle and steady rippling against the shore line.

Nearby, white bathers stared with apprehension. A group of three fellows and two young girls who had been splashing and ducking close to the shore saw them, and immediately left the water and walked down a hundred yards to re-enter it. Alfred seemed to wince, and then his face again became hard and intent. Booker saw various white bathers picking up their bundles and moving away from them, and still afraid of these white men, he hated them.

Alfred trotted gracefully to the shore line, and plunged into the water, followed by Booker. They cut outward, and Alfred suddenly paddled around and playfully ducked Booker. They again hit outward. Catching his breath and plunging beside his companion, Booker told Alfred that they had made a mistake coming out here where they were two against a mob. Alfred retorted that he was not going to whine and beg the white man for anything. Some black men had to be the first to come, if they wanted to have the right of a place to swim. And he wasn't scared anyway. Booker shook his pained head, caught a mouthful of water, and splashed to keep himself up. Alfred dove under water and reappeared a number of yards away, laughing, snorting, glorying in the use of his body. After they had swum around, Booker again chattered that he was afraid.

"Here is one black boy that's not going to be mobbed," Alfred said.

II

Buddy Coen and his friends emerged from the water laughing, shaking their wet bodies and heads. They found a space of sand within the enclosure of the regular beach and dropped down, hunting for the cigarettes they had hidden.

"Well, boys, I was just going to say, if you lads want to provide the bottle, I'm all set for a bender tonight," Buddy said after lighting a cigarette.

"If you'd go back driving a hack, you'd have dough enough for your own liquor," fat Marty Mulligan said.

"What the hell have I got a wife working as a waitress for? So that I can drive a taxi all night. See any holes in my head, Irish?" Buddy said tauntingly.

"After the fight Buddy started last Saturday night with two dicks, I should think he'd stay sober once in a while and see how it feels," Morris said.

"Say, there's plenty of neat pickups around here, even if most of them are Polacks," the big Swede said.

"Boys, my girl is out of town tonight, and I'm dated up with a married woman I met out on my territory. Her husband works nights, and brother, she's the stuff," Marty bragged, following his statement with an anatomical description of her contours, charms and sexual technique.

The big Swede began talking about the old days, and Marty told anecdotes of how he used to get drunk when he was going to Saint Stanislaus high school. They talked on until suddenly from a group close to them they heard a lad say:

"There's niggers down a way on the beach."

They became tense, and Buddy asked was that straight stuff.

"Bad enough having Polacks dirtying up the lake without diseased shines," the big Swede said in hate.

"A few weeks ago, a coal-black bastard tried to get into the lockers here, but he was told that there weren't any free. Then a couple of us boys just talked to him outside, you know, we talked, and used a little persuasion, and he's one black bastard that knows his place, and knows that this is a white man's park and a white man's beach," Buddy said.

"Say, I just need to sock somebody to make the day exciting and put me in good spirits for my date tonight," Marty Mulligan said.

"Well, then, what the hell are you guys waiting for?" Buddy said, jumping to his feet.

They followed Buddy to the water, swam out around the fencing that extended along the formal beach limits and walked along the shore line in search of the Negroes.

"I know I don't mind pounding a few black bastards full of lumps," Norton said.

"Me now, I ain't sloughed anybody since Christ knows when, and I need a little practice," Morris said.

III

"Alfred, I'm tired," Booker said.

"Nigger, shut up! Nobody's going to hurt you," Alfred said.

"Well, I is, just the same," Booker said, his voice breaking into a whine.

Ignoring Booker, Alfred turned over on his back and floated with the sun boiling down upon his coppery limbs. Booker paddled after him, afraid to go in alone. He turned and looked back along the avenue of sand filled with so many white people. Blocks and blocks of sand, populated with all these whites. The fears of a mob assailed him. He wished that he had never come. He thought of Negroes lynched in the South, of many who had been beaten and mobbed in the Chicago race riots of 1919. He remembered as a boy in those times how he had seen one of his race, dead, hanging livid from a telephone post in an alley. He was afraid, and with his fear was hate, hatred of the white man, hatred because of the injustices to him, to his race, hatred because he was afraid of the white man. Again he glanced along the avenue of sand filled with white men, and each small figure along it was a potential member of a mob to beat him and Alfred. He turned and again looked at his friend who was floating, unconcerned. He wished that he had Alfred's courage. With chattering teeth, he shook his head slowly and sadly, feeling, sensing, knowing that they were going to pay dearly for this venture. He treaded water waiting for Alfred, wishing that he was out of it. He saw a group of white bathers stand at the shore and look out over the water. He had a premonition.

IV

"There they are," Buddy said, curtly nodding his head toward the water, and they saw two kinky heads and two Negro faces, diminished by distance.

"Let's drown the bastards!" Morris said.

Buddy said that they would walk off a little ways and wait until the two shines came in. They moved a few yards away, and waited, keen and eager. Buddy lashed out contemptuous remarks, keeping them on edge, and Marty remarked that they had driven the white man out of Washington Park, and that if things went on, soon the whole South Side would be black.

"If they want Jackson Park, they got to fight for it!" Buddy sneered.

"Just think! Look at all these white girls bathing around here. With niggers on the beach, it ain't safe for them," Morris said.

"And do you fellows know, my sister nearly came out here swimming today?" Morris said.

They saw the two Negroes coming in and heard the smaller one trying to convince the big one about something, but they could not catch enough of what he said. The two Negroes walked slowly toward their small bundles of clothing, their wet bodies glistening in the sunlight. After they had sat down, Buddy arose and led the group toward them. Seeing the white fellows approaching, Booker grabbed his clothes and ran. Four of the white lads pursued him, yelling to stop that nigger.

With a sulky expression on his face, Alfred arose at the approach of Buddy and Morris.

"The water nice?" Buddy asked, his voice constrained and threatening.

"Passable." Alfred answered, his fists clenched.

"Been out here before?" Buddy continued.

"No. . . . Why?" Alfred said with unmistakable fearlessness.

A crowd gathered around, and excitement cut through the beach like an electric current because of the shouts and chase after Booker. A white bather tripped him as he ran and joined the four other pursuers in cursing and punching him, mercilessly disregarding his pleas to be let alone. They dragged him to his feet, knocked him down, kicked him, dragged him up, knocked him over again while he continued to emit shrill and helpless cries.

"Anybody ever tell you that this is a white man's beach?" Morris asked Alfred.

"You know we don't want niggers here!" Buddy said.

Buddy went down from a quick and surprising punch in the jaw, and Alfred countered Morris' left swing with a thudding right that snapped the white lad's head back. Buddy sat down, rubbed his jaw, shook his dazed head, leaped to his feet, and went into Alfred swinging both hands. While the Negro fought off the two of them, others dragged back the howling Booker to the fight scene. The big Swede broke through the crowd of spectators and clipped Alfred viciously on the side of the head. Two other white bathers smashed into the attack. Defending himself, Alfred crashed Morris to the sand and was then battered off his feet. A heel was brought against his jaw, and as he struggled to arise, five white bodies piled onto him, punching, scratching, kneeing him. Spectators shouted, females screamed and encouraged the white lads, and Alfred was quickly and severely punished. Booker opened his mouth to beg for mercy, and a smashing fist brought blood from his lips, and another wallop between the eyes toppled him over backward.

A bald-headed Jewish man with a paunchy stomach protested, and a small, pretty blonde girl screamed that he must be a nigger lover. A middle-aged woman with a reddish bovine face called in an Irish brogue for them to hit the black skunks, while a child strained at her waist and shouted.

A park policeman hurriedly shoved through the spectators, and the slugging ceased. The two Negroes sat in the sand, their faces cut and bleeding.

"You fellows better go home!" the policeman said roughly, sneering as he spoke.

They slowly got up, and Booker tried to explain that they had done nothing.

"Don't be giving me any lip," the policeman said. "I said you better go home or do your swimming down at Thirty-ninth if you don't want to be starting riots. Now move along!"

He shoved Booker.

"And you, too," he said to Alfred who had not moved.

Booker hurriedly put his trousers on and Alfred did likewise slowly, as if with endless patience. They wiped their bleeding faces with dirty handkerchiefs, and Booker sniffled.

"Go ahead now!" the policeman roughly repeated.

"We will, but we'll come back!" Alfred said challengingly.

The crowd slowly dispersed, and the six fellows stood there near the policeman.

"Shall we follow them?" asked Marty.

"They ain't worth hitting, the skunks, and the dirty fighting they do, kicking me that way," said Collins limping.

They turned and walked heroically back toward the enclosed beach.

"That black bastard had the nerve to hit me," Buddy said, pointing to his puffed eye.

"Like all niggers, they were yellow," said Morris.

"Well, we did a neat job with them," Norton bragged.

"Boy, I caught that big one between his teeth. Look at my hand," Marty said, showing his swollen knuckles.

"Look at that, fellows! There's somethin'. I say there sisters!" the Swede said to three girls who were coquetting on the sand.

Looking covertly at legs and breasts, they leered.

[1934]

The Oratory Contest

I

Facing the bathroom mirror, Gerry O'Dell practiced for the contest, and he imagined the thunder of applause that would greet him at the conclusion of his oration. His mother called him, and he said that he was coming. He met his dad in the hallway, and Mr. O'Dell looked at his narrow-faced, small, sixteen-year-old son with a mingling of pride and humility.

"Well, Gerry, how do you feel? The old soupbone in your throat loosened up?" the father asked.

"Yes, Dad," Gerry nervously answered.

"Gerry, your mother and I are mighty proud of you, and we'll be giving you all the . . . the moral support we can tonight. Don't get worried because you're speaking in public, or because of the size of the crowd. Ah, anyway, Gerry, oratory is certainly a great gift for a boy to have," the father said, putting his hairy hands into his blue trouser pockets and rocking backward on his heels. "Gerry, if a man has the makings of a great orator in him, he need have no fears of getting ahead in life."

"George, don't be making the boy nervous. Gerald, supper is ready," the mother called.

"Martha, I was only explaining to him," the father apologetically explained.

"Father, you mustn't be saying any more now," she said in a nagging tone.

The father followed his son into the dining room, and he seemed to have been hurt as the family sat down for supper.

"Well, Sis, how did school go today?" the father asked, cutting into his lamb chop and looking at his pig-tailed daughter while Gerry talked with his brother, Michael, about Sister Sylvester, the eighth-grade teacher at Saint Catherine's grammar school.

"I was spelled down," Ellen said.

"What word did you miss, Sis?"

"Interest, Daddy."

"Maybe you'll do better the next time."

"But, gee, Daddy, I tried so hard. I could have cried right then and there like a baby," she said.

"That's just too bad! Too bad that you couldn't show off before Georgie Schaeffer," Michael said, making a wry face at his sister.

"Is that so!"

Mrs. O'Dell told her younger children to stop arguing and eat their supper. It was no time to be disturbing Gerald. The family ate, and the father cast continued glances of approval and pride at his oldest son.

"Gerry, where did you learn the things you're talking about tonight? You must certainly have studied a lot to learn them," the father said.

"I read the Constitution, and the editorials on it that have been printed recently in *The Chicago Questioner*. And then, of course, there was my civics course, and Father Robert gave me lots of suggestions, and he spent an awful lot of time helping me rehearse my speech. He helped me get it written and to get my delivery set in my mind," Gerry said.

"Gerry, when I heard you give your oration at the semi-finals, I was a mighty proud father, I was."

Gerry smiled self-consciously.

"After you finish high school, you'll have to go to college. I want you to get a fine education."

"But, Dad, how can I?" Gerry said, looking hopefully at his father.

"You ought to be able to get a job and study law in the evenings downtown at Saint Vincent's."

"That's what I'll have to do," Gerry said disconsolately.

"Of course, something might turn up," the father said.

"George, that is what you've been saying for twenty years," Mrs. O'Dell said sarcastically.

"Martha, you can't say that I ain't tried. I've provided for you and the children as well as I could, and I always brought my pay home to you untouched. I don't see where you have any right to complain when a man has always done his best."

"George, I'm not complaining. It's just that after all these years I'm tired out. Look how long we're married, and we don't even own our own home."

"We will yet. I mean it! I swear we will! A fellow at the barns was telling me yesterday that he can get a ticket on the English Sweepstakes. Now suppose I should win that! One hundred thousand dollars! Say, we'd be rolling in wealth. You know, Martha, you never can tell what will happen in life. Now last year, I remember reading in the papers where some foreigner, a cook in some New York hotel, won over a hundred thousand dollars on a sweepstakes ticket."

"And you're not that cook. You've been talking yourself blue in the face about winning in baseball pools almost as long as I can remember. And what have you won? What?"

"Didn't I win twenty-five dollars on a baseball pool last year?"

"Yes, and how much did you spend buying tickets during the year?"

"Gee, give a man a chance."

"Give you a chance! That's all I've ever given you."

"Have it your way then. But three years ago Tom Foley, who runs a car on Western Avenue, won five hundred, didn't he? If he can have luck like that, what's to stop me from having it?"

"You're not Tom Foley."

"Aw, Ma!" O'Dell whined, causing Gerry to glance at him quickly in disgust.

"I can't be listening to all your nonsense, George. I got to see that the boys get ready for tonight," she said when they had finished their tea and dessert.

"Gee, Ma, are you sure you can't come?" Gerry said as she arose from the table, a small, broad, fat-cheeked woman in her forties whose stomach was swollen out.

"Gerald, your mother isn't feeling up to snuff this evening. But I'll be thinking of you, speaking, and saying a little prayer to the Lord that you'll win the prize. Your mother knows that her son is going to take the prize, and she'll be just as happy whether she hears you or not, just as long as you telephone me the minute you get out of the hall," the mother said.

"Ma, can I go?" the sister asked.

"You got to stay home with your mother," the father said while Gerry kissed Mrs. O'Dell goodbye and left.

II

Mrs. O'Dell sat knitting baby socks in the dining room, and the daughter was bent over her school books at the table. The father entered the cramped room and asked his wife for some money. She slowly arose and waddled to their bedroom. She drew a two-dollar bill from a large leather pocketbook and handed it to him.

"George, I get spells. I'm afraid," she said.

"Don't worry, Martha. Gerry is a chip off the old block, and he has the makings of a fine orator. Why, he already orates better than a lot of lawyers and politicians I've heard," he said.

"It's not that, George. I'm too old now and this one is going to be a harder ordeal than when I was younger and had the others. Oh, George, I'm afraid! I can't bear to think of leaving you and the children without their mother."

Worried, he gently patted her back, tenderly caressed her unkempt black hair.

"I feel as if I can't carry the load inside of me. And my back gets so sore. I had a dream last night, and it's a premonition. I fear I shan't be pulling through. Oh, George, hold me, kiss me like you used to a long time ago! I can't bear it, the thought of dying and leaving you with an infant baby."

She sobbed in his arms. Holding her, he felt as if paralyzed. He sensed in her the mystery of woman which enabled them to bring forth a man's child. He was filled with respect, awed into speechlessness. He kissed her, clasped her tightly, his feelings reverential. He thought of how they were going along now, and of how they were past knowing and feeling again what they had known and felt in those first burning days of their marriage. Now it was just having sympathy with each other, being used to one another, having their family, their duties, and the obligations which they had to meet together, the feeling of liking, more than loving, each other, and wanting to be proud of their kids. He kissed her again.

Michael called his dad from the doorway. The parents blushed with embarrassment. They turned their heads aside. The father gruffly told his son that he was coming. He kissed his wife a final goodbye.

III

It was a muggy, misty March evening. Walking to the street-car line with his son, O'Dell turned memories of other times over and over in his mind. He remembered his courtship and the days when he was younger and had worked nights, and of how at this time, on this kind of a night, he would be driving his car along Ashland Avenue. He wished that it were still those days and that he were young instead of a motorman rapidly getting old as his family was beginning to grow up. It was strange now to think of himself in other days, to think of what he had been, to realize how he had not at all known what life had in store for himself and his young bride. And now they both knew. And just to think that there had been a time when this boy, Michael, beside him had not been born and neither had Gerry. Gerry had once been in his mother's womb just as the latest newcomer was at this very moment. He remembered the coming of his three children, Martha's shrieks and agonies, his own apprehensions and worries, the helpless feeling that had come over him, the drowsy tiredness on Martha's face after each delivery. He was afraid for it to happen all over again, afraid that this new one was going to mean trouble. *Death*! He wished that it were over with. Yes, and he wished that he were a young motorman again, instead of being pretty close on toward the declining years of middle age. He shook his head wistfully, thinking of how now, for years, day after day, he had driven street-cars. And he had been driving them before the boy at his side was born, and even before Gerry had been on the way. Gerry had turned out fine, but not just exactly what he had imagined Gerry would be. Ah, nothing in life turned out just as a man imagined that it would turn out. And this new one? When it would be Gerry's age, he and Martha, if the Lord spared them both, they would be old. He trembled at the thought of this new one, and it turned his mind to thoughts of the years, of death, the end of them both.

"Mickey, you always want to be good to your mother. Help her all you can while you've got her, because you'll never realize how much she means to you until she's gone," he said.

"Yes, Dad," the boy dutifully replied, the father's words merely giving him the feeling that the old man was just preaching a little in order to hear himself talk.

"You won't have her with you always, you know."

They boarded a street-car and stood on the rear platform talking with the conductor who was a friend of Mr. O'Dell's. O'Dell told his friend where they were going and why. The conductor told O'Dell that one of his girls was a smart one like that, too, and she had just won a prize button in school for writing. But anyway, that girl of his, she was a great kid, and a smart one, too. Then they had to get off at Sixty-third Street and change for an eastbound car.

IV

O'Dell became increasingly timid as the car approached the school auditorium of Mary Our Mother. He tried to force a feeling of reassurance upon himself, thinking that he was just as good as any man, telling himself that he was a free-born American who earned his living by honest work. He had just as much right as any man to come to this contest and hear his own boy whom he was educating out of his hard-earned money. He was an honest man, and work was honorable, and what if he was a motorman and some of the fathers of Gerry's classmates were higher up on the ladder than he? No, there was no need of his being ashamed. America was a democratic country. Still, he was shy. He knew that he would feel out of place. But he was proud of his son, and he knew that Gerry was going to win out over the sons of richer fathers, and . . . he felt that he just wouldn't be in place, and that maybe he shouldn't have come.

And he realized that Gerry, instead of waiting for him and Michael, had gone ahead. Gerry, he suddenly felt, was ashamed of him. He argued with himself that the boy had had to get there early, and that, anyway, he had been nervous about the contest and restless, like a colt before the start of a race. But still, no, he could not rid his mind of that thought.

He noticed other people on the sidewalk, walking in the same direction as he, and he heard them talking. Some of them sounded like parents, and he was sure that many of them must be the fathers and mothers of boys who went to Mary Our Mother. Did any of them, he wondered, have thoughts such as he? Well, before this evening was over they were all going to know about Gerald O'Dell.

And at home, there was Martha, her body big and swollen. He wished that she had come along. And she was at home, knitting away. He was responsible for her condition, and if he had curbed himself, well, they wouldn't be having this worry and this danger, and all the expense and sacrifice that it would involve, and she would be at his side, and they would both be so proud and happy, hearing Gerry win with his oration. How good it would be to have Martha at his side, both of them hearing the whole auditorium applaud her boy, her own flesh and blood. And she would not be granted this pleasure. He could just see her at home, knitting, silent, afraid. And she was going to be hurt, and this new child was going to be, maybe, so hard at her age, and oh, God forbid that she should die.

In front of the auditorium, he saw boys of varying ages, some only a year or so older than his Michael, other lads of seventeen and eighteen in long pants. He looked about to see if Gerry were among them, but he wasn't. He would like to tell them who he was, the father of Gerry O'Dell.

"Mike, here we are," he said in an attempt to be whimsical.

He handed two complimentary tickets to the lad collecting them at the door, and in a humble mood he followed the usher to seats in the center of the auditorium. He looked shyly about the lighted hall, seeing a confusion of strange faces, the people moving down the aisles to seats, and he was excited and expectant. He wanted it to begin. He glanced up toward the stage, with the stand and a row of chairs in front of the drawn red curtain. The boys, judges and the honored guests, including a number of priests, some of whom might be Gerry's teachers, would all sit in those chairs. And again he felt out of place, humbly so. He felt that in the auditorium there must be the fathers of many of Gerry's classmates, men who had gone so much further in the world than he had, men who could afford to send their sons to good colleges.

He remembered the sight of the lads outside, and it caused him to think of how Gerry must have an entire life closed out to his father and mother, a life they could never get their little fingers on. He glanced sidewise at Michael, who was awkwardly twisting in his seat and looking about at faces with a boy's alive and curious eyes. And what did he see? What? Michael, too, and the girl, they had their lives that were closed to their father and mother, and as they grew older they would both drift further and further away.

"Like it, Mickey?" he asked, wanting to get close to his son, to be like a pal with him.

Michael smiled, muttered an absorbed uhuh.

"Some day you'll be going to the school here, too, and maybe, like Gerry, you'll be winning oratorical contests and prizes."

"I'd rather be on the football team."

"Maybe you can do both."

Michael smiled frankly, and the father suddenly found his mood dissipating under the smile. He did not feel himself to be such a stranger to Michael.

V

He was conscious of the movement of people, priests in the rear, the hall filling up, and he guessed that it was going to start. Suddenly the orchestra began a scratchy prelude, and O'Dell told himself that it must be fine music. Like those around him, he sat quiet, a little hushed. Glad, too, that it was starting. He waited, entertained but anxious, through the elocution contests, when first-year students recited pieces. The junior contest followed, and four boys delivered famous orations. O'Dell thought that the tall boy who delivered a speech of Senator Hoar's defending the retention of the Philippine Islands, had been the best. All of them had been good, but his boy would be better. And that was what he was waiting for.

He heard more music, idly reflecting that the priests here at Mary Our Mother must be giving the boys a good education. Anxiety was working within him like a pump. Right after the music Gerry would speak. He gripped and clasped his hands. Michael stirred. He tapped him, whispering to be quiet and to act well-mannered. The music, carried through by violins, seemed like the distant sounds of a waterfall, and they lulled within him. Dreamily he visualized Gerry speaking, imagined the lad's future as a great lawyer, and he thought of how boys in oratorical contests such as this one would, in years to come, be delivering the famous speeches and orations of Senator Gerald O'Dell. Gerald O'Dell, his son, the boy whose education had cost him sacrifices.

And now Gerry, small and freckled, was on the platform. He seemed so calm, as if there was not a worry in his head. He stood there, straight, dignified, and, ah, but wouldn't he be a pride to his father in the years to come. He was speaking. O'Dell leaned forward, listening attentively as his son's deep and full voice carried down the auditorium.

So the first step is, what is the Constitution?

O'Dell was in a spell, completely under the sway of his son's words, and he nodded his head as Gerry's voice rose in the final introductory statement which suggested that the United States and the Constitution are inseparable, and that without one there could not be the other.

And to all of us who are true Americans, our Constitution is sacred, the creed of those rights which are guaranteed to every one of us as an enduring pledge of our liberties.

Gerry spoke without halt, retaining not only the absorbed attention of his father but also of nearly everyone in the auditorium. He continued, declaiming that the defense of the Constitution, and of the principles which it embodied, was a sacred duty to be held inviolable, and that he who did not, nor would not, uphold these principles did not deserve to be called an American. He added that he who holds public office and willingly betrays his trust cannot be called an American. But in his talk he was not primarily interested in such men, even though they wantonly betrayed their public trust. He was concerned with something more vital, the betrayal of the fundamental principles on which the Constitution was founded, that of state's rights, individual liberty. And men, men in public affairs, were, because of ignorance or perversity or even malice, seeking to destroy that principle by advocating the passage of a Federal Maternity Act and a law establishing a Federal Educational Department. These men wanted to abolish child labor by an act of Congress, even though the Constitution did not grant this prerogative to Congress.

O'Dell smiled when the boy quoted the late Champ Clark.

If the groups seeking Federal assistance would put their burdens on the state legislatures where they belong, Congress would have time for the work which, under the Constitution, belongs to Congress.

Continuing, Gerry referred to this tendency toward centralization, seeking to prove that it was unjustified. And then, with cleanly contrived gestures and a rising voice, he concluded:

Should we allow our rights to be taken from us? No! Wherever this tendency to centralization shows its serpentine head, we shall fight it, because it is a menace to us, to everyone who is a liberty-loving American, and we must fight this menace. And defending our liberties, we shall take a slogan from some recent words of a Cabinet member, Herbert Hoover: "It is time to decentralize." Our forefathers, Washington, Jefferson, and Madison, fought to give us our rights. Shall we let them be stripped away from us? Never! We will defend our rights. We will raise our voices until we are heard and our voices resound. Yes, we will even shout: It is time to decentralize.

Gerry O'Dell bowed to the audience. He turned and walked to his place among the others on the stage, while the applause thundered. The father clapped himself weary, restraining strong impulses to shout and stamp his feet. Tears welled in his eyes. He smiled with a simple and childlike joy. Unable to check himself, he turned to the man on his left and said:

"That's my boy."

"Smart lad."

The remaining speeches in the senior oratorical contest seemed dull and uninteresting to him. His boy had it all over these other lads. And he felt himself justified in these impressions when the judges announced their decision, and amid a second strong burst of clapping Gerald O'Dell was announced the winner of the gold medal in the Senior Oratorical Contest. O'Dell rushed out to a drugstore to telephone the news to Martha. Then he and Michael went back. The tag end of the crowd was filtering out. Boys were coming out in groups, standing, talking, dispersing with the crowd. He searched for Gerry. Gerry would certainly have waited. A boy came out. It was Gerry. No! He searched again. Gerry must be inside, being congratulated. He went in, but found the stage empty. Gerry must have gone. He told himself that Gerry had known that his father would wait to see him, congratulate him, buy him a treat, and that then they would go home together. And Gerry had not waited. He still looked anxiously about at the disappearing faces. Where was he? He asked a boy in a lingering group of students if any of them had seen Gerald O'Dell. They hadn't. He said that he was Gerald's father. They said Gerald had spoken well and deserved his victory. He stood with Michael. Only a few scattered groups remained in front of the hall. Feeling blank, he told himself, yes, Gerry had gone. He solemnly led Michael away, both of them silent. He asked himself why Gerry hadn't waited, and he knew the answer to his question.

[1935]

Precinct Captain

I

O'Malley was a stocky man in his forties, with a solid brick-like face, thinning reddish hair and narrow blue eyes. He had an air about him. He walked, he talked, he sat, he stood, he gesticulated with an air of authority. He was always playing his role in public, the role of a man who had been in the political game for twenty years. The fruits of his public service were a job as deputy sheriff in the county building and the title precinct captain in his neighborhood near South Shore Drive and Seventy-first Street.

The primary fight put O'Malley on the spot. In the previous election, he had gone around and told all his people to vote for Kline for Governor. He had said that Kline was as fine a man as they would ever find in public life in the whole state of Illinois. He told them that Kline had a fine record. He said that it showed you what a fine country America was when it would elect a Jew. Many of his voters were Irish, and he told them that the Irish and the Jews had to stick together. Look what happened to the Irish in the old country. And look what happened to the Jews in, where was it, Jerusalem? Anyway, look what happened to them. He had thus argued that the Irish had to vote for Kline for Governor because he was a fine man, because he had a fine record, because he was a good Democrat, because the Party and the organization were behind him, and because it was a fine thing for the Irish and the Jews to stick together. If the Irish voted for a Jew, the Jews would return the compliment by voting for a mick. And to Jewish voters in his precinct he had said that they had to come out and stand by a man of their own race and repay him for his public service rendered to them, and to all of the people.

Now, O'Malley was in the hole. All those whom he had lined up to vote for Kline had now to be lined up to cast their ballots for Anderson against Kline. It was a hot primary fight, and the organization needed every vote it could garner in the entire county because Kline was certain to roll up a large downstate plurality. O'Malley was working night and day, ringing doorbells, rapping on doors, trying to compose letters to his voters, handing out cards and cigars, hiring one gang of kids and young men to put Anderson literature into mailboxes and another group to take Kline literature out of the same mailboxes.

Easter Sunday came two days before the primary election. He was still busy, with more people to see, more cards to dispose of, more Kline literature to be destroyed, more Anderson literature to be distributed. The organization was fighting for big spoils, and the machine was built up of such rank-and-file corporals as himself. They had to do the producing. If they didn't, the machine was sunk and they were sunk with it. In every ward the Kline people were putting together an organization. If they won, they could have their own ward committeemen, their own precinct captains, and then, where would O'Malley be? He had to hop to it, and he was doing the hopping. He went to an early Mass on Easter Sunday, received Holy Communion, and then, after a quick breakfast, he was out working. He had to see a printer and arrange for the printing of more cards and for the mimeographing of a letter for distribution to the voters, on Tuesday morning. He had sat up almost all of Saturday night composing this letter. It told the Democratic voters of the precinct that their friend and neighbor was Patrick J. Connolly. He had served them long and well. He had guarded the public interest as if it were his own property. He had never turned a deaf ear to their needs and their appeals. And now Patrick J. Connolly needed them as they had needed him. He needed their votes so that he could be returned as ward committeeman, in which capacity he would continue to serve them as he had done in the past. O'Malley was pleased with this letter of his. It convinced him that the big-shots down in the City Hall weren't the only fellows who knew a trick or two. None of them could have written a better letter, a letter that would win more votes than his would. But it had been hard work. He had gone to confession, and after midnight he could not eat, drink, even take a sip of water. He had done the job, though. After arranging with the printer, he had his rounds to make. The ballot was so long, and he had to give instructions to the people on how to vote, what names to skip on it, what men to vote for. It was a tough job, and no matter how long he spent explaining the ballot, he still could not be sure that the idea had been put across. And some of his voters were so damn dumb! They might vote for Anderson, but not for Connolly. They might give a vote to some of the traitors on the ticket who had waited until their names were printed on the organization's list on the ballot before they had changed and come out for Kline. Ah, yes, his job was all grief during an election fight.

About four o'clock, tired and weary, he got around to the Doyles. The Doyles were nice people, and he was glad he had met them. He knew that Mr. Doyle must have once been a well-to-do man. He acted and talked like a gentleman. Now he was having hard times and the breaks had gone against him. And the boy, he was all right, too, a fine chap. They were poor because of hard times, and too proud to go on relief. He was going to try and see what he could do for them by way of getting a job for Doyle if he could manage it. The Doyles were the kind of people you called the worthy poor.

He walked in on them in their one-room furnished apartment over a store. The apartment gave the sense of overcrowding, and the furniture was old and scratched. It seemed almost to breathe out a feeling of its own unliveableness. O'Malley smiled and handed a box of candy to Mrs. Doyle, a fat, beefy-armed, bovine woman. He pulled out cigars for Doyle, a tall, thin, graying man whose blue trousers were frayed at the pocket and their narrow, worn cuffs were out of style. He also handed two cigars to the son.

"Well, Mildred, here's the best precinct captain in Chicago," Doyle said as Mrs. Doyle was dusting off the best chair for O'Malley.

"No, just the most worn out," O'Malley said.

"You poor man, you must be so tired. Here, let me make you a cup of coffee," Mrs. Doyle said.

"Please don't, Mrs. Doyle. I only got a minute. There's still a long list of people I got to see," he said.

"You work so hard. It'll be a shame if everybody doesn't turn out and vote for you," she said.

"You don't think they will?" he asked, his brows beetling in worry.

"Certainly they will," Doyle quickly said.

"Don't be giving me heart failure, Mrs. Doyle. After all, a man of my advanced age can't take too much," O'Malley said, smiling grimly.

"It looks good, huh, O'Malley?" said the twenty-five-year-old son, a rather emaciated, characterless young chap with badly decayed teeth.

"I think I got it pretty much set. Now, how have you folks got the people managed in this building?"

"Skipper, you needn't worry about this building. Say, it's in your vest pocket," Doyle said.

"That's the way I like to hear you talk," O'Malley said, smiling and lighting a cigar while Doyle and his son puffed on theirs.

"Mr. O'Malley, are you sure you wouldn't take a cup of coffee? It'll only take me a minute to make it for you," Mrs. Doyle said maternally.

"No, thanks. Now, about this fellow across the hall, the Polack?"

"I'm getting up at six in the morning to see him. He's hard to catch," Mrs. Doyle said.

"Be sure and do it. We got to get every vote we can. We got a fight on our hands this time."

"You'll win. Everybody else in the building is going to vote for Anderson. And you know, Mr. O'Malley, there was somebody around putting folders for Kline in the mailboxes."

"There was?" he exclaimed, glancing angrily at Mrs. Doyle. "Say, I'll bet he was one of these birds with a fishhook for a nose."

"But wait until you hear the rest of the story. I spoke to him. He asked me who I was for. I said, why I was for Kline. But now wait a minute until I tell you all of the story, Mr. O'Malley. I said that I was for Kline and so was everybody else in the building. I said that I had talked to them for Kline. So he put his folders in the mailboxes, and I asked him for more. He gave me some. I said, 'Oh, Mister, give me a lot more. I want to give these to all of my friends in the neighborhood.' So I got a great big pile of Kline literature. And right after I saw that he was gone, I took the stuff out of the boxes and threw the whole shebang into the garbage can," Mrs. Doyle said.

"Good for you! Good for you, Mrs. Doyle! If all people were like you folks here, I'll tell you, my job would be a good deal easier than it is and I wouldn't be getting early gray hairs from worry."

"Say, what the hell, Skipper! Don't have such a low opinion of yourself. You're the best precinct captain in Chicago," Doyle said ingratiatingly.

"I only wish I was," O'Malley said with almost histrionic dejection.

"Why, of course you are, Mr. O'Malley," Mrs. Doyle said.

"Sure, but let me tell you something. Roosevelt's the best precinct captain we got."

"My, but isn't he a wonderful man!" Mrs. Doyle exclaimed.

"He's a real bird, all right, fine man. He's done a lot for the people and the country," Doyle said.

"Best president we had since Woodrow Wilson," young Doyle said.

"You're damn tootin', he is! Damn tootin'! And he's the best precinct captain we got. But I ain't worried none about putting him over in my precinct in the fall. What I'm worried about is the primary election this Tuesday. Now, are you sure you got everybody in the building all set?"

"Oh, yes, of course. There isn't one Kline person in the whole building," Mrs. Doyle said.

"Here's the way I handle them. I say that, of course, now, Kline is a fine man. He's governor. A fine man. Sure. But so is Anderson. Anderson is a fine man, and he is the one we got to put over. Kline has that Oriental strain in him that's in his blood. He's not one of us, and he doesn't understand our problems."

"Say, Mr. Doyle, you ought to have my job. You're a smart man. That's the ticket, and I'm going to use that line myself. Say, I wish everybody in my precinct was like you. And you got mostly Irish in this building, haven't you?"

"Yes, Irish and Catholic."

"Of course, there is the Polish man across the way, and Mrs. Hirsch. I don't like her. She's too dirty, and, say, she would talk a leg off you. Now the other day—"

"Who's she for?" O'Malley interrupted.

"Why, Anderson, of course."

"Well, tell her to stay that way. And don't forget to nail the Polack," O'Malley said.

"Of course, I will," Mrs. Doyle said.

"You know, folks, I can't understand an Irishman who would vote for Kline after what he done to us. It was us who put him in, and then he is a turncoat. Why, four years ago I went around and told everybody to vote for him. Why, I got out a bigger vote for Kline in this precinct than I ever got out for anybody except Roosevelt. The Irish didn't go against him because he's a Jew. And what does he do? He turns on us," O'Malley said, his words and tone giving expression to a puzzled, wounded feeling.

"He gave us the can, didn't he? But he ain't got a chance, has he?" the son said.

"Not a chance of a snowball in hell if all the others around the city get out the vote the way I'll do it. Now, take that big apartment building down the street here in the next block. There must be a hundred voters in that buildin'. Well, I got every Democratic vote in the joint," O'Malley proudly said.

"Good for you," Mrs. Doyle said.

"The woman who works in the renting office there, I spoke to her and lined her up. So when some dame comes around for Kline, why, this woman, she says to the Kline dame, she says that the tenants in the buildin' have just gotten sick and tired of everybody and his brother comin' around about votin' and puttin' cards in the boxes. She says to the Kline dame that she can't let anybody else go around botherin' and annoyin' her tenants, because if she does, a lot of them will move out on her. So this Kline dame, she is dumb. You know, she ain't never been in politics and thinks she can come in and lick somebody like myself who has been in the political game all my life. She's dumb, see! She asks the woman, are her tenants for Kline. The woman says of course they are, sure, because everybody is. She takes the Kline literature from this dumb dame and throws it all in the ash-can, just the same as you did, Mrs. Doyle."

"That was clever," Doyle said.

"You ought to meet that woman. She's a fine woman," said O'Malley.

"Well, she helped. And on this game, every little bit helps," the son said profoundly.

"You're a smart young fellow. Every little bit, every vote does count. Every one. And to think of how many votes I swung to Kline four years ago. For him to go and turn his back on the organization and the people that made him, bitin' the hand that fed him. Well, don't worry! I'm cookin' the goose for him in my precinct. We don't waste our time with traitors to us when we're the fellows that made them somebody," O'Malley said vindictively.

"Mr. O'Malley, I'm just so certain that Anderson will get the nomination," Mrs. Doyle said.

"So am I. But we can't take any chances. Every vote counts. Now, are you sure you got every voter in this here buildin'?"

"It's in the bag," the son said.

"Yes, we guarantee it," Doyle said.

"All of the people have promised me already, except that man across the hall, the Polish one. I'm getting up in the morning to make sure of him," Mrs. Doyle said.

"That's the way I like to hear you talk. And if we win, I won't forget how helpful you've been to me," O'Malley said.

"We're doing everything we can," Mrs. Doyle said.

"That's the ticket," O'Malley said.

"And, Mr. O'Malley, what about election day?" Doyle nervously asked.

"Here, I brought these sample ballots," O'Malley said, arising and pulling out long pink-sheeted ballots, one of which he spread out upon the narrow dining-room table. "Now, I got this all marked up just right." The family gathered around him. He became official, and almost coldly professional. His tone of voice changed. "You can all study this after I go, and I'm gonna leave some of these here for you to show to the people in the buildin' and to get them to study it. Now watch me carefully. See, you start here with Anderson's name at the top of the ticket. Now you go straight down until you get to Hogan for sheriff. You skip him. Any man that would turn on his friends the way Hogan did, he doesn't deserve a vote. Coming out yesterday and sayin' he was for Kline like he did on us. Be sure to skip Hogan, and tell your friends in the buildin' here to. And then you go straight down the list, Kaczmarski, Moran, Cogan, Connell, and then, here, you skip Schulman for county clerk. See, I got it here, and there's no X after Schulman's name. He is another one who turned his coat and betrayed his friends and the organization. And now here, don't forget, Connolly. See, right here! Tell all your people, absolutely, to mark an X after Connolly's name. See it, for ward committeeman. When you mention Connolly, you say: 'Your ward committeeman.' You see, what good is it going to do us if we get in the top of the ticket but don't get our own man, our own friend and neighbor, in for ward committeeman? So, don't forget it. Above all else, we got to get Connolly in." O'Malley said.

"Of course," Mrs. Doyle said with assurance.

"Now it should all be clear. See how they are marked with an X, and then, I got rings around the names of those you skip, like Hogan. You won't forget this and go votin' for the men I got ringed, will you?"

"Holy Moses, no!" Doyle said.

"You can study this sample ballot carefully after I go. And you know, you can take these into the booths with you when you vote, in order to see how to vote. We just got the rulin' on that, and it's O.K. to take sample ballots into the booth."

"We'll study it, Skipper, and show the neighbors what to do," Doyle said.

"If you're sure you can do that, you'll save me a lot of valuable time," said O'Malley.

"Of course we can. And we're glad to do it. You poor man, you must be so tired," said Mrs. Doyle.

"Well, I've been doing this for twenty years. I'm used to it, but, golly, a man does get tired toward the end of a hot primary fight," O'Malley said.

"And what about election day, Mr. O'Malley?" Mrs. Doyle asked.

"I've just been demonstratin' it to you, and I thought you all said you got the dope straight?" O'Malley asked, his expression changing.

"Yes, we understand that. But what I meant is, what time should we come to vote and, you know, Mr. O'Malley, you said something about your wanting us working around the polls, because you said we were so helpful to you," Mrs. Doyle tactfully said.

"Sure, you come around at six, and I'll get you fixed up."

"We'll be there," said Doyle.

"Then, if we win, as I fully expect to, well, as I just said, I don't forget them that sticks with me. If I did, I wouldn't be worthy of the name of O'Malley."

"Oh, we know it. And Mr. O'Malley, you look so tired, haven't you the time for a cup of coffee?" said Mrs. Doyle.

"Gee, no, I spent more time talkin' than I meant to. I'm so busy. I got to get these cards distributed," he said, taking out a stack of Connolly cards and giving some to Mrs. Doyle.

"You better leave a little more than that. I can distribute them," Mrs. Doyle said.

"Ah, that's the way to hear you talk," O'Malley said, handing her additional cards.

Leaving more cigars, he went out, followed by profuse farewells from all of the Doyles.

II

"He's such a nice man," said Mrs. Doyle.

"He's a sketch," the son said.

"We don't care what he is, as long as he gets us a job," said Doyle.

"I wonder? Maybe it would have been better for us if we had gone for Anderson, but let Arty here be a Kline man. Then we might have gotten somewhere either way," Mrs. Doyle said.

"Catch me voting for a Jew," the son said.

"Listen, Arty, we don't care what in the name of Jesus Christ he is, if he gives us a job. God, we want to get a job for one of us, or we can't go on! We can't be such choosers," said Doyle.

"Here, he brought this candy, and it's filling. If you watch it, Papa, so the sweets don't get in your teeth, and you do the same, Arty, it's filling," said Mrs. Doyle.

"I can't eat chocolates, not with these molars I got," the son said, as his father took a chocolate and chewed it carefully.

"I'm glad that he didn't take the coffee. We hardly have any canned milk left," Mrs. Doyle said.

"Yes, we'll vote for Kline, Anderson, or the Devil himself for a job," Doyle said.

"That's why I talked like I did, about the people here. You know, some of them won't talk to me if I say Anderson. They're Republicans. But we might as well let him think that we're doing everything in our power," Mrs. Doyle said, eating a chocolate.

"Yes, and we'll give him our votes. Golly, I hope that we put Anderson over," Doyle said, grabbing a caramel.

"We got to! If we don't, we won't be anywheres," said Mrs. Doyle while the son enviously watched his parents eating the candy, his tongue playing around in his decayed teeth.

"Damn it, I meant to pray for Anderson's success this morning at Mass, and I forgot to," Doyle said.

"You would! You're just like an absent-minded professor," said Mrs. Doyle.

"Couldn't help it. I meant to. And I can still pray until Tuesday," said Doyle.

"Well, I think that the Lord will provide for us by electing Anderson so you can get a job," Mrs. Doyle said, dividing the last two pieces of candy with her husband.

"And after election, Tuesday, we can get a swell meal. We'll have five dollars each. And, Ma, I think that we can spare ourselves a movie. Shirley Temple will be at the show that night," Doyle said.

"But, Pa, we'll have to watch that money. You know, the agent told us last month that he was giving us our last chance. If we get evicted, we got to have a little something, or where will we sleep?" said Mrs. Doyle.

"Goddamn it, Anderson has got to get in," said Doyle, pacing the floor nervously.

[1936]

The Professor

I

The Professor slanted his reddish, bull-dog face and frowned. He rubbed back a few strands of graying hair from his thick forehead. He slammed his pudgy fist against the desk and glowered.

"This morning I am going to be a tough guy like O'Neill," he announced brusquely.

The class laughed, and heads turned to simper at unkempt O'Neill, who occupied a rear seat.

"Ordinarily, I am a peaceable citizen, but this morning I cannot hold myself responsible for any belligerent activities which I may commence with the male students of this class in Advanced Composition. It is to be understood, however, that regardless of my disposition, I am too gentlemanly and chivalrous to strike any of the ladies. . . . Um. . . . Now that I have given fair warning, and in case any of the young men present are trembling lest I descend upon them like the wrath of Carlyle, they may leave the room. . . . I see that no one is leaving. . . . Well, you remain at your own risk, because after everything is said and done, a man over fifty cannot be held morally accountable for his deeds on a morning when the prunes he has eaten have not agreed with his stomach."

The Professor fumbled through the manuscripts before him while the class appreciated his humor. When it quieted down, he read a thriller by Harry Cogan, the neat, goggled, never-smiling young man who sat in the first row. After the reading, he blessed the story with banalities and opened class discussion. Two commonplace girls paraphrased his banalities, and Mr. Cogan agitated upon the precipice of a modest smile. The Professor asked Mr. Scroggins for his opinion.

"Well, Mr. Saxon . . . ah. . . . Now, on the whole . . . I think that the story is pretty good, and that it had many passages that are truly professional. . . . But I think . . . I think that Mr. Cogan has been careless in spots, using some very bad clichés such as . . . 'The steel dagger gleamed above green eyes in the hushed and lightless room.' That's bad."

The Professor nodded agreement, but added that such slips could perhaps be partially forgiven in one who could write sentences like "The night crushed speechlessly about them."

Frail Miss Durham timidly objected to the story because of the author's lack of sympathy with his character, Bastian McGraw. After hemming and hawing, the Professor countered that the character of Bastian McGraw was so weak and so vicious that a writer could scarcely be decently sympathetic toward him. The class then went dead, and Mr. Cogan took occasion to ask would it be all right if, after he had rewritten the story, he tried it on *The Saturday Evening Post.* The Professor answered that it wouldn't do any harm.

"Mr. Saxon, do you really approve of that story?" lean, ascetic, Adam's-appled Abe Ginsberg asked.

"Well, Abe, that depends upon what you mean by approve."

"I want to know if you approve of it," Abe repeated excitedly.

"Um. . . . Considering that the author is a beginner, yes, I do. I believe that it shows promise. To the contrary, I don't approve of it in the sense that I would approve of a story by Poe, Kipling, O. Henry, Bret Harte, or Chekhov. Mr. Cogan is only starting out."

"You approve, then?"

"As I explained."

Abe smirked in arrogant derision, and the Professor asked O'Neill's opinion.

"I agree with Abe that it's lousy," said O'Neill, some of the girls tittering at his bluntness.

"But Abe didn't say precisely that."

"I do now!" Abe said, provoking added tittering.

An argument concerning the plot short story quickly developed. Abe, morally indignant, and O'Neill, youthfully cynical, attacked the Professor.

"Of course, you two are free to stick to your own views," the Professor began when the discussion had stumbled into an impasse, "although I should like to assure you that they will never get you anywhere. If a story hasn't plot and pattern, what can it contain? What can be its meaning? What can it offer as a bid to reader-interest?"

"It can have life, the Misery, the Rawness, the Squalor, the Tragedy, the Beauty, the Glory of Life!" Abe said loudly and in the manner of a zealous prophet.

"But, Abe, plot does not exclude that. For instance, have you ever read the stories of Wilbur Daniel Steele?"

"He's one guy I can't stomach," O'Neill interrupted.

"Well, may God have mercy on Mr. O'Neill's soul," the Professor remarked.

"I loathe Wilbur Daniel Steele's work, and I scorn all trick writing," Abe declared.

Losing some of its log-like lethargy, the class laughed. Abe denounced his fellow students, along with O. Henry. Mr. Scroggins asked the Professor to summarize and repeat his views on the technique of the short story. The Professor replied, giving a good paraphrase of any number of textbooks and commonly accepted views on the subject. O'Neill waved a book in the air, opening it on a page where a diagram was printed.

"That sounds just like this book. I picked it up because I thought it was a textbook on bridge-building. But I discover that all these diagrams are to tell you how to write a short story," O'Neill said.

"That's not funny," Scroggins said.

"No, it's a scandal," O'Neill said.

"It's sad!" Abe said, jerking nervously to his feet.

The Professor was secretly thrilled by Abe, his brilliant baby of a student, and he thought, too, that when he could stimulate Abe to such enthusiasms he wasn't doing his job of teaching so badly. The spirit was there, and Abe was possibly a genius, even if his ideas were wrong. In his own undergraduate days, the Professor had been similarly wrong, but ah, the lost zest and spirit and enthusiasm of those days, their hopes. Ah, the pathos of distance!

Continuing to argue with his two prize students, he suddenly seemed to hear himself talking as if he were two persons, one repeating the formulas of twenty-seven years, the other an uncomplimentary and dissatisfied listener. He winced inwardly, and halted the discussion by asking Miss Slocomb to read her story, *The Justifying Moment.* The story described a witty and sophisticated young author and a beautiful and charming girl who drove through moonlit woods, wittily and incisively discussing Life, Beauty, and their own souls. Suddenly the author revealed that he was disgusted with his level and boresome existence, and determined that he would experience one moment of high, abandoned, and romantic living, even though it caused his death. With unrestrained jubilation he drove the automobile into a tree and, arising from the wreckage, he declaimed to the high heavens that now all his life was worth while, because he had had his one grand and justifying moment.

Only half-listening, the Professor dwelt upon his own past, recalling ghosted memories that were cloaked with a consoling melancholy. Ah, those undergraduate days when he had thrilled with the ambition to become a great writer! And those fevered nights when he had written, written, written! And Muriel Smith, the girl whom he had thought he loved. She walked slowly into his mind, her each light step pressing the heaviness of loss upon him. He held her before him, a pale memory-image dripping bitter nostalgia, and he thought of her chestnut hair, her blue eyes, the lips that he had kissed farewell on many a zero winter evening when the moon was a frozen chip of snow in the sky and he was setting out for that long return journey back south to the campus dormitory. Ah, Muriel, and the manner she had had of resting her dimpled chin in a white palm. And those six months of anxiety after he had determined to propose, and he had slaved to write out his proposal in Shakespearean blank verse. And that night when he had read it so well, and the cruelly gentle feminine kindness in her rejection. Ah!

God, that girl's story! Ye gods and little fishes! A pity for her to think that she could write, almost a maniacal delusion! But it would be too cruel to hurt the poor thing's feelings by telling her so. And still, what in the name of all the gods there be could he say to her about it? What? Great Caesar's Ghost!

Sometimes he played bridge with Muriel and her husband, an advertising man, and all that was now merely a prank out of the irrevocable past,

just as it should be. Neither of them regretted that she had rejected him.
No, his regrets were merely the pathos of distance, regrets for a lost state
of his own feelings.

That girl's story! Atrocious!

Miss Slocomb's watery eyes begged for praise. In veiled words he cau-
tioned her about the use of scenes that might impress the reader as being
exaggerated, because if a young writer was not careful, he or she was liable to break a leg in the pitfall of melodrama. He opened class discussion
and permitted his students to wander on. He thought of Muriel, her of the
dreams of his young manhood, of some of the best thoughts and emotions
of his whole life. Lost to him! Ah! The loss was that of the emotions, and
similarly he had lost that first emotional state for his wife whom he had
loved, too, as a young man loves. He had slept in the same bed with her
for twenty-five years, and she had borne him three daughters, and he had
looked across the breakfast table into her bony face for an eternity of mornings. They had an indifferent affection toward each other, a casualized sympathy. Out of each other's sight, they did not think much of one another.
They accepted each other. That was perhaps as it should be, and yet, ah,
the pathos of distance. She had been a good wife, and Muriel could have
been no better. But his wife had been at best only half sympathetic to all
the things he had cherished the most. Now, old age was creeping upon both
of them. He thought of *Modern Love,* Meredith's incomparable poem. Ah,
how well it described emotions which many a couple must have!

"Don't you think, Mr. Saxon, that there are too many figures of
speech in that story? Ones like . . . 'The moon was a newly minted dime
cemented in the cloud-tiled floor of the sky' . . . now that, of course, is
good. But just the same, the total effect is bad because there is so much
imagery, particularly in the climax where swift action is called for," Mr.
Brennan said.

"Quite so, George, good criticism," the Professor said.

Through his mind ran the lines:

At dinner she is hostess, I am host.
Went the feat ever cheerfuller? She keeps
The Topic over intellectual deeps
In buoyancy afloat. They see no ghost.
With sparkling surface-eyes we ply the ball:
It is in truth a most contagious game.
HIDING THE SKELETON, shall be its name.

"I tried to infuse feeling and poetry in my story, the tones of woods and sky, and that was why I used so many images," Miss Slocomb said.

"The intention, of course, is laudable, but the trick is to get them in without putting bumps and obstacles upon the hill of rising action," the Professor countered.

He seemed to be listening calmly to his students. But feelings cracked and burst inside of him, falling into a weltering chaos. He knit his smashed feelings together with more lines from Meredith:

Thus piteously Love closed what he begat:
The union of this ever-diverse pair!
These two were rapid falcons in a snare.
Condemned to do the flitting of the bat.

Yes, he and his wife, and many other men and their wives, too, were all not so rapid falcons in a snare, condemned to do the flitting of the bat. And soon, relatively soon, would come . . .

"That's a bully suggestion, Miss Durham, and I think that Miss Slocomb should adopt it."

"I will, Mr. Saxon. I like criticism like that, because it tells me where I fail, and it is constructive," Miss Slocomb said.

Soon . . . last night he had again foundered over those headings in the biography of British authors. . . . Soon . . .

"And now, Miss Durham, will you please read that sketch of yours, *Pinkish Dust*?" he asked.

Miss Durham coughed with embarrassment, arose, read from the poetry of Rupert Brooke to explain her title, and slowly went through her sketch.

Soon! Last night, those prophetic headings! . . . Oliver Goldsmith (1728–1774), William Cowper (1731–1800), William Blake (1757–1827), Newman (1801–1890), Robert Browning (1812–1889), Ruskin (1819–1900), Robert Louis Stevenson (1850–1894), Thomas Carlyle (1795–1881), Matthew Arnold (1822–1888) . . . all his dead giants and poets.

And once in the springtime of another century, the young undergraduate, Paul Saxon, a boy from a small town in Indiana, had stood under an oak tree in Washington Park brooding upon life, chanting hopeful lines from Robert Browning. And then, young Saxon had not been so afraid. He had shaken his fist in the face of life, daring death. Then he had anticipated the grave as the last dark and adventurous tower to which he could come, like Childe Roland. Young Saxon had been brave in the springtime of another century.

The bell sounded, ending the class hour.

II

The chimes stridently tolled *Nearer My God to Thee* as the Professor and Abe walked across the campus. Abe glanced at the sun-polished ivied towers, the well-groomed lawns and blooming lilac trees. He remarked that it made him think of the middle ages. The Professor, noticing the lilac trees, thought how they seemed like shy and blooming virgins, opening their arms to their lover, the sun. And he suddenly reflected on how he had grown old teaching at this institution. He loved it. And some day he would have to leave it.

"Abe, you didn't understand me today. I don't think that a fellow like Cogan can write, or that he ever will. But he's a nice boy, sincere, and well-meaning, and I just can't hurt his feelings by being the one to tell him that he might as well give up the idea of writing now when he's young. I just can't be that cruel and tell him."

Abe was absorbed in his own thoughts. They passed through the campus men's club, one of the buildings in the northeast quadrangle. A poster announcing the Professor's play, *Sorry Old Fellow,* which was to be produced by the campus student dramatic association, stood in the corridor. The Professor hoped that Abe would comment on it, but the student was silent. Perhaps he even guessed that fear of rejection had prevented the Professor from submitting it to commercial producers.

They walked along a sunny street, and the Professor spoke of his own undergraduate days when he had known the grand infliction of the divine afflatus. He had piled work upon his instructors in every composition course, and after graduation he had been determined to become a writer. But first he had married and gotten a job in order to establish himself in emotional and economic security. He had written several novels that had been fair successes commercially, and he had contributed to *Lippincott's* and the other magazines of the day. One of his stories had even been reprinted in several anthologies. But after having completed the manuscript of still another novel, he'd destroyed it. Stealing a glance at Abe, he sensed that his student might be pitying him, and changed the subject, speaking in that witty, slangy manner that had given him local fame.

Smoking a cigarette, he rode downtown on an Illinois Central Suburban train. His attention wandered from the morning newspaper to his great Victorians. Sighing, he reflected how the scientific work of Darwin had crashed into the Victorian world like a comet, smashing all values and certainties. All its poets and writers had awakened in a universe that was crumbling. Persistent and terrifying questions had stared them in the face. Is there a God? Is there an after-life? Or is the universe blind matter and a brute survival of the fittest? Do we ascend from lower species, or do we come trailing clouds of glory from God Who is our home? Like graveworms these questions had, he thought, crawled through the pages of Victorian writings, making it, for him, the saddest period in all English literary history. And he had been nursed in that world. Its values were his values. He was too old now to be casually agnostic like so many of his students. Too old! He was sadder than his poets. His Carlyle, mighty mind, knifed by Doubt. Newman, always with a skeleton in his closet. Poor Walt Pater, wearily obsessed with anticipations of Death, stretching the tired arms of his emotions toward Rome when the brain could not follow. Great Browning whistling to keep up his courage. And grand and wistful Robert Louis, also whistling. Tennyson, pitting his genius against unanswerable eternal problems in *In Memoriam*. Matthew Arnold hearing in his inmost ear only the melancholy, long, withdrawing roar of the River of Faith. Ah . . . for the world which seems

> *To lie before us like a land of dreams,*
> *So various, so beautiful, so new,*
> *Hath really neither joy, nor love, nor light,*
> *Nor certitude, nor peace, nor help for pain;*
> *And we are here as on a darkling plain*
> *Where ignorant armies clash by night.*

Doubt, doubt had been the cancer of their spirits, as it was of his. Would it always be so? Would men never know? Always life going on, and man never knowing? Always! Never?

The train ran parallel to the lake that was plated with sunshine, its waters churning, the white caps and waves slashing against the beach. Ah, how fresh and young the lake! How lightly it bore the weight of the many centuries that had walked over its back! If man could only bear the weight of the eternal years thus! Alas! And Matthew Arnold's sleepless ministers of Nature were out there

> *Their glorious tasks in silence perfecting.*

Ah, sad, how all men came questing to the shingles where the waters halt, questing, asking, begging an answer. They stood at the seashore before the mystery of life. And the waves roared and broke, speaking no word of certitude or consolation. And . . .

Paul Saxon (1876–19??) . . . Percy Bysshe Shelley (1792–1822). . . . Paul Saxon (1876–????).

Yes, Paul Saxon, sorry old fellow. . . . One day he would be alone in a six-foot coffin, under the ground for the worms and the rats of Graceland Cemetery. His farewell from life and man and his poets would be shovelfuls of dirt rattled on his coffin, first one shovelful rattling, then others plumping in heavy succession. The seasons would roll on, and springs would come, and the suns of many, many Maytimes would shatter over his mounded grave. But it would be calm and peaceful down there, no, no, no, it would be lonely. Tonight he would have dinner with Louise, his oldest daughter, and he would see one of his little granddaughters. There would be an excellent meal, and afterward a lively round of bridge. Louise was no longer named Saxon. He was the last Saxon, the last of his line, and when the gravediggers would have heaped fresh dirt upon his coffin the sun of Saxon would have set. And it was going to be lonely there, under the ground, away from the sunlight, with only the worms and the rats.

Foolish to worry like that. . . . Foolish defeatism! Unnecessary morbidity! He was still hale and hearty, his teeth were healthy, his limbs flexible. Many of life's goods were still in store for him. And he had the right attitude toward life. The idea was to keep busy and active, not to contemplate black thoughts. He did that. He had his teaching, his newspaper work, his social life, golf, bridge, his interest in college athletics, brilliant students like Abe to nurture, first nights at the theater with people pointing him out and saying there goes Paul Saxon, literary banquets where he met interesting people, plenty of excellent meals, books to read, conversations. Conversation itself was an art, and he had mastered it. Many considered him one of the best conversationalists about town. Ah, no need for pessimism. All these things got him through his days tolerably well. . . . But at night, those few minutes when he lay awake, unable to take his eyes off those headings. Ten or fifteen minutes before sleep . . .

George Meredith (1828–1909) . . . Paul Saxon (1876–19??).

III

In his private office at *The Chicago Questioner* the Professor wrote the daily piece for his column, *Contrasts.* It was a review of a book by Gladys

Fairchild Kennilworth, a member of the Gold-Coast society set which the Professor had never quite completely attained. He contrasted her volume with *An American Tragedy*. Unlike Dreiser, this local author was sincere. She did not write a somber portrait, false to life because it represented people as will-less automata, like rats in a maze. Rather than being so unbalanced, Gladys Fairchild Kennilworth presented human beings as free, exercising that independence of will which was the bounty of their Creator. And her writing was sheer beauty. In each of her gemlike tales the meaning had transcended the local and the immediate, swooping up, like a glorious bird on the wing, into the empyrean realm of the universal, and thereby becoming fine art.

Reading his piece over, he decided that it was good, and that the author would appreciate it, too. And he breathed easily because Andrew Aiken Fletcher, owner of *The Questioner*, was a very erratic man. Employees on any of his papers throughout the country never knew when he would take a dislike to something one of them wrote. The Professor felt that at all events his job was safe for one more day, because there was nothing in this column that was likely to displease the erratic Mr. Fletcher.

Lighting a cigarette, he looked at his fan mail, letters containing challenges to fights and games of golf, notes assuring him that he did not know the simple ABC of bridge, corrections of his grammar, appreciations of his common sense, decency, and capacity for leadership, suggestions for future columns, praise from former University students for a recently written eulogy of Coach Harry Haggin Jackson, the grand old man of the gridiron, requests for autographs written in feminine handwriting. Out of the batch he suddenly found a letter from one of his former prize students, a boy whom he liked, and in whom he had placed great faith. It concluded:

> *Both you and Harry Haggin Jackson are getting more pathological every day. Look out or the freshmen and the sophomores will get wise to you.*

He maintained his equilibrium with an effort. He sat motionless. He grew angry. But then he decided that the letter was mean, petty, unfair, warped. He lamented that youth was so hard, and cold, and unsympathetic, and brutal. Youth, ah, youth! Because these cruel strains were in the very grain of youth, it lacked understanding and rarely accomplished anything genuinely human. He decided that this was a good idea for a column one of these days.

He went to the window and nervously glanced down at the diminished specks of human beings on the sidewalk. He termed it the urban ant heap, and decided that it, too, would serve as a column he might write.

He returned to his desk and stared at the wall calendar. Another day for him who was the last of his line, whose name was writ on less than waters, writ on the pages of a yellow journal that was drowned each noon hour, whose name was writ not on waters, but on oblivion, and whose sun was setting in the west of life. Ah, me!

Ah, many a time and oft in these last years he had fumed, to revolt and abandon everything. He thought of Browning's poem on the lost leader. Had he, too, sacrificed everything for a few handfuls of silver to make life comfortable? Suppose he should write a novel laying naked his soul, a human document to drip tears through the ages as the record of one defeated man? But he lacked the ability and the courage to destroy and burn all his bridges, and to speak out in hard truths. A man of fifty doesn't usually revolt. That was just the theme of *Sorry Old Fellow*, and it was a good play, too. He had to play the game. Hadn't he written recently that playing the game was the ethical basis of sports and also of life? His words turned and came back on him like retched-up food.

To be, or not to be; that is the question.
Whether 'tis nobler . . .

Hamlet Saxon smoked another cigarette. His face seemed to have become suddenly old and worried and mean. It carried an expression of smallness, cheapness and spite that was rarely noticeable. Aging Hamlet Saxon sat in the newspaper office, smoking a cigarette.

Too late now! No one would see Paul Saxon, last of his line, taking the dusty road at daybreak, walking to the far horizon with only the city of God at the other end of the road. That was merely poetry. He sat at his desk, thinking that he had often been called *The Happy Warrior*. He sat. The Happy Warrior sat, his cigarette ashes dropping over his littered desk.

Kelly Malloy, city editor, waddled in, interrupting the Professor's thoughts. Younger than the Professor, Kelly looked more shopworn. He had several unnecessary chins and his stomach bubbled out ridiculously. His eyes were the blue eyes of a mischievous boy corpsed in lazy fat. His manner was familiar, much to the Professor's discomfort.

"Professor, I'd like to talk to you. Say, do you know you're the only professor I ever met who talked and acted like a human being?" Kelly said, a remark he had been making ever since Mr. Saxon had been on the paper.

Kelly spoke of a perplexing problem in bridge which bothered him.

The Professor provided an analysis that was acceptable, because Kelly always accepted the Professor's analyses on such matters. Then Kelly spoke of the latest gang murder, but the Professor could not suffer him. He grabbed his hat, pleaded a luncheon engagement, and was gone.

For teaching two classes and doing his newspaper work the Professor received seventeen thousand dollars a year. His day's work was done, and he stepped out of *The Questioner* Building just as the one o'clock whistles blew. Joining the flow of pedestrians, he felt less spry than usual. He was troubled, and tried to forget himself by observing the passing people. He noticed bleary-eyed men and women moving furtively, many of them looking pinched, underfed, crass. An aging woman with powder in the sad creases of her face. Ah! Sometimes the city streets seemed to him like walking morgues. He informed himself that the people on the downtown streets were dabs of mud spun against his perceptions by the perpetually revolving and sometimes cruel wheel of life. He told himself that the passing people were an inundation of human beings whose faces were breaking waves of joy and sorrow. But in the souls of all these men and women there was the compensation of Faith. In the souls of all these people, Faith endowed them with dreams and hopes which they hugged tightly within the manger of their hearts. Ah, there was another crackerjack column he would soon write!

He tried to douse his mood by laughing at himself. He had always prided himself on having a real sense of humor. Now it would not work. He realized, as if finally, that he had come to a point in life where he could no longer be light and gay. He had to be serious, to squeeze sustenance and hope from every one of his little doings. He was a failure, and, yes, something of a clown. But he must be serious and feel that he was importantly contributing to the things that were human and valuable. Life was no longer a game, a race to be run, an experience to be exploited, a gilded rack upon which to hang figures of speech and poetry. It was something very, very precious, and he wanted to clutch that preciousness tightly within himself . . . forever. . . . And some day his grip would relax, weaken, stiffen, and the preciousness would drop like some beautiful choked thing. Dead!

Weep for Adonais!

[1932–37]

The Bride of Christ

I

Sister Bertha, a shriveled corpse, lay in a simple coffin, garbed in the black habit of her order. Her face, with all the wrinkling deformities of old age printed on it, was ashen and hard, almost like stone; there was a bag of skin under the pointed, shrunken chin. Her bony hands were folded over her stomach, and in her stiffened fingers was entwined a pair of rosary beads.

Sister Bertha lay dead before the small altar of the convent chapel, the same chapel in which, these last five years, she had daily heard mass during the school year. Her coffin had been placed in front of the altar rail at which she had so frequently knelt to receive the Blessed Sacrament. And in the front pew of the dim and small chapel, two nuns knelt on watch, their lips moving noiselessly in prayer for the repose of the soul of the departed member of their community. They occasionally lifted their eyes and glanced at the casket, the burning candles, the flickering red altar light before the tabernacle.

The minutes passed slowly and quietly, accompanied only by the occasional rustling of the heavily clothed nuns and by the muffled echoes from other parts of the convent, or from that distant foreign world beyond its walls.

For forty years Sister Bertha had performed the work of a nun, and all during those years death had been almost constantly in her consciousness. For those four decades she had labored in the Master's vineyard so that when she died she would be united with Him, gaining honored admittance into the Communion of Saints in Heaven. And now she lay before His altar, the embalmed remains of a withered old woman. That goal for which she had pointed her days had been attained: she had died in the state of Grace. She was, if her faith were justified, now joyous in Heaven.

All memories, all acts of devotion, all thoughts and aspirations, all fears of sin, all prickings of conscience, every impress of life upon her was wiped out of the decomposing brain within her skull. All that remained of Sister Bertha lay as a simple prediction, as a strong and certain prophecy of the destiny of all living matter. All memory of her was now lodged in living brain cells and in dusty records. In time, these living brain cells would be dead. In time, these records would fade into illegibility. And then, even memory of her would be obliterated.

Thus Sister Bertha lay in death, while two of her sister nuns kept silent and prayerful watch over her corpse.

Scattered over the world were many men who, as boys, had been the material, the souls, on which she had worked. As boys they had sat, straining and awed, tortured into attentiveness in the classrooms she had querulously ruled with a loud voice, a frowning sour visage, and a firm ruler. Although these thousands of men had known her at different periods, and in different towns and cities, the majority of them had known essentially the same teacher. They had known a tall nun whose voice was high-pitched. Some of them had known this nun when her face had begun to wrinkle. Others had known her as a middle-aged woman. But wrinkles had only signified that she was aging, not mellowing. They had signalized no change in that capricious disposition of hers. These men had, as boys, known essentially the same woman and the same classroom routine. She had acquired many nicknames from them in her forty years of teaching, but over and over again boys in different towns and cities and even sisters in her own community gave her the same nickname: Sister Battling Bertha.

In this long period she usually had taught seventh- and eighth-grade boys. She had taught in small towns scattered through Indiana, Michigan, and Illinois, as well as in various neighborhoods of Chicago. But her manner and her method had always been unvarying. She usually had swept into the classroom with an angry frown on her face. As she had grown older, her face had become chalky, and in her last year she had seemed almost ghostlike. Each of her days she had similarly dedicated to Christ, her Master, with hastily murmured prayers. Then would begin her daily struggle with her pupils—catechism, bible history, arithmetic, grammar, history, reading, Palmer Method in writing. Year after year she had taught these subjects from the same textbooks, rigidly following the course, page after page. She would shriek at disobedient boys and at the dunces who could not grasp the lessons easily. Sometimes her voice rose to such a pitch that she disturbed other classes, and her sister nuns would rush to her classroom door to discover whether or not Sister Bertha were having a riot on her hands. She used sledge-hammer methods of teaching. Pupils were required to know the assigned lessons by rote. If not, she bullied them, screamed at them, predicted that they would be failures in life who might even end up on the gallows. Often when boys whispered or threw spitballs in the schoolroom, or when an incorrigible dunce did not know his lesson, she would fling herself from her dais, sweep down the classroom aisle, shrieking, her beads rattling, her habit swishing. She would pound the erring or guilty boy on the back of the neck with her ruler or clapper, and as she administered punishment she would shout in that rasping voice of hers. As she aged, she became increasingly nearsighted, and often, due to this condition, she would strike the wrong pupil. Almost no pupil was safe in her classroom. And when she beat her pupils, a gleam of almost passionate satisfaction would come into those small, weak, watery eyes. She would grab a boy by the scruff of the neck, shake and pound him, and as she did this, the muscles of her face would tighten. Her expression would be that of a fanatic swept with joy. If appearances were not deceiving, the happiest moments of her life must have been those during which she was punishing bad little boys. She terrified her pupils, the innocent and the guilty alike. Few boys ever liked school while she was their teacher. When she was ill, they were happy. When they learned that she had been transferred to another school, they hurrahed. Even the brightest of boys, those who had sometimes earned the nickname of "Sister's pet"—even such pupils were overjoyed when they learned that she would teach them no longer.

Thus for forty years she had taught. During her last years she was half blind. Her memory began to fade. She sometimes showed the symptoms of a person sinking into a second childhood. Her pupils suffered more from the advance of age upon her than she did herself. Her hearing began to fail as had her memory and her eyesight. She screamed more violently, more shrilly, more whiningly. She became, in these last years, like raw energy. She would often suddenly and without provocation descend on a boy and beat him until he screamed for mercy, perhaps to leave him for the remainder of his life smarting under the memory of an unjust, unfair, undue punishment.

She was equally a source of tribulation to her sister nuns who had to live in the same convent with her. She quarreled with them over trivialities. She constantly accused them of being lacking in piety, devotion, and in being lax in the observance of religious duties and obligations. When angered with one of them, she would hurl accusations of impiety and even of heresy. Any sign of simple and harmless levity, any human foible or failing, any little indulgence in gossip which was, almost by necessity, the principal amusement and recreation of the nuns—these led her to offer sharp and curt criticisms and complaints. She would unexpectedly catch two young nuns giggling over some item of gossip and she would sink to her knees and sanctimoniously and melodramatically bless herself and pray loudly to God to save their sinful souls. She would arise from her prayers and even accuse them of having been guilty of a violation of the sixth commandment, a charge, she was convinced, that was true of many of the grammar-school boys and girls whom she happened to be teaching. She would even accuse the young nuns she had caught giggling as having been a bad influence tending to lead pupils in the school to commit the dread sin. She would rant and rage and then go off in a fury to complain to the Sister-Superior to lay charges against the younger nuns. She upset and unnerved the entire convent wherever she was. Life within the convent walls became then a kind of armed truce. She herself stimulated more gossip. She caused dissension. She became the source and inspiration for many an un-nunlike squabble.

Sister Bertha had entered the convent when she was in her early twenties. She had been, at that time, a tall and homely young woman, graceless in stature and mind, awkward in movement, unpopular almost everywhere. She was the daughter of a small-town storekeeper. Shortly before her entry into the convent she had been courted by a middle-aged barber. Her parents, to whom she had become a tribulation because of her carping religiosity, her extreme and rather histrionic piety, had favored her marrying the man. Friends, neighbors, gossipy townspeople had all taken an interest in the prospective match. They had waited in expectation for the news that it had resulted in an engagement. But she had rejected the proposal. She loved Christ, not mortal man. And sex was an ugly cancer in her mind, a hideous unmentionable. Marriage would have meant experiencing this terrifyingly ugly thing. It would have meant sleeping with a man in sinful and disgusting intimacy. It was vulgar, earthly love. Her love was spiritual and Heavenly. She began to pray with an intensified fervor. She devoted long and perfervid hours to God, often remaining on her knees until she suffered pain and physical torture. She made novenas to the Blessed Virgin Mary. She heard mass daily. At length, she became convinced that she had been honored with the call to serve Christ. During a sultry summer evening when she was in bed, her mind became disturbed and distorted. She became feverish with excitement. She was convinced that she was having a vision. She believed that she saw Christ by her opened window, His feet and His hands bearing the marks of the crucifixion nails, a rent in His side exposing His bleeding Sacred Heart. He told her that hers was a mission to go forth in His name, and to teach and guide the little ones who were beloved by Him and whose tiny footsteps needed to be guided into the paths of virtue, piety, and holiness.

She entered the convent. At thirty, she began teaching. And that had been forty years ago. During these forty years there had been all the little trivialities of the schoolroom, her explosions, beatings, harsh words, instruction in the so-called basic subjects, the hearing of lessons, the telling of parables for the added inculcation of moral lessons, the repetition of the same distortions and simplifications of American history, the same problems in percentage, the same answers to catechism questions, the same sentences to be diagrammed, the same rules of grammar to be explained, the same routine continuing year in and year out. She had had few contacts with the outside world. She had scarcely read newspapers. She had voted twice on instructions from her bishop. There had been daily prayers and hours of meditation, and regular confessions. All the natural impulses of a woman had been canceled in love of and devotion to Christ. Always, Christ had been in her mind. She had imagined and relived His life over and over again, His crucifixion, the vinegar and gall which He had been given to drink, the wiping of His face by Veronica, the forgiveness of Saint Mary Magdalen from her sins of the flesh, His Resurrection and Ascension into Heaven—the life of Christ, her Christ. How often had she not prayed to Him? How many times had she not knelt, wishing that she were a Veronica who was wiping blood from the pained, bloody, suffering face of the tormented God! How often had she not visualized Him crucified, wincing from her vision of the nails piercing His tender and holy flesh. She had lived with Christ in her mind for forty years. She had sought to serve Him in her way by teaching the young to live with Him, and to be worthy of Him in Heaven.

And now she lay dead. Those who had been her pupils were scattered over the world. Whenever most of them dwelled nostalgically and reminiscently on their boyhood days, she became integrally interwoven into their memories. Often, when they did not image her in such moods, she remained an unseen, unimaged terror stalking these nostalgic moods and contemplations. Many of them remembered her with resentment, almost none with understanding. They could not forget her blows, her shrieks, her rigid classroom discipline, her unfairness. None of them loved her. And now she lay dead.

II

A solemn high mass for the dead was celebrated over her corpse. Sacred church music was sung. The nuns in the community knelt in devout attendance. In back of them were the school children and a few parishioners. The music was slow, sad, solemn. The parish priest delivered a brief sermon. He spoke of how Sister Bertha had labored in the Master's vineyard for forty years. She had heard the call of the Master as a young woman, and she had heeded that call. She had taught the Truth, inspiring in young hearts the faith and the goodness of Christ, our Lord. Year after year she had taught the Word to those little ones whom Christ Himself had singled out as the special lambs who were to be protected above all others in His flock. Who knew how extensive her influence for good had been? Who knew on what spot of earth at the very minute that he was preaching over her poor earthly remains—who knew but what some one of her many boys was remembering in the tabernacle of his heart, remembering her teaching, her inspiration, profiting from that atmosphere of holiness and devotion that had permeated her classroom? Who knew but at what corner of God's earth, at this very moment, some one of her former boys was being steered clear of sin and temptation because of the good example she had set for him years ago in a little modest classroom?

Yes, hers had been a quiet life, peaceful. It would not furnish the material for even a slender book of earthly drama. No. But it would for a book of good and holy deeds for the next world. And how large and bulky that book would be, that book of the good and holy deeds of Sister Bertha! For daily, hers had been a life in Christ. It had begun with meditation and prayers in the morning and it had progressed through the classroom, to conclude with prayers and meditation before sleep in the evening. Her first thought in the morning had always been of God. Her last thought in the evening had also always been of God. Yes, hers had been a simple and undistinguished life as this world measures a life. But a holy and a wonderful life, as life is measured in the kingdom of God. A life of sacrifices here! A life of eternal joys above! And now in Heaven the angels must be smiling, and there must be the joy of paradise reigning. One of their own, one of the real Communion of Saints, had come home. And the joy of Heaven, it was a consolation for those on earth, sisters, parents, little boys, who were missing her with heaviness of heart. She was departed now. Her soul was flown aloft. She was taking her proper place in Heaven as a true and rightful bride of Christ.

And thus was Sister Bertha buried. All her petty tyrannies, her unjust punishments, her prejudiced utterances against those not of the True Faith, her shrieks and shouts, all was of the past, buried and forgotten; and her thousands of former pupils scarcely remembered her, scarcely carried with them in life any example learned in her classroom, scarcely remembered anything connected with her except the fear that she had driven like a spike into their hearts. This was the Sister Bertha who was buried as a Bride of Christ.

[1934-38]

Street Scene

"Say, do I belong to the human race?" the old man asked himself aloud as he stood at the corner of Ninth Street and Michigan.

It was an Indian summer afternoon. Across the street, in Grant Park, there was a playograph recording the World Series baseball game between the St. Louis Cardinals and the New York Yankees. The old man wore shapeless clothes; his shirt was gray with dirt, and the toes stuck out of his army boots. He shuffled along and stopped in front of the gold and bronze entrance to the Nation Oil Building.

"Hell, I give up," he told himself.

He yawned. He stretched his arms like a sleepy man. He took off his coat, rolled it into a bundle, and laid it on the sidewalk. Heedless of those who stopped to gape at him, he slowly went through the gestures of un-dressing, putting on pajamas and getting ready for bed. He mumbled instructions to an imaginary valet, remarking that he wouldn't need a bath in the morning because he had decided to lie down and die.

He lay down on the sidewalk and carefully drew imaginary covers over himself. He made loud, snoring noises.

A small crowd immediately gathered about him.

"Nighty, night," he said.

Strangers gaped at him. He stared vacant-eyed at the sky. More pedestrians stopped to cluster curiously about him.

"Are you hurt, fellow?"

"Hell, he's just full of canned heat."

"What's the matter with you?"

"He was knocked down in a fight."

"Who is he?"

"You can see, he's coked up with wood alcohol."

"Somebody call a doctor."

"Where's the police? They're never around when they're needed."

"The man was knocked down by an automobile. Somebody call for an ambulance."

"Here's an officer."

"The law."

A burly, red-faced policeman pushed his way through the growing crowd. He looked at the old man, who met his gaze with innocent eyes.

"What's wrong?" the policeman asked.

"Hello, officer."

The policeman looked at him dubiously. He pushed his cap back on his head and scratched his head.

"What's the matter with you, huh? Come on, what's the matter?"

A woman tried to tell the policeman what had happened.

"I'm all right, officer. I've just laid down here because I feel kind of tired. I thought maybe I'd just like to lay down and die, that's all. I only want to be left alone so that I can lay down and die."

Some of the on-lookers laughed.

"What?" the cop asked, angry and bewildered.

"Can't you let me alone? Can't you let me alone to die in peace?"

"Come on, now, none of this wise stuff. Move on! Get up and move on! Do you hear me?"

"Can't I die in peace? I tell you, all I want is to die in peace."

"You heard me! Move on! I don't want any monkeyshines here. This is a public place."

He grabbed the old man's arm and tugged at it. The old man didn't resist when the policeman pulled him.

A portly police sergeant appeared on the scene.

"What's wrong, Mike?" the sergeant asked.

"There's nothin' wrong, sir. I'm only trying to die in peace."

The policeman let the man drop back on the sidewalk.

"Shut up, you!" The policeman turned to the sergeant.

"He's disturbin' the peace."

"What's the matter with you? You can't die there," the sergeant said angrily.

"Jesus Christ, can't a man die in peace, even in a free country?"

"Come on, quit blasphemin' and move on," the sergeant ordered.

"Move on!" the policeman commanded, prodding the old man with a club.

The old man didn't move.

The sergeant grabbed his sleeve and tried to lift him. Then both the sergeant and the policeman shoved him.

"I told you to be on your way," the sergeant shouted.

The old man rose. The crowd laughed hilariously. He limped on for about ten feet. He turned around and told the crowd:

"I only want to die quietly."

"Go on or I'll run you in," the cop bellowed as a number of spectators continued laughing.

The old man moved down a few more paces. He again stretched himself out on the sidewalk.

More people stopped to see what was happening.

"I'll run yuh all in," the sergeant said, turning to glare at the amused and voluble crowd.

The sergeant and the policeman stood over the old man, not knowing what to do.

"I only want to die in peace. That's all I want. You can't make me work. I'm too tired. This is a free country."

"Shut up, you!" the policeman snapped.

"I only want to say, work is too hard for me."

"Get up!" the policeman said, putting his foot against the old man's ribs. "Get up, I say! This is a public street and not a sanitarium. Get up and be quick about it! Do you hear me?" the policeman bellowed.

"I want to die in peace. Can't you leave me alone?"

"Are you going to get up?" the sergeant asked.

"No, I'm dying. Let me die in peace."

"Officer, that man's sick. Call an ambulance," an indignant lady cried out.

"Lady, move on and tend to your own business."

The sergeant turned to the policeman.

"Come on, let's get this bum out of here."

They bent down and tried to lift the old man. He stiffened his body. They dragged him along the sidewalk on his buttocks. Some of the on-lookers laughed. A few protested, but the police paid no attention to them. Still more pedestrians stopped to watch. The policeman and the sergeant continued to drag the old man along the sidewalk. His shirt was unbuttoned. Freeing himself from the police, he lost his shirt. He lay on the sidewalk, naked and dirty from the waist up. His ribs showed.

"Get a tow wagon," a wit from the crowd yelled.

"No, get Big Bill Thompson the Mayor over here," a second wit said.

The policeman and the sergeant puffed, tired from their exertion. The old man watched them with innocently twinkling blue eyes. He turned and winked at the crowd. The policemen again tried to lift him. He relaxed, refusing to cooperate. They let him drop back onto the sidewalk. He shivered. His feet dangled over the edge of the curb. Automobiles had stopped, tying up traffic. Automobile horns made an incessant racket. The crowd now filled the sidewalk.

"Dunning for that bum," someone in the crowd said loudly.

"I don't care what happens. Let a truck run over me. I don't care. I don't care. I give up. I wanna die," the old man said. His teeth chattered. "No, sir, you can't make me work. I'll die instead."

"Get an ambulance," someone called.

"Let him alone, officer," someone else demanded.

The sergeant talked to the policeman, and then the cops went off.

"Come on, button up, you! There's ladies passing."

Another policeman showed up.

"Get them people back," the sergeant ordered. The policeman began edging the crowd back. When he succeeded on one side, they pressed forward on another.

"Just let me alone."

"Why don't you go to work, you bum?" a man yelled.

"It's too hard," the old man answered.

"Shut up, you!" the sergeant said.

A fat policeman joined the other cops and helped to push the crowd back. The sergeant stood over the old man.

"You gonna get up?" he asked.

"Officer, please leave me die in peace."

"The wagon is on the way," the sergeant said.

Suddenly the old man stood up, picked up his clothes, and put them on. He started walking away.

"Oh, no, you don't," the sergeant said, grabbing his arm.

The policemen escorted the old man southward. The crowd followed. Near Roosevelt Road they allowed him to sit and wait on the steps of an old building. He paid no attention to his audience.

"I'll be dead soon," he soliloquized. "Then let the world go to hell. It can die after me. It can die five minutes after me. I don't care. I don't even belong to the human race anyway. I don't care. I'm gonna die in five minutes. I won't work. All I want is to die in a little peace. I'm goin' West. Go West, young man. Ha! Ha! Everybody's goin' West, even cops. Ain't that right, officer?"

He looked up at the fat policeman.

"Shut up!"

"Even cops die. Everybody's going to die."

He looked down at the sidewalk for a moment and then, with a twinkle in his eyes, he looked up at the policemen.

"That's a good joke, isn't it? Everybody dies, even cops."

The patrol wagon arrived.

Two policemen lifted him roughly, while the others kept the crowd back.

"Well, I must belong to the human race. They didn't send the dog catcher's bus after me," the old man said.

They shoved him into the patrol wagon. It went off.

The crowd slowly broke up. A stranger asked one of the officers what had happened.

"Nothin' much. Another bum cooked on canned heat. He's gone coo-koo. The stuff makes 'em all that way. Well, he'll get thirty days in the Bridewell, but it won't do no good. Them bums is jus bums. They're just bums."

"You're right, officer."

The cop strolled back along Michigan Boulevard. There was a cheer from the crowd by the playograph, and it broke up. The Yankees had won the world series from the Cardinals in four straight games.

[1930–43]

The Hyland Family

> When virtue displays itself solely as the individual's
> simple conformity with the duties of the station to which
> he belongs, it is rectitude.
>
> —Hegel

I

It was a radiant Sunday morning in July. Ten o'clock mass was just over at the Church of Mary Magdalen on the southeast side of Chicago. The crowd had begun to dwindle when Andrew J. Hyland, Sr. loomed in the center doorway with his two daughters and his son beside him. This was always a moment of quiet gratification for Andrew, Sr. He glowed inwardly with that sense of pleasure that only the good man can experience when he has done his duty. Andrew, Sr. knew that he was one of the leading members of the parish, and he accepted, as an obligation, the responsibility of fulfilling all his religious duties without laxity. He was one of the largest contributors to the annual church collections. He received the Sacraments regularly. He strove, in every possible way, to be a model Catholic layman. And for years he had required his family to remain kneeling for a few moments after mass, saying extra prayers, while others hastened and scuffled out of church. With the regularity of a clock, the Hyland family usually appeared in the church doorway at the same time every Sunday. They walked with dignity of bearing, conscious that they were the cynosure of many eyes. Even in their movements they seemed to reveal a sense of their own worth. But they did nothing to call attention to themselves. They dressed expensively and in fashion, but with good taste. If they stopped to talk with friends, they never raised their voices, nor did they laugh too loudly. They minded their own business. But their brief promenade out of church on Sunday mornings had become a parish event—in fact, an unmentioned but recognized family tradition.

Andrew, Sr. was a tall, thin man with a long, straight, almost hawklike nose and a tight, rather constricted, face. He was gray around the temples, but he looked well preserved and in the best of health. In every sense of the word, he appeared to be a solid and respectable citizen. Pleased as he was after Sunday mass, he also felt a twinge of pain. Five years before, his dearly beloved wife, Ellen, had passed away. All his memories of her were inextricably associated with the Church. She had been a pious woman. They had always received the Sacraments together, and it had been during her lifetime that he had begun the habit of kneeling to pray for a few moments at the end of mass. In church he missed her more than he did at home, and there were moments when he had to exert force of will to concentrate on the mass rather than lose himself in reveries of her. Sensing her beside him in spirit while he knelt in his pew, his sorrow was softened into resignation. No more than Job would he question the will of the Almighty. And yet the pain of her loss cast a somber hue over his emotions. Genuine as was his sense of gratification, it was nonetheless restrained. He remembered her and he missed her. And he drew from her death the lesson that even the happiest of lives, even the finest moments of joy are touched with sorrow.

Ruth Hyland was twenty-six; Helen was twenty-two; Andrew J., Jr. was twenty. The girls had attended the parish grammar school, Saint Paul's high school, and Saint Mary's of the Woods in Indiana. The son had been graduated from Notre Dame the previous June. The children were all fair of hair and skin, as their mother had been. Ruth was rather tall and thin, a bony, angular girl with high cheekbones and a pale complexion. Her face was drawn, but at times, and with the help of the clothes she wore, she looked attractive. Helen was plump and buttery, with rosy cheeks and vapid blue eyes; she still retained the virginal bloom of girlhood. Even when she was solemn it seemed as though her face would break into smiles. Andrew, Jr. was small of stature, bony like Ruth and his father, and prissy in his gestures. His lips were unusually thin, and he rarely smiled.

In public, the Hylands tended to act alike, as if by instinct. At times they even seemed to look alike. Promenading out of church, they walked in file. They knew they were on display and could not permit the slightest irregularity, even of gesture or expression. Ruth, haughtier than the other children, swept strangers with a gaze that verged on contempt. Helen, the most spontaneous of the Hylands, was tense with the necessity of being on good behavior. She was acting in imitation of her sister and in unconscious acceptance of the unmentioned family custom. Andrew, Jr. was dreamy, absorbed, and when he was in such a mood he appeared to be singularly pious, as if he carried outside of church the emotions, the feelings, the solemnity which were appropriate in the presence of God.

On this Sunday morning, Andrew, Jr.'s appearance was deceptive. It was his alertness which saved him from the embarrassment of having to speak to Marie Considine. She had had a crush on him ever since grammar school, and he had never reciprocated it. Because of her inability to hide her feelings, he had contempt for her. Although most people thought her pretty, she was a drab thing in his eyes. Her family didn't amount to anything, and her father had gone to a drunkard's grave. He saw her edging diagonally toward him and lifted his brows in annoyance. Years ago he had made it clear to her that he would have nothing to do with her. It was utterly preposterous of her to imagine he could admit her to his world. Withal, she was so lacking in character, so shameless, that she persisted in trying to attract his attention. And here she was, up to her old tricks. He saved himself from the discomfort of saying good morning to her by turning to Ruth and remarking in high seriousness that the morning was splendid. The weather was interesting to Ruth at the moment, because she was concerned in not seeing a former high-school classmate who was *gauche*. She spiritedly told her brother that the sun was shining. Helen was flustered, because she saw Jimmy Norgrove, who persisted in asking her to go out with him even though he knew she was engaged to Jimmy Barry. She didn't even care a tiny part of the fingernail of her little finger for him, but he always pestered her in the most impertinent manner. Every time she saw him she was confused and didn't know what to do. She joined in conversation with her brother and sister, saying it was a wonderful morning, wonderful. At the very same moment, Andrew, Sr. noticed his poor relation, third cousin Ed Nolan, gazing at him with searching, hurt eyes. Looking away from Ed Nolan, he confirmed the judgment of his children concerning the weather. Having thus escaped those who would intrude upon their dignity and self-respect, the Hylands stopped by the curb to converse with Old Tom Gregory, the millionaire chainstore man, and his wife. They inquired of the health of the Gregorys, exchanged a few words, and concluded by expressing perfect agreement with Old Tom when he said that it was a fine morning. Then they marched off to their Lincoln limousine and drove home to their nine-room apartment in a new building near South Shore Drive.

It was a comfortable home, spotlessly clean, and furnished by Ruth in what she considered the best of taste. The furniture was all new, and one could almost see the price tags on it. In the parlor there was a large Baby Grand piano. There were oil paintings on the wall, including a large one of the Holy Family. Along one wall there was a large bookcase. On the shelves were an odd assortment of novels, school books, the works of G. K. Chesterton, and a complete set of Sir Walter Scott in red morocco binding with gold stamping.

When the family returned home, Andrew, Jr. immediately went to his room, changed to flannels, and left to play tennis. Ruth brought slippers to her father, and he read the business section, the news section, and the sports section of *The Sunday Clarion*. Helen giggled over the comic section, Ruth curled up on the sofa and pored dreamily over the society news.

II

"Ruth, you always see to it that everything is just jack-dandy for Sunday dinner," Andrew, Sr. said as he ate a hearty meal.

The table was attractively covered with a spotless heavy linen tablecloth, and the silverware gleamed.

"Somebody has to see to such things," Ruth answered with a slight neurotic tremor in her voice.

They all went on eating as if they had not observed this tremor in Ruth's voice. Ruth pecked at a small helping of food. She thought it was vulgar for a girl to eat too much, and everyone said she ate like a bird. In consequence, she was always hungry and munched candy and sweets constantly. No matter how many sweets she ate, she never gained weight. At times her slimness was a source of pride to her, but at other times she was troubled and wished she were a little more plump. She was often displeased because Helen had such a good appetite, and frequently warned her sister that if she were not careful she would become fat. Helen worried about her weight and she was continually going on diets and then breaking her fine resolutions.

"Did any of you notice Ed Nolan hanging around outside of church this morning like a dog without a bone?" Andrew, Sr. asked.

They shook their heads negatively.

"He was waiting to buttonhole me. I suppose he wanted to make another touch."

"I wish he'd move to another parish," Ruth said.

"Do you know, I think I'd pay the cost if he would. He's always parading himself as my cousin. He embarrasses me. I've told him many times that I can't afford to loan him money. He had many chances, and he's done nothing with them."

"He's common," Ruth said, as if this were the most damning judgment that could be made of her cousin.

"He's a darn fool. He had a little money saved up, and I advised him to buy a house. But do you think he took my advice? You remember how he invested his money in Imbray stock?"

"Yes, we all remember," Andrew, Jr. said.

"He's the kind of a fellow who courts bad luck. But who wants another helping?"

Helen passed her plate, and Ruth cast a disapproving eye on her.

Andrew, Sr. served Helen a second helping.

"Ruthie, you?" he asked.

"No, thank you, Father."

"Oh, a little more won't hurt you."

"I've had enough," she said decisively.

"Well, I haven't. This roast beef is jack-dandy. Ella sure knows how to cook."

He served Andrew, Jr. and then gave himself a second helping.

"Helen, did you notice Fran Sweeney's dress at church?" Ruth asked.

"Yes, I did. She wore brown shoes with a black dress."

"She's as common as Marie Considine."

There was a lapse in conversation.

"Father Kilbride preached a good sermon, didn't he?"

"Did you notice, Dad, that he mentioned G. K. Chesterton?" Andrew, Jr. asked.

"Yes. I'll have to read that fellow sometime."

"Dad, I wish you would. Read his book, *The New Jerusalem,*" Andrew, Jr. advised.

"What's it about?"

"The Jews. He says the Jews are an Oriental people and that they should live and dress like Orientals instead of Occidentals."

"Say—that's not a bad idea," Andrew, Sr. exclaimed, the light of knowledge dawning in his eyes.

"Fran Sweeney is going steady with that bootlegger's son—Castano—think of that," Ruth cut in.

"I guess the old man wants her to marry him. Perhaps he smells the mazuma there. Old man Sweeney is in a bad fix these days. I heard the other night that he might lose some of his buildings," Andrew, Sr. said.

"Gosh, I wish I could understand why there has to be a depression," Helen said.

"Girls shouldn't trouble themselves about it," Andrew, Jr. told Helen.

"I wouldn't get anywhere if I did," Helen said.

"I was talking to Mr. Ames at the office the other day. He agreed with me that things would be a lot different if Al Smith was in the White House. But that's too much to expect. You see what they did to Smith here in Chicago last month?" Andrew, Sr. said.

"But, Dad, why are they all against us because we're Catholics?" Helen asked, a questioning look shadowing her face.

"Bigots," Andrew, Sr. answered with positiveness.

Noticing that they had finished, Ruth pressed the electric button for Ella, the colored servant. Ruth enjoyed this. She had had it installed after her mother died. Ella, a fat Negress, appeared, wearing a fancy organdy apron. She quietly removed the dishes and served the dessert and coffee.

Conversation became desultory. When they had finished, Andrew, Sr. bowed his head, and his children followed suit. They said grace aloud.

III

Ruth sat in her bedroom with the door closed. She was nervous. She wiped away a tear. She had just reread the letters of Joe Fontanna. Then she had put them back in the drawer where she kept her sacred mementos: Joe's letters, favors from parties, pictures, crushed flowers, dance programs, and other souvenirs.

She had a slight headache. Ever since Joe had died of a heart attack over two years ago, she had had headaches. She had strange aches and pains, too, and rarely felt well. She believed she was destined to die young, and yet she was not afraid. After what she had gone through, what terrors could there be in life, or in death?

As a girl in high school, Ruth had never been popular, and most of her friends had had more dates than she. For years she had lived for the night and the dance that would change her life. And while she was away at school, she had been invited to a Notre Dame homecoming victory dance by Tommy McGrew, a grammar-school classmate. He had lived in the same dormitory as Joe Fontanna, one of the ends on the Notre Dame football team. She had been introduced to Joe. Joe had exchanged dances with Tommy, and it had been love at first sight. Ruth, a frigid girl, had blossomed out. During the subsequent Christmas vacation, she had had several dates with Joe. After his graduation, they had become engaged, and three months before their expected marriage he had died suddenly of a heart attack.

Ruth knew there could never be anyone else in her life to take the place of Joe. He had been a tall, well-built, dark-haired, handsome Italian-American boy whose father was a wealthy wholesale grocer. Gruff and inarticulate, he had been a real diamond in the rough. She realized that she had had no real girlhood, no true happiness in life until she had met him. Most girls had not liked her. At Saint Paul's, she had usually been treated rather coldly. She had not been understood, and some of the girls had meanly thought her a snob. In her senior year, she had hoped to be on the Senior Prom Committee and thus get her name and her picture on the society pages of the newspapers. The girls had not voted for her, and her disappointment rankled even now, almost ten years afterward. It was only with Joe that she had truly been happy. Before that, she had wanted love but had been afraid of it, even disdainful of it. When boys had taken her to dances, she had been rather aloof, and when they had tried to kiss her, she had frozen up. But from the first moment she had set eyes on Joe she knew that he was different. She had melted. And then this tragedy had happened.

The way she had received the news had been a terrible shock. She had been expecting a telephone call from him. She had rushed to the telephone and had been told the news of his death. She had fainted. For a week she had been in hysterics. The doctor had kept her on sedatives for several months. Long after his death she would still burst into tears, even in public. She felt incomplete. She could not maintain her interest in anything. She rarely smiled. She brooded over him, going over and over again in memory the days of their courtship and engagement. She had so reconstructed her memories of their love that she could no longer distinguish what was fact and what was fantasy. She dreamed of him continually, and even events from her dreams became mixed with memories. At times, when she heard the name Joseph mentioned, or read it in print, tears would well up in her eyes. Although she knew it was sinful, she often regretted she had not given herself to him and even taken the initiative in order that it might have happened. For now she could never know the fruits of love. Now she must go to her grave a virgin. And had she sacrificed herself, she could have confessed it, atoned for it, devoted her entire life to doing penance for that one sin. She consoled herself by visualizing herself as a tragic person. She saw her destiny as one of nobility and suffering. And yet she revolted against her destiny. The minute-by-minute reality of her life was hard to bear. Why, why had such a tragedy been hers? She wanted to live. She was only twenty-six. She could see nothing ahead of her but a barren future. She had nothing in life but memories of Joe.

She devoted herself to the care and management of the home. She did the shopping, attended to such matters as laundry, decided on what meals were to be served, strove to take the place of her mother. All this was not enough. She wanted her own home. She spun out every domestic chore, making it take as much time as possible. She complained that she had too much to do. She took needless time in shopping, in checking on prices, in finding bargains. She was continuously rearranging the furniture and looking for new things to buy. She read fashion magazines and bought dresses, coached Helen in what to wear, talked endlessly of style and clothes. She hunted for recipes for new dishes which she had Ella cook. She read romantic love stories and books about royalty with yearning sadness. All this was not enough to fill her life. She lived in her memories.

Now she heard Helen singing gaily in her room next door. She had sung to herself that way when Joe had been alive. The mere presence of Helen, who was so much in love, made her memories more unbearable, exacerbated her nerves, and produced frightening feelings of envy and jealousy. Bitterly, she complained to herself of her fate, voicing over again the same laments she had voiced to herself ever since his death. She knew it was not fair of her to feel this way about her sister. She didn't want to be jealous of Helen or spiteful toward her. Such emotions rose within her without having been willed. What could she expect Helen to do? Helen was in love. And how well she could imagine Helen's feelings, her dreams and all the delights and hopes that filled her mind. When a girl was in love, when she had found the one and only person, every minute of the day was saturated with joy. Then she lived on wings of joy and expectation. Helen was feeling that way now as she sang in her bedroom. Ruth's sadness became overpowering. She wanted to cry. She struggled with herself not to. She sobbed softly.

Helen stopped singing. In a moment she knocked on Ruth's door.

"What do you want?" Ruth cried out impatiently.

"It's me. If you aren't doing anything, I just wanted to talk," Helen said.

"I was taking a nap. I have a headache. Can't you people let me alone," Ruth answered.

"Oh, all right. I'm sorry," Helen said in disappointment.

Ruth immediately regretted her impulsive action. She had spoken before thinking. But her eyes were red from crying, and she hadn't wanted Helen to see her. She should have talked with her sister. Perhaps the kid had something on her mind. Helen needed a mother. She had to be like a mother. Oh, she didn't want to. Why was this her fate?

Weekends were always the worst for her. This was the time when girls had their big dates. With Joe, Saturday and Sunday nights had been so divine. And Helen was a constant reminder of these. She had used to fuss on Sundays, just as Helen did now, in order to pass the time until Joe called for her.

That was the past!

A cold horror came over her. Nothing in life was more awful than the past. The very word was like ice laid on one's spine. She had to forget. She had to live in the present. She had to live.

She stared at the wall with tear-stained eyes. She imagined herself talking to Joe. She explained to him how she felt, poured out her heart to him in imagination. Her feelings dissolved into a soft melancholy. Her tears dried. She slipped into a mood of consoling sadness.

The telephone rang. She had a vague notion that it was for her. She heard Helen rush past her door to answer the telephone.

"It's for you," Helen called.

Ruth didn't answer. Helen knocked on the door.

"Who is it?" Ruth asked, annoyed.

An intense wave of anticipation gripped her. She suddenly believed this was a telephone call that would change her entire life.

"It's Teresa."

"All right. Tell her I'll be right there," she said sharply, her hopes collapsed.

IV

Andrew, Sr. awoke from a nap about three-thirty. The children were out. Opening his heavy-lidded eyes, he was momentarily disorientated. For a few seconds he didn't know where he was, what time it was, nor even what day it was. He was weary. Always, when he took an afternoon nap on Sunday, he would awaken in this way. And he would then be stricken with the horror of old age and of death. Now he was terrified. He felt a pain in his left armpit. It spread downward along his arm. It had come and gone all day, but he hadn't paid much attention to it. He guessed it was probably a touch of neuralgia and that a man of his age must expect a few such pains. However, you would expect neuralgia pains in winter rather than summer. Yawning, he sat up in bed and tried to reason away his fear. The pain seemed to disappear. It gave him a premonition of death. He laughed at himself. He knew that he was in good health and that there was no cause for worry. His feeling of weariness began to fade. He blinked his eyes. He sat rigid because he had a sudden heartburn. He reclined, sweating in fear, until this pain passed. A man of his age must watch his diet. He had eaten too much for Sunday dinner. He mustn't do that.

He sat up again. His pains were gone. He resolved to eat more cautiously and assured himself that he had no cause for worry. He'd been checked up by the doctor only a few months ago and he had been all right then. His acute fear changed into a state of vague depression. He went to the parlor, sat down in a comfortable chair, and tried to relax.

During the week, he always looked forward to Sunday. The idea of being away from his office at the drug company, of Sunday mass, of dinner with the kids, everything about Sunday appealed to him in anticipation. And then he would be disappointed when Sunday came. The day would be long, drawn-out. Time would creep by. He would keep wondering what to do with himself. He always expected something out of the way to happen on Sunday. But usually Sunday would crawl by, and he would be glad when it was over. But then, he got a rest. A man needed a rest. He was vice-president of a wholesale drug company and had many responsibilities, many things to attend to. They were doing a big business in warehouse receipts, and the responsibility and handling of these rested on his shoulders. He had to be very careful about them. This part of his work sometimes worried him. Yes, Sunday was refreshing, even though it was sometimes a little dull. A man needed to do nothing and to have no worries one day a week.

On Sunday he missed Ellen the most. If she were alive, they could do things on Sunday just as they used to. They could take drives about the city and into the country, go to a moving picture show, take a walk. How often he longed to stroll in the park with her, taking her arm, the two of them thinking of the past, of their youth. And this was all gone. Ellen was dead. At times it was still difficult for him to realize this, to realize the terrible meaning in the fact that Ellen was dead. He no longer had her to talk to. The girl he had loved, the girl who had so enthralled him in his young manhood, his lifelong partner and helpmate—she was dead. The mother of his grown children was no more on this earth. He was saddened by regret, a feeling of loss. Sunday without Ellen was so empty.

The afternoon was slowly passing. The minutes seemed long. It was as if time had such a feeble pulse. And yet time flew so quickly, rushing by until one was no longer young. He brooded over this thought as he lit a cigar and gazed out the window. An automobile passed. People walked by. It was warm and sunny. He turned away from the window and sat in a chair.

He was vigorous and in fine health, thank the Lord. That pain in his shoulder and the heartburn were nothing serious. But somehow he was getting so little out of life. The children had their own lives, their own thoughts, their own friends. Helen would be married soon. The others would, too. Ruth would get over Joe and she would meet some fine lad. His kids were sensible, and he took pride in them. He couldn't think of them not marrying. What young fellow wouldn't want his daughters? What decent girl wouldn't be more than proud to marry his boy? They would all marry, and then he would be alone. He didn't want to spend his last years alone. At times he wished the kids would marry and that he would meet a sensible and attractive woman with a good head, one who was neither too young nor too old. He'd marry her. It was no slur on Ellen's memory to want this. Lord have mercy on Ellen's soul! Looking down on him from Heaven, she would even approve, want him to marry again, if he found the right sort of woman. Would his children approve? But a man had his own life to live. He had vigorous years ahead. He was lonely. The kids could not fill up the emptiness of his life for him.

The past crowded back on Andrew, Sr. He thought of how Ruth resembled Ellen. That was why she was his favorite. Ah, yes, both of them, his dead wife, his daughter—they were thoroughbreds. If only she had been spared him! How often had he not thought in their happiest days, even in the rapturous days of their honeymoon, that some day one of them must go. How this thought had occasionally frightened him! And it had happened. Ellen had gone.

He picked up his newspaper and read it in order to forget. He wanted not to think. He was dreamy, and as he read he forgot everything he had just perused. He liked his Sunday paper. There was more to read in it than there was on weekdays.

V

Ever since he had been in grammar school, Andrew, Jr. had thought that some day he might write. At Mary Our Mother high school and in college he had always received excellent marks in his English courses, and his teachers had told him that he had talent and should go on writing. After his graduation from Notre Dame, Andrew, Jr. faced the problem of deciding what he was to do about his future. He had been voted the young man of his high-school class who seemed most likely to succeed, and he had never for one moment doubted that he would be very successful. In his moments of greatest self confidence he imagined he would even be a famous man. Graduation had posed the problem of his future. He had no inclination for business, and with the depression ravaging the land, there were not many business opportunities for young men just out of college. Some of his classmates from Notre Dame had had great difficulty in finding work. Had he chosen to follow a business career, the only opening would have been in the wholesale drug company of which his father was vice-president. And since he believed he would be wasting his talents in the drug business, his choice of a future had narrowed down to law or literature. He had not made up his mind which of these alternatives he would take. Now he favored one, now the other; at times he thought he might follow both careers simultaneously. He was, however, faced with no need of arriving at a decision hastily. He could spend the entire summer thinking out the problem carefully. He had already discussed the question briefly with his father. Dad wanted him to return to Notre Dame and study law. This prospect was attractive. He had had a good time at Notre Dame and he had been a good student, graduating with an excellent average. Study was not a burden to him as it was to many young men. And to be able to answer questions in a classroom, proving that he had studied, was a pleasure. It enhanced his sense of his own worth and superiority. He was unable to make up his mind because he believed that writing was his first love, and he wanted to begin his literary career immediately. He hoped that he would become an overnight success and that his stories would be published as quickly as he wrote them. Were he to return to school and study law, he would have less time for literature. But when he would decide to devote himself to literature, he would begin to have doubts. Granting that he might succeed, how long would it take? If he had to wait too long for fame and money, how would he live? His father had educated him, and he could not expect his father to go on supporting him for years. A legal education would be very fine training in thinking, and it would be something to fall back on.

In the meantime, he did try to write. Since June he had been working on a story he considered a good exercise in style. Superficially, it seemed like many stories that were printed in *The Saturday Evening Post* and other magazines. It would recount how a young Catholic lawyer went to Havana on a vacation and there met a beautiful señorita who was the daughter of one of the best families of Cuba. He had never been to Cuba, but had read enough about it in the library to gain what he considered the necessary background material. He had chosen Cuba as his setting because it was a tropical island. The tropics were associated with romance. Romance would permit him to use and develop his style. But his main interest in this subject was that it gave him a chance to write beautiful descriptions. He was working on the story and had reached a point where he was describing the young lawyer alone in the moonlight, gazing out across the harbor after he had first met the heroine.

After dinner on this particular Sunday he had gone to his room to write, but he faced a snag. Rack his brain as he would, he was unable to think up a new and original metaphor with which to describe the moonlight glittering on the waters of the bay.

After he had conceived and discarded about twenty figures of speech, Andrew, Jr. began to feel sleepy. He went out for some air. Strolling aimlessly and thinking of his story, he happened to pass the home of Jerry Davitt, a high-school and college classmate. He dropped in and saw Jerry and Mr. Davitt for a few minutes and then he strolled back toward home. He decided that he need not make up his mind about the future immediately. The postponement of his decision affected him as much as an actual resolution would have. He felt released. He would drift along for a while, writing, reading, enjoying himself. And he would finish his story and might even sell it. It might be printed in a Catholic magazine, and then he would see his name in print. He prided himself, as if it were a personal merit, because he need not go out and seek work. His thoughts shifted from writing to friends of his who were struggling to get ahead. He felt sorry for them. He revelled in a sense of his own superiority. He was one person who need not worry about grubbing in the market place. Despite the depression, Dad drew a good salary from the drug company and he had not invested money unwisely on the stock market. In fact, his father seemed to be as well off now as he had been before the stock-market crash.

He suddenly quickened his pace, wanting to get back to the story.

The girls had gone out, and his father was alone in the parlor.

"You home?" Andrew, Sr. asked him, looking up from the newspaper.

"I took a little walk and stopped in to see Jerry Davitt."

"How are they?"

"They're all right. Mr. Davitt told me to ask you if you can help him get some of that Bourbon."

Andrew, Sr. looked worried for a moment.

"He understands, doesn't he, that I'm not in that kind of business and do it for him only as a personal favor?"

"Yes, I think he does, Dad. I explained it to him."

"Well, then, I might. But, Andy, are you sure he doesn't talk about it to anyone?"

"I don't think he does. I told him not to, and I think he understands that you're doing it merely to oblige him."

"The girls have gone out. I wish Ruth went out more. I'm worried about her."

"She'll be all right."

"Yes, I think so. She's less nervous than she used to be."

Andrew, Jr. turned to leave the parlor, saying he was going to work.

"How's the writing?" Andrew, Sr. asked.

"Very good," Andrew, Jr. answered, leaving the parlor.

VI

Helen stood naked before the long mirror in her bedroom. She was proud and joyous at the sight of her body, and she was ashamed. She ought not to do this. If Ruth should catch her, Ruth would bawl her out, or even laugh at her. Ruth had always been an older sister and still wanted to treat her like a child. She was not a child. She was a pretty young woman who was engaged to be married to the one man in her life, the boy for whom she had been made. She thought of Jimmy Barry, but not in a sinful way. She was going to marry him. When she did, it would not be a sin. It was blessed, wasn't it, when you were married, and you did it to have children? She was afraid that it would hurt, awfully, to have children. She blushed, realizing that to have children you had to do that. Why was life the way it was? Why couldn't love be like it was now between Jimmy and her, dancing and kisses, and, oh, such wonderful, wonderful feelings? Why did there have to be this other thing? She was afraid of it. What was it like? How did it feel? This question popped up in her mind all the time, and there was no one she knew to whom she could go and find out.

Gosh, when she was married, what would she do? How could she find that out? She was really ashamed of herself because she had such thoughts. But she couldn't always help herself. These thoughts and questions would always come into her mind now. In a dream last night she had asked these questions of herself. She wanted to talk to someone. Today she had made up her mind to talk to Ruth, and she had knocked on Ruth's door. But Ruth had been cranky, probably crying about Joe. She was so sorry for Ruth, but she didn't know what she could do to help her. And even if she did ask Ruth, would Ruth know anything? She was sure Ruth had never done it.

She told herself that she was pretty, and not too fat. She felt good. She was bathed and warm, fragrant with perfume on her body. She posed naked in front of the mirror, holding her hands over her small upright breasts. Then she turned away and sat down on the silk coverlet over her bed. She wished she were dressed and that Jimmy had already called for her. Oh, she had such wonderful evenings with Jimmy. She was so happy. It made her feel sorry for poor Ruth.

But, gee, it was so wonderful to be a young girl in love. And just think, now that she had found the right person, her whole life would be like this. Oh, life was wonderful, wonderful, wonderful.

If there were only not *that* to make one so afraid, so ashamed of oneself. Why must she be so curious? Curiosity killed the cat.

Was it really sinful to think the way she did and to look at herself naked in the mirror? She couldn't help herself sometimes. Jimmy liked her figure. Whenever he had told her that he did, she blushed and was ashamed, but, oh, it was wonderful, wonderful, wonderful, hearing the words from his lips. It was like hearing music you loved. Jimmy had the most wonderful voice. She always used this word. Wonderful, wonderful, wonderful—it was a wonderful word.

She gazed at her image in the mirror again. Boys always liked to look at girls. Often when she walked down the street they would stare at her. Sometimes they'd have such a funny look in their eyes that she'd get all flustered and embarrassed. Was her brother that way, like some boys were? He went out with girls. Might Ruth possibly have ever done this when Joe was alive? Ruth had been so different then. Now she understood why. She'd like to tell Ruth that she understood, but she was afraid to, because Ruth was sometimes so peculiar, and Ruth didn't like to talk about Joe. Her figure was nicer than Ruth's. Ruth was too thin and bony. But, goodness, wasn't she mean to have such thoughts? She was sorry that she had thought this, this proud thought, and she wanted to erase it from her mind.

Erase it! Erase it! Erase it! she told herself silently, because that was what she always said when she wanted to get rid of a bad thought.

When she had been a little girl, she'd been jealous of Ruth going to parties. And now, just think, she went out with the one and only person in the whole world. Think of it, how for years she had wanted to be grown up and engaged, and now she was grown up and engaged.

In three months I'll be a married woman, she told herself, with uncontained joy, but immediately she shuddered with fear.

Oh, she wanted to be Mrs. James Barry so much, and she was so afraid of it.

She opened her mouth wide and her eyes popped in excitement. My goodness, it was almost time for Jimmy to call for her, and she wasn't even dressed. She started dressing in nervous haste.

VII

Jimmy Barry was talking with Andrew, Sr. while Helen finished dressing. He was a ruddy young man of twenty-eight, healthy, good-looking, and well-mannered.

"How are the plans coming along, Jimmy?" Andrew, Sr. asked.

"Fine, Mr. Hyland. That's what I want to tell you about. I thought of a great slogan today. It hits the nail on the head. I think it's going to assure us success. I cracked my brain for the right slogan for over a week, and I didn't have any luck. Then, just like that, I was walking home from church this morning, and it came to me out of a clear sky. I wonder if you'll like it."

"What is it?" Andrew, Sr. asked as Jimmy paused.

"A dime a dog," Jimmy said proudly.

Andrew, Sr. leaned back and looked at the ceiling and reflected. Jimmy sat on the edge of his chair, tensely waiting for Andrew, Sr.'s reaction.

"Sounds pretty good, Jimmy."

Jimmy relaxed. He smiled charmingly and with gratitude.

"Dad likes it. Now we're all set. Dad's signing the contracts this week, and we'll be in business next year. We're going to start with twenty-five hot-dog stands all over the South Side, and as things warrant it, we'll expand and cover the whole city with Barry's hot-dog stands. We're going to have

Neon lights, modernistic decorations, and we'll employ good-looking girls with high-school educations to serve."

"Fine, fine. I like your plans."

"After we get going, Dad wants me to run the business myself. Until then I'm going to do the promotion. A fraternity brother of mine from school is an advertising writer and he's working on a swell ad. We're going to take a big ad in the papers, announcing Barry's Hot-Dog Stands. My picture is going to be at the head of it. We want to get the personal touch in it, you know."

"That sounds good. You ought to make a go of it."

"I know we will."

"I must say, Jimmy, I'm mighty proud to hear you tell me this. I always knew you had enterprise. If more businessmen did what you and your father are doing, we'd snap out of this depression in no time. Before we can get back to where we were, everybody has to get out of the rut they're in. They have the wrong psychology."

"We're starting, too, at just the right time. Costs and wages are at rock bottom, as you know. This thing's going to be done right. I think our slogan is enough to make this proposition a knockout. It's just right, the kind of a slogan that sticks in people's minds. You know, it's been running through my head all day."

"A dime a dog," Andrew, Sr. said.

"Gee, it does sound swell." Jimmy grinned. "A dime a dog."

At this moment Helen shyly entered the room. Jimmy jumped to his feet. Andrew, Sr. gazed at them benignly.

He talked with them a moment, and they left. Then he lit a cigar and puffed at it contentedly. He grew nostalgic, thinking of when he had courted Ellen. That pain in the inside of his arm returned. It radiated down to his little finger. He grew pale with fright. Men his age often had strokes. He bent his little finger and then dug his thumb into it. He felt the nail, and this gave him reassurance. It couldn't be a stroke. It must be neuralgia. Come to think of it, he'd had a touch of neuralgia last April. He sat still for a while, and his thoughts became vague. The pain went away. The best thing in the world for neuralgia was a nice medicinal drink of Bourbon. He got himself a drink. It was good stuff and warmed him.

He turned on the radio, but didn't listen. He turned it off. He heard Andy in the hall and asked where he was going. Andy said that he was going to see a movie. Andrew, Sr. decided that a good movie was just what he needed for relaxation. He said he'd go along.

At a movie he could forget all the troubles of the world, and then he thought that some pancakes would hit the spot. He had a sudden craving for pancakes.

He got his hat, while Andrew, Jr. waited. As they were leaving, Andrew, Sr. remarked that Ruth might want to go with them. They knocked on her door and asked her, but she answered that she'd rather stay home and read. She didn't mind being home alone.

They left.

VIII

Ruth was glad that everyone had gone out. She was sad and lonely in the large empty apartment. But she was by herself. She wasn't afraid. The door was locked. And whatever happened to her could be nothing compared with the tragedy she had already suffered. She curled up on the parlor sofa and munched chocolates while she read the memoirs of a Russian Grand Duchess. The book took her out of herself and her sorrows. Her mind was filled with magnificent court scenes. She saw herself moving amid the royalty of Europe. Reading on, she thought that perhaps it would have been better if there had never been an American Revolution. For if there hadn't been one, America might be part of England today. There would be royalty in America, and royalty always gave a better tone to society. She became bold. She imagined herself as the Princess Ruth, moving among kings, counts, dukes, barons, and princes.

Princess Ruth, she repeated to herself as if this were a magic formula.

Her happy fantasies made her attractive, although there was no one to see her.

She gazed around the room, blushing as if she feared someone were watching her and knew her thoughts.

Oh, I am silly, she told herself.

She tried to laugh. The emptiness of the apartment seemed to frighten her. She turned pale. She imagined she heard noises and remained rigid for a moment. Then she ran to the front door. It was bolted, all right.

It was her nerves, that was all.

She returned to the book. But she grew sad and put down the book and stared gloomily about the parlor. Was she as tragic as these Russian princesses and grand duchesses who had suffered so because of the Russian Revolution?

Her thoughts returned to Joe. They seemed unbearable. She went to the piano and played "None but the Lonely Heart" over and over again.

IX

In the Tivoli Theater, Helen and Jimmy had held hands. When she came out of the theater, she scarcely remembered the picture she'd seen. Jimmy got a cab and as soon as they were inside took her in his arms. They went to the Neapolitan Room at the Westgate Hotel. They danced and had chicken sandwiches and coffee. They looked at each other with moon-struck faces, and there were periods when they scarcely talked. When they danced, Jimmy nestled his cheek against her hair. Helen pressed herself closely to him on the dance floor. She was too breathless to talk, and her heart palpitated.

"You look so pretty tonight," Jimmy said to her at the table after another dance.

"You think so?"

"You know I think so."

"What kind of furniture do we want?" she asked, changing the subject because she was afraid of her love, afraid of it as something sinful.

"The best we can get. That's going to be your job."

"Ruth wants to tell me what we ought to have. She always treats me like a big sister. Not that she doesn't want to be helpful—but, gosh . . ."

Helen became inarticulate and couldn't go on speaking because she wasn't quite sure what she wanted to say.

"Never mind her. It's going to be your home—our home."

They danced again. Would he think her bad because she pressed so close to him? She couldn't help herself. And he seemed to want her to.

"Jimmy?" she murmured demurely.

"What?"

"Tell me you love me."

"You know I do."

"Tell me again."

"I love you."

Jimmy held up his head proudly, wanting to be seen, wanting strangers to know they were in love. When he held her in his arms, he wanted her, wanted her damned badly. He wished they were married already. She was so sweet, so pure, that at times he felt as if a fellow like him, who had

had a little experience, was lousy even thinking of wanting to marry her. And he always thought of what would happen on their first night. He had to control himself not to go too far as it was. He pressed her tightly to him.

They danced.

In the cab they kissed again, and they kissed in the hallway until Helen was disheveled. She didn't want to leave him. She had no control over herself. She clung to him and kissed him fiercely.

"I wish we were being married tomorrow," he said, suddenly leaning against a mailbox.

"I do, too," she said.

He looked at her tenderly.

"I suppose you think I'm terrible," she said.

"Why, sweetheart, I'm crazy about you."

"Just think, we'll always be together."

They kissed again, and finally they reluctantly parted.

Outside the door, Helen straightened her hair, smoothed out her dress, and then she went in quietly. There was not a sound in the house. Everyone was asleep. She hurried to her room and stood in the darkness.

Why am I so happy? she asked herself.

Poor little me, I don't deserve this, she told herself as she got ready for bed.

X

Andrew J. Hyland, Sr. discovered himself walking along a dim and narrow street toward a frame house with a red light over the doorway. Although he did not know how he had come to this street, he accepted it as if it were as familiar to him as his own home. He passed darkened houses; their strange, angular shapes jutted out of blackness. Without warning, he became troubled by the memory that he had committed some crime somewhere in some world. His mind clouded with guilt. His face grew grim and fearful. He lowered his head. He walked on, painfully sensing the imminence of an approaching horror. In vain he tried to recall a crime which he now knew he had committed in the desert of some unremembered world. He knew that he had to repent, and how could he repent what he did not even remember?

He came to the dismal wooden house with red light over the doorway.

His white-robed, twelve-year-old daughter, Ruth, rose up at his side, with the wings of an angel.

Don't do it, Father, she pleaded.

I am going in to denounce the iniquitous and to warn them of the Judgment Day, he answered.

Don't lie, Father, she said in tears.

I do what I must, he said, brushing past her.

She knelt in prayer, and her tears watered the ground.

He entered a dimly lit room where men, women, and devils were sinning on the floor in a wild debauch, while other devils laughed raucously and played tinkling music on phallic-shaped banjos.

He watched the sinning men, women, and devils with mounting excitement.

Shame, disgusting shame! he cried out feverishly.

A whore, with the horns of a devil, came to him, swayed her abdomen, and leered. He fixed his eyes intently on her navel. He must sin and he must not sin, and he wouldn't sin, and he took a step forward, wanting her, and he knew that he must not sin, and he told himself that he would not sin.

He fell on his face before her and, groveling, he told her in a weak, cracked voice:

Yes.

The men, women, and devils lined the wall and watched him grovel.

There is more joy in Hell for the ruin of one virtuous man, a devil said in a fiendish voice.

And Andrew J. Hyland, Sr. knew he had gone to Hell.

He rose. He took a step toward the door to flee, and he was where he had been before he took a step. The whore with horns rushed to him with opened arms.

No, he told her feebly, his eyes on her huge navel.

It's too late, she answered with a leer on her scrofulous face.

And there was a loud clamor. A huge rent appeared in the ceiling. The sinners shrank into corners and cowered. Andrew J. Hyland, Sr. looked up and saw the Sacred Heart of Jesus, its precious blood dripping onto the floor beside him.

I am saved, he exclaimed in exultation.

The sainted man has worked miracles, a girl cried out, trembling with fear as the sinners rubbed their faces in slime.

Get down in the slime! the voice of God thundered from the ceiling.

And Andrew J. Hyland, Sr. crawled through slime to join the men, women, and devils, and the whore with horns was beside him.

I was worth it, you old hypocrite, she sneered.

He groaned.

He knew that he was in Hell, damned forever, forever damned. He dare not even lift his head. Damned, damned for the crime he could not remember, damned forever and forever and forever and a day. He was dead, and he was damned, and he was alone in Hell and it was dark. A terrible sadness overcame him. There was nothing left. Only his regrets, regrets without end . . .

Andrew, Sr. woke up in his darkened bedroom. Momentarily remembering his terrible dreams, he was relieved. The dreams faded from memory, and he was troubled by vague regrets. He could not shake off a feeling of regret, and he did not know the reason why he felt this way. He sank back into his pillow and tried to sleep. He was unable to. He wished he hadn't eaten pancakes with Andy after the movie tonight. A man of his age shouldn't do that so late at night. He tossed in bed and began to worry about his health. He was over fifty. He didn't have too many years ahead of him. He had to be very careful. A cold sweat of terror broke out on his body. He became rigid. The very darkness frightened him. He felt a heartburn and he belched. Well, it was just a stomach upset. Nothing to worry about. In fact, he seemed to be feeling better already. He wouldn't worry. And if he were not all right by morning, he'd take a mild laxative. He closed his eyes. He would lie quietly until he fell asleep. He counted sheep and grew drowsy. He drifted into sleep, remaining vaguely conscious of himself lying in bed.

He awoke suddenly, gripped by a crushing pain in his chest. It tightened like a vice around his heart. It seemed as if there were some force within him crushing his lungs into the shape of pancakes. With mounting intensity the pain tore into his fluttering heart. His heart seemed to shrink and shrivel up within him. He sensed the pain as some powerful force, as strong as steel, closing its bands about his lungs to cut off the air from entering them. Then, in his agony, he imagined that a man of enormous weight was sitting on his chest. He grew weaker. He feebly tried to sit up. He lay back in bed. All his attention was focused on the pain, the constriction of heart and lungs within him. He did not cry out. He did nothing. He suffered in silence.

The pain slowly ebbed. He felt a burning sensation inside his chest and in his stomach. He sighed and breathed more easily as air seemed to be entering his lungs. He was taut from the shock of his pain. Another cold sweat of fear broke out on his forehead. He believed that he had almost died. He cowered. Without thought, he hid his head under the sheets. He pulled the sheets down. He lay still, gratified to feel the still ebbing pain. But it seemed to spread out from the region of his heart. He knew that he must lie perfectly still. Perhaps he ought to call his children. He decided not to. The attack had come and gone. He had survived it. The sense of survival in the imminency of death caused him to feel pleasure. He lay unmoving, enjoying even the dying pains within him. Yes, it had been a narrow escape. In the morning he'd see a doctor. God had spared him.

He must pray. Just as he formed the words of *The Act of Contrition* silently to himself, he was torn by another sharp and violent pain. He groped out of bed, switched on the light, and looked at himself in the mirror. He saw the image of a sick man who had, almost in the space of a night, seemed to grow old. Yes, that image was of him, and he had become, without warning, a sick old man. He was too weak to stand. He sat on a chair. Automatically, his head sank until his chin rested on his chest. The constricting fingers of pain were pressing on his heart like pincers controlled by an all-powerful and relentless force. He could not cry out. He could not move. There was no strength left in him. The beating of his heart was a weak and irregularly murmuring whisper, fading, fading into an awful quiet. His whole past life seemed to have been so short, and each second of this silent and tortured present seemed endless. The pain was now so intense that it seemed as if his lungs were crushed. His consciousness was a burning rhythm of pain. In one final instant of lucidity he tried to cry out to his children. Then his trembling thoughts broke up into small fragments. And with one final, violent spasm of pain, one last burning agony, he slumped forward. And Andrew J. Hyland, Sr. slid off the chair, crashing into eternity as his lifeless body hit the floor.

[1933-43]

Lib

I didn't go to school that morning. I sat by the parlor window and looked out at Washington Park. It was like a picture. It was early May. There was no sun, and the deepened green of the park absorbed all the sorrowing colors of my boy's mood. I sat and stared through frames of trees at the lagoon; it seemed like a smooth surface of dirtied glass. Tears came to my eyes, but I wiped them away and continued to stare out of the window.

About ten-thirty, I called my dog Lib and took her for a walk in the park. She was a shaggy airedale, with a fine pedigree and a long record of illegitimate puppies. I let her run loose instead of leashing her. Lib was sprightly. She ran and scurried, cocking her ears, barking after birds, rolling in the grass, laughing as dogs laugh. I ran with her, had her chase sticks, and sent her through the bushes to find tennis balls. She came out with three balls, one of them almost new. Then I took her over to the lagoon. Lib liked water. On summer days, she used to sneak away from home and go over to the park for a swim. If no one called her back, she would swim all the way across the lagoon. She also chased the sheep, and they'd run, baa-baaing. Lib rounding up the sheep was always a comical sight to me; at the same time, I was always proud of her when she did this. But it didn't appeal to the park cops. However, she had got to know them. She could tell a park policeman at a good distance, and she knew how to avoid them. All the park flatfoots used to vow that they would kill her on sight. But they never could catch her.

I thought about the things Lib would do. Once, I had taken her swimming over by the muddy waters near the stepping-stones. She had frisked out of the waters and run up to a lady dressed immaculately in white, playfully jumping at her, pawing the spotless dress. When my grandmother went to the store, Lib used to expect her to come back with cakes or liver. If she returned without these, the dog would lie in a corner and refused to go near her. She was not an obedient dog. Whenever I took her out, she ran about wildly, and usually refused to obey any summons until she was fagged out. All the kids in the neighborhood used to kid me about the way I called her. They'd shout at me: "Here, Lib!" In winter, she would pull kids along the ice; but if you took her near thin, dangerous ice, she would smell at the shore line and then shy away.

Nobody in the neighborhood seemed to like Lib. They used to say she was a goofy dog. Our neighbors were always complaining to the real-estate agent. Once the crank next door threw a milk bottle at her. He was living there, and the family renting the apartment had a little girl who was brought up to be afraid of dogs. Whenever she saw Lib or heard the dog bark, she screamed. Now, finally, in order to pacify the neighbors, we were getting rid of Lib. We were sending her to a farm near St. Louis. Lib would like that. She could do all the running she wanted to. She wouldn't be cramped and confined. There would be no flatfoots to chase her. We were sending her away that very day.

I took her over to the lagoon and made her stand up for one of the balls she had found. I threw it well toward the center of the lagoon. She swam out for it and returned, dropping the ball at my feet. I threw it again. She swam for it. I continued this until she seemed to be fagged out. I sat by the bank. I wished the sun were out. I remembered how I used to take her out early in the morning. Then the park would be pleasant. I would go barefooted, and the dew would be cool and wet under my feet. There would be the song of birds and sweet early-morning odors. Now and then a squirrel would come shyly out of a bush and scramble up a tree. Lib would chase the squirrel. She would chase sparrows, too. Slowly we would go around onto the island. Sometimes I would sit on a bench and watch the dog ramble. The sun would be so warm. An iron-faced Slav would often be in the lagoon, snaring weeds. I would watch him and wish I had hip boots like his. I would think of the country up in Michigan and wish I could take Lib up there. I would sit and watch the dog, the grass, the sunlight, the trees, the sparrows. The sparrows were like noisy old women. Lib seemed to hate them.

I sat by the shore line and watched Lib. She was on all fours, looking at me. I told myself that she was almost human. I stood at the threshold of a mystery. Why did dogs seem so human? It did not occur to me that dogs possess, in a cruder form, a consciousness generally similar to our own, and that they probably or possibly experience, in an unrefined or primitive form, a type of imagery similar to our own. Hence, when they are in contact with human beings for a long time, they should take on some human characteristics. I didn't think of that. I looked at Lib's sad face, with her seemingly melancholy dark eyes, and wished I could talk to her, wished that she could speak to me. I said, "Hello, Lib." I said, "Lib, you're going away; I won't see you any more." I said, "Hello, Lib," and she rose, wagged her tail, cocked her ears, and came close to me. I petted her and rubbed my cheek against her nose. I took some dog biscuit from my pocket and made her stand up and speak for it. Then she sat by herself, held the biscuit between her paws, and chewed it. I watched her. I said, "It's good-by, Lib." Every time I started to cry I wiped the tears away and said, "Yeah, it's so-long, Lib."

When the dog finished the pieces of biscuit, I made her sit up and tossed the ball in the air. She caught it. Lib knew a lot of tricks.

We walked around to the wooded island. I thought about many of the things she had done. Often she would go down into the cellar and kill a rat. She would cart it up on the porch and wag her tail at us for approval. Sometimes she hid dead rats on the porch. She was a wise dog. She would carry the paper home, too. Or she would play dead dog.

I looked at my watch and saw that it was time to be returning. I said, "Hello there, Lib." I watched her cock her ears. It was fascinating to watch a dog cock its ears. I wished I could do something about it, paint a picture of it, have the dog tell me why it cocked its ears, why it could get so happy. I wasn't happy. I took Lib home.

My father and I took her to the Englewood Express office in a taxicab. Lib had never ridden in an automobile before, and she seemed confused. She kept jumping about and looking out the window. My father sensed that I didn't want to lose the dog. He kept telling me that it would be better for the dog in the country; he said a city was no place for an airedale, and that it wasn't really fair to the dog. I said, "Yes."

At the express office, we crated Lib. She was confused, docile, and trusting. We placed a pan of water, a bone, and a biscuit in the crate. She looked out of the crate and howled. I remembered when Lib first came to us. She had been only a few weeks old, and she had whimpered on that first night. The neighbors had been disturbed. When she had become acclimated, she would run all around the house, searching for slippers. Once she had chewed my grandmother's slippers and had been whipped. After this, she never went into my grandmother's bedroom again. I looked at Lib and wiped away a tear.

"Well, she's set now," my father said.

"Yes," I said.

"Don't take it so hard," he said. "She'll be better off in the country."

"She was a nuisance," I said.

"Yes," he said.

"Take in summer. She shed hair and got it all over the parlor rug, and I never could get the rugs clean," I said.

"I know," he said.

"Good-by, Lib," I said, my voice a little choked.

"Come on. I'll buy you a soda," he said.

"Heck, I won't miss her," I said.

"She's as comfortable as we can make her," he said.

"Yes," I said.

"The train don't leave until five," he said.

"Gee, she'll be in the cage a long time," I said.

"I'll tip one of the men around here to be sure they feed and watch her," he said.

I looked at Lib. I patted her head. She stopped moaning. She looked at me. Her face seemed so trusting. We left her. I looked back at Lib. She was watching me and she seemed bewildered. "Good-by, Lib," I said.

"What kind of soda do you want?" my father asked.

"I don't care," I said.

"We'll go to the ball game," he said.

I didn't answer. I thought that Lib would be in a cage all night. I noticed there wasn't any sun out. We walked down to a drugstore on Sixty-third Street. But I didn't want any soda.

[1930-46]

Young Convicts

They were the children of Slavic immigrants and lived in the manufacturing district around Thirty-fifth and Morgan. Their fathers worked in the factories located in the area. Their sisters, even before they started to bloom and lose their gawky pre-puberty figures, also joined the ranks of those who trooped to the factories at six and seven in the morning. At six, seven, eight o'clock, rain or shine, morning after morning, their fathers, mothers, older brothers, sisters, all became part of the long line plodding to work.

There were six kids in this gang. Tony, the eldest, was a boy of twelve, and Stanley, the youngest, was eight. They all liked candy. They liked to go to the movies, especially on Saturday afternoons, when the serial was shown. They liked serials and movies of that type best because there was danger and adventure, shooting, robbing, train wrecks, bandits, outlaws, Indians, Mexicans, battles. And they scarcely ever had money for candy or for movies.

But they liked candy and they liked movies. And they liked to do dangerous, brave things, to pull off stunts like those pulled off by the older fellows in the neighborhood. They wanted to fight and steal, and then brag about it, just as they heard their older brothers bragging. They could be heroes just like the older boys. And when they could steal, they could have money for candy and the movies.

Home to each of the kids in the gang was much the same. A wooden shack, one or two stories high, with an outside privy that smelled you out every time you wanted to take a leak. Three, four, five rooms, generally dirty, full of rags, papers, the smell of kerosene lamps. Dark bedrooms, old beds, dirty sheets, two, three, four, and five sleeping together in the same bed, and on cold nights there was always a fight for the blankets. A mother and a father who were generally overtired from work, and from raising a family. And the mother and father didn't speak English. They were greenhorns. And once every week, two weeks, three weeks, the mother and father would get drunk. They would curse and fight, throwing things at one another, shouting, even brandishing knives and cutting one another up, until the police came with a paddy wagon. These kids' homes were alike.

They didn't like school very much. They didn't like their studies, and in the classroom they groaned, twisted, squirmed, itched, dreamed of high deeds like those of the movie heroes and villains in the Saturday-afternoon serials, like those of the older fellows, like those of Al Capone. In school, they waited for the end of class. They were afraid of their teachers, and they neither liked nor trusted them. The teachers, some of them young girls from good families who were waiting until they found a husband, did not like the bad boys much either. Sometimes, in the hallways, the kids would hear one teacher tell another that she wished she would be transferred to another school where there was a better class of pupils than these incorrigible Polacks and Bohemians.

Often, they didn't learn their lessons. They bummed from school regularly, and went scavenging through vacant lots and streets, keeping their eyes peeled for the overworked truant officers. Or they went to the railroad yards with sacks and wagons for coal that was needed at home. In fact, they learned to steal in the railroad yards. The parents would send them out at night to get coal, and they'd go down to the yards and get it, one kid getting up in a car and throwing chunks down to the others. From the railroad yards they went to the stockyards, going over the fences and leaving with anything removable that could perhaps be sold. They stole everything they could, and finally stealing got to be a nightly occupation.

They knew about hold-ups. They knew that some of the older guys in the district had pulled off hold-ups, and that made them heroes. So they determined that they too would be heroes and pull hold-ups. That would get money for candy and movies. And they would be living like the heroes they saw in the movies. One night, Tony, the gang leader, picked out the Nation Oil filling station on Thirty-fifth Street. They played across the street from the station for two nights. They goofed about, ran, played tag by a closed factory, getting a line on what time the station closed and what time the cop on the beat passed by after it had closed. When they were sure of their time and their layout, they went to work. Young Stanley tossed a house brick through a side window. Tony then stood on a box, put his hand through the broken glass, and unlatched the window. He went in, followed by the others. The money was in the safe, and that could not be touched. So they tore the telephone box from the wall and scooted with it. They broke it open in a vacant lot and divided the nickels that were in it. The loot was three dollars, and, although it was to be divided evenly, Stanley was cheated out of a quarter.

Successful in their raid on the filling station, they made other raids. They robbed every filling station in the district, always running off with the telephone box, and they enjoyed the fruits of their robbery in candy, cigarettes, and movies. Tony liked it. He bossed his gang with an iron hand. Night after night he drove them in raid after raid. If they complained, he kicked them in the pants and slapped their faces. If they talked back to him, he cracked them. He saw himself as a young Al Capone. He dreamed of shootings, gang fights, submachine guns, robberies, money, automobiles, everything the gangsters had in the movies, everything Al Capone had in real life. And he always planned out the raids, instructing each kid in what he should do, going to the place in advance to get the lay of the land. He always had money and gave some of it away to younger kids, to girls whom he would try to bribe in order to get them alone with him in basements. He hung around the corners and the poolrooms late at night, watching the older fellows. He imitated them in walking, talking, gestures, held his cigarettes as they did, borrowed all their remarks. He pushed and pressed his gang constantly, always discovering new places to rob. One night they robbed a chain restaurant. Stanley threw a brick through the back window and they entered and ran off with the cash in the till. Two nights later, they returned to the Nation Oil Company's filling station and again ran off with the telephone box full of nickels. This time they noticed that the attendant had gone home, leaving his safe open. In it, they saw bills, many of them, dollars and dollars, more money than they had ever seen before. They were so surprised by the sight of the money, so afraid, that they did not take it, satisfying themselves with only the small change in the safe. And on the night after this robbery they returned to the chain restaurant. They were caught by a watchman and a city policeman.

They were brought before Judge Katherine Henderson in the Juvenile Court; she was a woman jurist who was known beyond the city for her good work. The court was crowded with its usual array of young culprits and harassed, shamed parents. The boys had to wait their turn, and they sat with other boys, cowed and meek, and with their shabbily dressed immigrant parents. Nearly all those waiting to be tried were the children of working people, most of them of immigrants. Some were released, some placed on probation, some sentenced to the Juvenile Detention Home. Judge Henderson spoke crisply, hastily, perfunctorily, often in a scolding tone. She hurried through case after case, disposed of it, making instant decisions, bawling out parents, often telling immigrant fathers and mothers that they were responsible for the delinquent conduct of their children.

Judge Henderson just didn't have the time. The cases had to be disposed of. Tomorrow there would be the same number. The juvenile problem was insoluble. There was no settlement of it. The same boys were warned, but they were brought back. Parents were warned, but they were helpless. There was nothing to do but rush through from case to case, let so many off, put so many on probation, send so many to the Detention Home. Day after day this must go on. The law must be upheld. There was no time for her to delay, study, probe into the causes of these delinquencies. All she could do was reach out and try, and hope that a few boys would be rescued from crime, and a few girls from the life of a prostitute. That was what she did. Lectures, warnings, scoldings, questions, sentences. Next. Next. Next. All morning. Next. All afternoon. Next. Tomorrow. More. Next.

Tony and the gang were called up. The bailiff rounded them up and prodded them in the back, his language curt and sharp. He shoved them up to the bar of justice. Judge Henderson read the papers on the case, closed her lips as she read, nodded her gray head. She raised her brows. Her benign face showed worry. She seemed to be wondering and thinking. She looked down sharply at the six boys before her. Their heads dropped. They were afraid to look her in the eye, just as they feared looking teachers, or policemen, in the eye. Her gaze shifted. She stared at their parents, who stood silently behind the boys. She asked each of the boys what his

name was. The first answered that he was Clement Comorosky. Where was
his mother? He shook his head. Again she asked where his mother was.
Again he shook his head. More stridently, she asked where his father and
mother were. He said that both were working and could not come down.
Stanley's mother then spoke in Polish. An interpreter was called, and she
spoke to him. He told the judge that the woman had said that the father
and mother of the Comorosky boy worked in a factory and were afraid to
stay out because they were too poor, and needed the day's wages, and they
were afraid that if they didn't report for work they might be laid off. Please,
she would take their place.

"All right. Now, do you boys know what you did?" the judge asked.

None of them answered. They stood with averted eyes.

"Can any of you talk? Can you talk?" she asked, sweeping her eyes from
one to another, fixing them on Clement, who was ten years old.

He nodded his head affirmatively.

"Do you know that it's a crime to break into other peoples' homes and
stores and to take things that don't belong to you?"

"I'm sorry . . . ma'am," Clement said.

"How long have you been doing this?"

"Just this time," Clement said.

She looked through the papers before her and called out Stanley's
name.

"You were here before, and I told you that I didn't want to see you
brought back. And why don't you go to school?"

He looked at her with large-eyed awe.

"Are your parents here?"

A small Slavic woman said that she was his mother; her face was lined,
and an old black shawl covered her head. The judge asked her if she ever
tried to keep her boy in at night. She shook her head, and said that she
tried, but that he went out anyway. The judge looked down at Stanley, glow-
ering.

"And what did you do?"

"Me? I thrun the brick through de window."

Many who heard him smiled. The judge continued to question them
in a brusque manner which inspired fear. Their answers came slowly. They
were evasive. They did not understand all of her questions. She became
more brusque. She seemed annoyed. She listened, with increasing irrita-
tion, while the watchman who caught the boys gave his testimony. Then
the gas station attendant testified that twice the station had been broken

into, and the telephone box had been ripped off the wall on each occasion. The restaurant manager gave testimony also.

"You boys have to learn that you can't go on breaking into places and stealing money. That is not right, and it is not permitted. Do you hear me?"

Six heads nodded.

"Well, why did you do it?"

Her additional questions brought out the fact that Tony was the leader and inspiration of the gang, that Stevie Lozminski was his lieutenant, and that the raids and burglaries had been committed under their direction. Both had been in the court before for truancy and burglary, and the truant officer testified that all her efforts to do anything that would keep them in the classroom, where they belonged, were fruitless. Their teachers and the principal of the school had turned in written reports describing them as incorrigible. The judge continued her brusque questioning, directing some of it at the parents, who stood in silent awe and fear. She lectured the parents about taking care of their offspring and insisted that the interpreter translate her remarks so that they would surely be understood. Tony, Stevie, and Clement were all sentenced to six months in the Juvenile Detention Home, and the others were put on probation. The mothers cried. They looked with bewildered grief at the judge, their pleading eyes almost like those of sick animals. The boys were pulled from their parents' arms and taken off. Two of the mothers cried.

The next case, that of a colored boy caught stealing, was called.

The mill of the court continued.

[1931, 1946]

Boyhood

Stepping on the cracks in the sidewalk, Jim English asked Danny
O'Neill when there was going to be a party. Danny, busy thinking his own
thoughts and also stepping on sidewalk cracks, didn't hear Jim. He liked
Jim, but felt sorry for him. Jim was poor, and everybody in the seventh-
grade class thought he was goofy. Danny was sometimes treated badly by
the other kids, but Jim was in a worse pickle than he. His father had run
away and left him and his mother alone, and she did housework. The other kids all looked down on Jim, and Jim wasn't bright in classes. Sometimes, all you had to do to get a laugh was to use Jim's words. But Danny
really liked him and felt sorry for him.

They walked along Indiana Avenue. Danny booted a tin can on the
sidewalk into the withered, unkempt grass. Jim gave it a kick. They went
out into the street and had a contest to see who could kick the can the far-

thest. Danny won. He was pleased. But then, it was easy to kick a tin can farther than poor Jim, just as it was easy to be less of a goof than Jim.

Danny kept kicking the tin can. He adjusted his gold-rimmed glasses.

Jim interrupted their silence by asking when there was going to be another party.

"I don't know. I don't *like* parties," Danny answered casually between swipes at the tin can.

"Why? You go to them, don't you?"

"Sometimes," Danny said noncommittally.

Jim looked at him, skeptical. "I don't believe you," he said shaking his head sidewise.

"I'm not kiddin'. I really don't."

Jim laughed with friendly doubt.

"I don't believe it," he repeated, laughing a second time.

"I don't care if you do or if you don't. I know if I care a whole lot for parties or if I don't."

"No, but I think you're foolin'. I really think you're foolin' me. What about all those parties you used to give?"

"There wasn't so many of them. Once in a while I like a party. Once in a while. And anyway I only gave one."

"I think you're kiddin' me."

"I'm not kiddin' you, English. I only care about parties once in a while. I don't care so much about parties. I only like them now and then."

Danny started stepping on cracks again. He took three steps to a square, but it was difficult. Jim was silent at his side. Danny kept watching how vacant Jim's face was, and he missed several cracks. "Goofy," he muttered to himself.

Jim asked Danny if he didn't honestly know when there was going to be another party.

"Don't know."

Jim seemed hurt.

"You're not gonna get sore because I didn't believe you, are ya?" Jim said conciliatingly.

"Oh, no."

Danny lost interest in stepping on squares. He began touching the railings that enclosed the plots of dried grass in front of the buildings.

"Say, Roslyn Hayes is sort of a nice girl, isn't she?" Jim casually remarked.

"Hm . . . Yes."

Danny caught Jim suddenly dropping his face in confusion.

"Well, there ain't no more baseball games until the war's over," Jim said hurriedly.

"No, there ain't," Danny said, smiling to himself.

"Maybe not for years."

"But, Jim, what makes you so interested in Roslyn Hayes?" Danny asked, thrilled to mention her name, happy to be able to talk about her without giving away how much he loved her.

"I ain't. I just wondered about her. Do you think I'm interested?"

"I dunno. You asked me a lot of questions, and I wondered."

"I'm not. I'm not interested in girls."

"I just sort of wondered," Danny said.

"Rube Waddell's one of my favorite ball players of all time," Danny said.

"I never heard of him."

"Ain't you never heard of Rube Waddell? Honest?"

"No, who was he?"

"Rube Waddell was the world's greatest southpaw, except maybe for Eddie Plank."

"Who did he pitch for, Danny?"

"Philadelphia, the Browns, Minneapolis in the American Association. And I think he pitched in the National League before 1900, but he jumped when they started the American League."

"Why's he your favorite?" Jim asked.

"He's dead," Danny answered.

"Is that why he's your favorite?"

"No. He did anything he felt like doing. That's the way he was."

"Is he really dead?"

"Yes, Jim. I guess he drank himself to death."

"Was he really good?"

"He still holds the strike-out record in the American League."

"Honest?"

"Yeah. Haven't you ever heard about some of the things he used to do?"

"No. What?"

"Go off in the middle of the season without telling Connie Mack. He might even be pitching, and walk off in the fifth or sixth inning, and then maybe some scout or newspaperman would find him a week later, fishing by a country stream, or even pitching for some scrub team in a hick burg. When he was feeling right, he would sometimes walk three men, and then call the side in to sit around the pitching box while he whiffed the next three batters. He could almost make a baseball talk."

Jim didn't know whether or not he should believe Danny.

"Honestly, did they have a pitcher like that?"

"Yes."

Jim gaped, dubious.

"They're always remembering things like that about Rube and writing them up."

Jim was still doubtful, wondering.

"Did you ever see a big-league game?" Danny asked.

Jim looked away, ashamed. Danny saw the queer, sad look in Jim's eyes. He liked Jim. He wished he could make him become something else besides the class goof.

"I seen enough," Jim said.

They came to Jim's home. It was a disheveled, unpainted, slatternly wooden affair between Fifty-eighth and Fifty-ninth on Indiana Avenue. They stood in front of it and didn't say anything for a while.

"Listen, do you want to wait and go to the store with me? It won't take me long, and then we can take a walk," Jim asked.

"No, I gotta hurry."

Jim looked disappointed.

"So long."

"So long."

Danny wandered on.

"Listen, Dan . . ." Jim called after him.

"Yeah," unenthusiastically.

"Wanna go to a show on Hallowe'en night?"

"No, I can't get out."

Jim looked more disappointed.

II

Danny walked along. Jim didn't even know about Rube Waddell. Nobody liked Jim. He was too big a goof, and he was a string bean. He was sissified and threw a baseball and batted like a girl. He would get killed in a football game. But he felt sorry for Jim. He got a funny kind of feeling being sorry for Jim, as if it were his fault Jim was like he was.

Danny picked up a broken twig and swished it as he walked along. He remembered Jim's questions about Roslyn. Jim would like to go to the parties the kids had, and he would like to have Roslyn for his girl. He was an awful pest with his questions about Roslyn. Jim liked Roslyn. That was funny. A goof like Jim liking a girl like Roslyn. Danny had to laugh. He swished the twig and laughed again. Jim would give a whole lot to know the truth, to know that Roslyn liked Danny O'Neill. She did like him. She liked him, even if she did snub him sometimes. Glenn had said that she liked him.

Danny was very sorry about Jim. He knew that Jim was poor, and he felt sorry he had asked Jim how many big-league games he had ever seen. Yes, he felt sorry for Jim, but, then, Jim was an awful pest and was always asking the goofiest questions and expressing the battiest opinions. He was always saying crazy things about baseball and girls and everything. And he got poor marks in school. What could be battier than to want to go to a show on Hallowe'en?

Danny kept on walking, swishing the piece of dead branch.

III

There was going to be a Hallowe'en surprise party for Billy Morris. Billy was out with the kids—Danny, Dick Buckford, Ralph Borax, Glenn, Tommy O'Connor, Walter Regan, and Andy Houlihan. They had brought Fat Mulloy along, so he could be used as a pretext for running away and going up to Billy's. They told Billy they'd ditch Fat and hide up at his house and have his mother make some hot chocolate, like she did on Hallowe'en last year. Then they said they would go out again and raise some more Cain.

They were straggling along a street. Danny felt creepy. He imagined he saw strange, funny things, witches the size of the Teenie Weenies in the Sunday *Clarion*, riding around the air on toothpick brooms, monstrous owls with fierce satanic eyes gleaming out of mysterious skies, demons from Hell dancing about fires like Indians on the warpath.

"You're a little goofy, aren't you, O'Neill?" Billy said.

He spoiled Danny's strange fancies.

"Not like you are, singing like a nut all day in school."

"Don't you wish you were able to?"

"Say, you guys, can that and let's do something," Fat Mulloy said.

"Let's kick in a window on George," Dick Buckford said.

"Let's not and say we did," Andy Houlihan said.

"Let's," several others said.

"But listen, you guys, we're liable to get in trouble doing that," Tom O'Connor said.

"Say, O'Connor, will you kindly go home and soak your head," Fat Mulloy bullied.

"Well, I don't wanna start out and land in jail," Tom said.

"You can't kick a window in on George. He's our janitor. We'll have to go someplace else," Ralph Borax said.

"What do you say about gettin' some rotten eggs or old tomatoes an' throwin' 'em in at the Chinks' laundry?" Billy Morris said.

"The Chinks are too mean and dangerous. They'll burn you with hot irons," Glenn said.

"What? Are all you guys yellow?" Fat asked.

No, they weren't yellow, they said, but—

"Well, then, let's do something," Fat said.

Everybody agreed with Fat. They straggled along.

"Wallio. . . . Walliwalli. . . . Wallioooooooooooooooo," Billy sang monotonously.

"Morris, you better have your head examined," Danny said.

"All right, I'll do that. I sort of like your company anyway. We'll have a lot of fun at Kankakee."

"Let's do something," Fat said.

"Diz is Diz O'Neill is Diz O'Neill is Diz O'Neill is Diz O'Neill is Diz O'Neill is Diz O'Neill is Diz O'Neill," Billy droned in sing-song.

"Yeah, he is that way," Walter Regan said.

Danny ignored them, but he was disturbed.

Dick Buckford joined their chorus of raillery, saying that Goofy O'Neill's suit was a monkey suit because the coat didn't have any belt.

"Any of your business what kind of a suit I wear? Why don't you change your head? It's three times too big for you anyway," Danny said.

Several of the kids laughed at Dick.

"It's brains. You couldn't have a head this big," Dick said, and he laughed in that goofy way of his.

"Brains, hell. Your brains are in your slats," Danny said.

"You haven't even got any brains in your can," Dick said, grinning sheepishly.

"Damn it, let's quit goofing and do something. You guys are worse than my grandmother," Fat said.

"O'Neill is as dizzy as Jim English," Walter Regan said.

"I'm gonna paste somebody in the mouth tonight," Danny said.

"Diz O'Neill is as goofy as goofy as goofy as goofy as Jim English is as goofy as goofy as goofy as goofy as goofy as Diz O'Neill is," Billy sang drily.

"Goofier than English," Dick said.

Danny was hurt and angry. He wanted to be one of the kids like the rest of them, and not the goof of the gang. He did not know why they teased him so much. If he could ignore them, they would stop. But he couldn't. He always lost his temper and wanted to paste somebody. He was going off the handle now. He stepped forward, sneering.

"Damn you fellows."

"O'Neill is a crazy hot-headed Irishman, who is even goofier than Jim English," Billy Morris said.

Danny went for Billy, but Billy was too swift for him. He darted away, chased by leaden-footed Danny. Billy stood across the street, taunting Danny, who had stopped the chase. Dick joined Billy. They shouted at Danny, until he rushed toward them. They waited. Danny went at Dick and Billy with swinging fists, but he succeeded only in catching Billy with a glancing blow on the shoulder before they clinched. They tumbled; Billy was on the bottom and Dick on top. Billy kicked and squirmed and shouted and cursed, but all this effort failed to prevent Danny from rubbing Billy's face against the hard ground. Dick tugged at Danny, slowly dragging him off Billy. The rest of the kids, headed by Walter Regan, rushed across the street, shouting "Pile on." They all yelled, "Get off," "Le-go," "Le-go my ear." "Take your finger outta my eye," "Quit sockin'." Then the scramble quieted down as quickly as it started. They moved on aimlessly, and Billy started kidding Fat Mulloy.

Danny lost his resentment following the free-for-all and the shifting of Billy's attack to Mulloy. He thought of himself as one of the gang and of Fat Mulloy as an outsider. He was going to the party and decided that spoiling the night by his hot-headedness was silly. He was going to the party— and Roslyn would be there.

"Hello, fellows," Jim English said, approaching them from the rear.

They greeted him coldly.

"Where you all goin'?" Jim asked.

"Don't know," Billy said.

"We're going no place," Dick said.

"We're goin' to hell. You wanna come along?" Fat said.

"Say, all foolin' aside, can I go along with you fellahs?" Jim asked.

"We're gonna smash windows and set fires to gates and barns," Dick said.

"Are you really?"

"Yeah."

"An' we're gonna tear down fences," Billy said.

Jim gaped.

"Yeah, and we're gonna throw rotten eggs and tomatoes in at the Chinks in the laundry at Fifty-eight Street," Billy said.

"You better not come along. Soapin' windows is your speed, English," Walter said.

"Can't I come? But are you fellahs really gonna do all those things?"

"Yeah, you better not come along," Danny said.

"We don't want you," Walter Regan said.

"You can't come along. You're nothing but a big string bean," Dick said.

They were in front of the Episcopal Church. They left Jim there, speechless, telling him he would be safe in church. Danny thought he had seen a tear sliding down Jim's cheek. As he walked on, he felt sorry for Jim. But he couldn't do anything. Jim was a string bean and a goof, and they couldn't bring him along on Hallowe'en night. He didn't belong with the gang. Danny didn't know what he could do about Jim, because Jim didn't belong.

"We can't be letting fellows like English come along. We just can't," Danny said.

"No, we can't," Walter said.

We. That meant the bunch, Danny and the others. He was one of We. They only kidded him good-naturedly. We included him, soothed his bruised vanity.

They walked on, and they met a tough bunch of kids from another neighborhood.

"Don't nobody say anything to this bunch. We don't want any trouble with 'em," Walter said.

Tom O'Connor and Glenn said the same thing. Danny sensed what would happen quickly. In a fight, they would lose, and he didn't want to fight. But he knew that this tough gang would crack wise, and, if he didn't call them, he would feel that he was yellow like Dick. If they cracked wise, he would have to call them. Anyway, tough gangs weren't always so tough when you called their bluff. They might trim this gang in a free-for-all. Fat would fight. Billy and Ralph would stick. Walter was big but yellow, and in a tight place he might fight like a cornered rat. No matter what happened, Danny would be the hero. He would bear the brunt of the fighting, and, when they got to the party, Roslyn would hear of his bravery. That was worth several socks in the jaw. But he didn't want to fight unless—well, it would make things easier with Roslyn. She would see that he was something more than the rest of them.

"Hey, you guys tough?" one fellow shouted at them.

"Any of you guys lookin' fer a fight?" a second yelled.

"We eat guys what are tough," a third hollered.

They bragged and cursed among themselves.

Danny's breath came jerkily. He was afraid. He didn't want to call their bluff. If he didn't, none of the other fellows would. He was afraid. But if he kept still, he would be—yellow—and Roslyn at the party would like him better if he was brave—and sometimes a good fight was a lot of fun. He was afraid, and his breath came in jerks.

"Hey, any of youse guys tough?"

"Yes," Danny said loudly.

"What?" from several of the other gang.

Three of them rushed across the street. They looked very tough. One of them, the smallest and most cartoon-like in appearance, was chewing a huge wad of tobacco.

"Where's de guy what sez he's tough?" from the tobacco-chewer.

"Lemme getta poke at 'im," a second said.

"Listen, fellows, we're not looking for trouble or for any fight. We didn't do anything to you fellows and we're perfectly willing to mind our own business," Tom conciliated.

"Yah better not."

"We like 'em tough. Where's de guy what's tough? De tougher dey are, de harder dey fall."

"Yeah, and we're pretty tough. We're so tough dat when we spit, rivers overflow," the tobacco-chewer said, plopping a silver dollar's weight of tobacco juice onto the sidewalk.

There was a brief, tenuous silence. Then the tobacco-chewer repeated his question and clenched his fist. The rest of his gang, noisy, motley, profane, joined him. They outnumbered Danny and the kids, two to one. Several of them poised soot bags.

"Where's the guy?"

"Lemme at him."

"You the guy what spoke?"

"Here I am," Danny said with forced dignity.

He faced them with a scowl that he felt was like Jack Dempsey's scowl when he kayoed Fred Fulton. The tobacco-chewer stepped closer, and his gang crowded in.

"Who are yah? What makes yah think you're tough?"

Danny clenched his fists tightly.

"What's your name?"

"You might tell me yours first—Pug Nose," Danny said.

Fists were clenched and teeth gritted. Five of them surrounded Danny. The others picked men.

"Wait a minute, Spud! . . . wait . . . WAIT!" a tall kid said, stepping in front of Danny.

It was Tim Cleary, who used to sit in front of Danny in school but had moved away.

"I know these guys. They're all right. Friends of mine," Tim said.

"Well, dis wise guy says he's tough."

"He is," Tim said.

"Well, I chew nails."

"Forget it, Spud. These guys are all right."

"Well, if they're friends of yours—but I like 'em tough."

The tobacco-chewer spit again.

"I'm always ready to 'commodate guys what are tough," he said.

"Forget it, Spud. They're a good bunch."

"All right, Tim, but—"

"And what do you say, Dan?"

"It's all right, then, with me, Tim."

The two groups became vaguely friendly. They talked of their evening's braveries, real and imaginary.

"We put an old tree through a window," Dick said.

"We got shagged by de dicks. One of 'em shot at us. We were knockin' fences down," a member of the Cleary bunch said.

"We were almost made into chop suey by the Chinks. Threw tomatoes at 'em. One Chink got plumped in the face. Gee, it was funny. Dick here threw the tomato, an' it hit him in the face," Walter said.

"Yeah, it was a lucky shot," Dick said.

"We caused a blockade by piling boxes on de cartracks over our way on State Street. Cars were stretched along the whole block," Spud said.

Then they separated, mutually refusing offers of uniting.

"Gee, you're crazy," Billy said to Danny.

"Listen, Dizzy, you can't be pulling that stuff with us. Only for Cleary, we'd of had our blocks knocked off," Walter said.

"O'Neill's goofy. Just because he's gotta hard head, and you can't hurt him, he thinks everybody's like that," Billy said.

"Well, anyway, I was all ready to lam the guy that was chewing tobacco," Dick said.

Walter and Glenn also said that if it had come to a fight, they, too, would have done some lamming.

Danny defended himself by declaring that he would have been yellow if he hadn't called them, and that he wasn't yellow, like some guys.

They fooled away an hour, going up one street and down another, placing a few ticktocks on windows, ringing doorbells, planning adventurous ravages. At about nine o'clock they decided it was time to ditch Fat Mulloy. Walter whispered to Billy. The plan was to have Fat break a window, and then in the shag to outrun him. Tom O'Connor and Andy Houlihan, who were slower than Fat, said they were going home and left the bunch. Fat said it was good riddance.

Danny was pleased with himself, planning to cop all the honors at the party. He knew Roslyn would hear of his courage and admire him. She was going to like him. He was going to kiss Roslyn.

Danny knew he was going to kiss Roslyn, and that it would be different from all the other kisses he had ever had at parties.

"Fat, you're afraid to kick in one of the Hunky's windows," Billy said.

"No, I'm not."

"Yes, you are. You're afraid. You're yellow."

"Why don't one of you brave guys do it?"

"We will, but you're afraid to do it."

The others joined Billy in questioning Fat's courage, even Danny. He was one of the bunch and not a Fat Mulloy or—a Jim English.

"I'm gonna punch one of you guys in the snoot," Fat said.

They looked at Danny. He said nothing, walking along casually. Fat looked at Billy and stepped closer to him. Billy retreated.

"I'll sock you in the jaw," Fat bellowed.

"Yes, you might do that, but you're yellow when it comes to kickin' in one of the Hunky's windows," Billy answered.

"Am I?"

"Yes."

"Well, come on. Then I'm gonna lay one on you."

They went to the corner building at Sixtieth and Indiana. Fat walked up to one of the basement windows, and the others ranged themselves close by, ready to run. They were breathless. Fat looked at the window and then glared at Billy. Fat retreated but returned when Billy laughed at him. He kicked viciously, and the glass hit the basement floor with a metallic ring. They fled, soon followed by the Hunky, a swarthy man, who yelled after them in angry foreign accents. They turned corners, dashed up and down alleys, climbed fences, cut through dark gangways, flashed in and out of secret courtways. Danny fell and ripped his stockings. Billy tore his trousers. Ralph was almost hit by an automobile. And Fat lumbered at the rear, puffing, after the Hunky had given up the pursuit, yelling for them to wait. They ran on wildly. Danny lost the others in an alley. But he was happy. He knew the party would be lots of fun. He thought how Roslyn would kiss him and admire him for his courage. He was going to have a good time at the party. Everybody would have some fun. They were all a good bunch of kids. They didn't mean anything by teasing each other. And he was one of the bunch, and not a Fat Mulloy or a Jim English. He was going to the party, a conquering hero. He was going to the party—going—to—kiss—Roslyn.

IV

Danny arrived at the party. The others were playing tin-tin and paid no attention to him. He found a seat in a Morris chair over in a corner and sat there, alone and awkward. He looked at Roslyn. She sat on the piano stool at the other side of the parlor, dressed in a worn gray suit of Glenn's. Natalie O'Reedy sat next to Roslyn. Natalie was the prettiest girl at school. But Danny watched Roslyn. He gazed around at the other girls, Helen Scanlan, Loretta Lonigan, Cabby Devlin, and fat Marion Troy. His eyes turned back to Roslyn.

The tin-tin game grew dull, and they talked. But Danny had little to say. He was an utter failure at thinking up things to say when there were girls around, particularly Roslyn. He watched Roslyn, and slouched further down in the Morris chair. He wished they would talk of the meeting with Tim Cleary's bunch. Several times he hinted at it, but no one followed up his hints. He kept watching Roslyn, until she caught him and squelched his spirit with a glance. He sat slouched and miserable, losing the last tatters of the feeling he had had coming here. He attempted to start conversations with several of the fellows, baseball with Dick, grammar with Tom O'Connor, dogs with Glenn. But they all had other people to talk to. Danny slouched further down in the chair and felt even more miserable.

The party dragged on.

"Le's do something," Danny finally said.

Something, he hoped, would be post-office.

"What?" someone asked.

"I can't play any kissing games. My mother told me not to," Natalie O'Reedy said.

Danny was not alone in his disappointment when Natalie spoiled all hopes of post-office.

"Well, let's do something," Danny said.

"Maybe you'd like to start another fight," Walter answered.

"Listen, Regan, don't get snotty."

Billy told Danny that he couldn't allow any fighting in his house, and also that girls were present. Roslyn stared at Danny with sudden scorn. He said nothing; he couldn't think of anything to say. He slunk further down in the Morris chair.

Tom O'Connor suggested dancing. Marion Troy played the piano, and the fellows who knew how—Tom O'Connor, Glenn, Billy Morris, and Andy Houlihan—danced. The others looked on.

After about six dances, Roslyn said, "Let's sing."

She took Marion's place at the piano, and they all gathered around. Danny stood directly in back of her, with his arms around the shoulders of Dick and Ralph. He felt like one of the bunch again, as he stood looking at her in front of him. She was not only good and sweet and pretty, but also talented, and she could dance and recite and play at a party.

He watched her playing, her small slender hands sliding from key to key with a soft grace. Somehow it made him think of the seagulls flying over Lake Michigan off Jackson Park. Her hands impressed him that way.

They sang *Mickey* several times. Everybody liked it.

Mickey, lovely Mickey,
With your hair of raven hue,
And your smilin' so beguilin',
There's a bit of Killarney bit of the Blarney, too.
Childhood in the wildwood,
Like a wild sunflower you grew.
Mickey, lovely Mickey,
Can you blame anyone for falling in love with you?

They sang other songs: *Just a Baby's Prayer at Twilight, Over There, America, Here's My Boy, We'll Knock the 'Ell Out of Kelly.*

Danny sang throatily, unable to carry a tune. He thought that now his dreams would begin to come true. For a moment, it seemed as though Dick and Ralph next to him were not real any more. Everything seemed shadowy, except Roslyn's white hands. He kept watching her hands. They were so vivid, white, beautiful. Then he daydreamed. He thought of wartorn French roads and towns, of airplane fights, sea battles in uncharted waters. And through all these came Roslyn, the girl with the white hands, to kiss him. He watched those hands, the hands of a wisp of a wonderful girl in a boy's suit, sliding from key to key and making him think of the seagulls over Lake Michigan. Roslyn.

Suddenly he grew intensely lonely. He felt out of place at the party, a misfit. The girl before him, with the beautiful white hands, was a stranger. She was worse than a stranger. She was an enemy, ready to hurt him every time she could. And no one could hurt Danny O'Neill as much as Roslyn. The whole room was full of strangers, half-sneering strangers who were jealous of him, afraid of him, hating him. They were all friends, but he remained on the outside. He had to fight against them all the time, and he was tired of it. He wished his folks would move to a new neighborhood, where he could start all over again. He looked around from face to face. He wanted to punch them all, to go from person to person and bust each one—except Roslyn. He was lonely, and he didn't belong at parties where there were a lot of girls. He belonged on a baseball field or in a fight. He was lonely.

"Just a baby's prayer at twilight
For his daddy over there."

V

Mrs. Morris called them into the dining room for sandwiches and hot chocolate. Danny thought she was very gracious.

"Eats, eats, everybody," Billy said.

"Tie Buckford up so the rest of us'll get a chance," Andy Houlihan said.

"Yes, we better tie him up," Danny said.

He didn't feel so lonely now. The whole bunch was so good-natured. He liked them all.

"Go on, O'Neill! At my party you ate six sandwiches," Dick said.

Roslyn gave Danny a sudden, darting look.

"Now, line up, and each boy select his partner," Mrs. Morris said.

Danny wanted to walk across the room and take Roslyn's arm, but he couldn't. He stood in a corner and looked at the geranium-patterned wallpaper. Tommy O'Connor was near him, and Danny felt awkward, and so he started talking with Tommy about diagramming sentences. Tommy wasn't interested. He went over to where Dick was standing and asked Dick about his uncle, a minor-league ball player. Dick was busy talking with Helen Scanlan. Danny had been in love with her until he began to love Roslyn in the sixth grade. He looked around the room, shifted his weight from foot to foot, and felt completely miserable and unnecessary. He wished Roslyn would come over and stand next to him. He glanced at her, and she glanced the other way. He watched her, standing demure and possessed. He wanted her for a partner, and he was afraid to ask her. The other fellows seemed equally hesitant about selecting a partner. They stood about the room and waited.

"Come on now, boys. Line up with your partners," Mrs. Morris said.

Finally Billy Morris lined up beside Natalie. Glenn pulled Roslyn by the elbow, next to him, behind Billy and Natalie. The others rapidly found partners, except Danny. He marched into the dining room at the end of the procession, feeling like a goof and a dunce and wishing he hadn't come.

The table was set with small, yellow-ribboned baskets at each plate, while orange streamers were draped from a pie in the center. More orange streamers hung down from the chandelier. Under each yellow paper napkin there was a favor.

They sat down and immediately began talking loudly. Everyone was curious about everyone else's favor, except Danny's. Glenn pulled out a small whistle, which he futilely attempted to blow, and they all laughed. Roslyn displayed a tiny automobile, which she rolled around her plate, and there was more laughing. Billy held up a miniature washing board and set the party into spasms when he rubbed on it with mock vigor.

"Washing, washing today. I'm forced to take in washing by my wife, Natalie." They all screamed with laughter. "She makes me work, washing for a living. Washing. Washing," he said.

Danny's favor was a dunce cap of reduced size. He put it on and grimaced awkwardly. No one noticed him. They continued to look at Billy, who was pretending to tear Dick's shirt in the washing.

"Gotta go faster and faster. Wife beats me when I loaf," Billy said, rubbing vigorously, utilizing his entire body in movement.

They roared.

Danny envied Billy. He wished he could think of funny things to say, like Billy did. He wished he could make people laugh and like him, as Billy did. He wished he wasn't something of a dunce. He never could think of anything to say. He sat and played with his dunce cap and tried to think of something funny, but couldn't. He played with his dunce cap and made funny motions with his arms.

"Look-it," Marion Troy said, noticing him and causing everyone to give him a passing glance of attention.

They all seemed to be having a good time except Danny. No one laughed at his jokes. The other fellows, particularly Billy, could have said the same things and made everybody laugh. Billy's description of how he brought Chinese laundry checks to school was a scream. Danny tried to have a good time, and he laughed with all the effort of a man laboring. But he kept telling himself that he didn't belong at parties.

Several times, as Danny tried to repeat how goofy Jim English was, he was hit in the eye with a peanut. The fourth time he was hit, he started shooting peanuts back.

"Cut out slingin' peanuts, O'Neill. You're not home now," Billy said.

"Yes, this isn't a barn," Dick said.

Dick had started the peanut throwing.

Danny blushed. He imagined Roslyn staring at him, with eyes that bored into his soul. He was afraid to face her. His cheeks grew redder and redder. He wished he had never come to the party and vowed that next week at school he would paste every fellow present in the snoot.

VI

As the party was breaking up, Tom O'Connor, Walter Regan, Dick Buckford, and Glenn commenced fooling around and wrestling in the parlor. Danny was caught in between them. They were shoving and pushing, and he stepped aside. He didn't want to fool around. He stood aside, with his back to the four of them. Suddenly he was shoved violently from the rear and pitched forward. Everyone laughed, laughter that burned like streaks of flame. He got up, angry. His glasses fell off. He picked them up bent. When he tried to straighten them, they split in two. He was angry. He was sure that Wallie Regan had pushed him, but he couldn't prove it. He put his broken glasses into his pocket.

"Who pushed me?" he growled at Walter.

No one answered. Glenn and Walter snickered.

"If I find out who pushed me and broke my glasses, I'll kill him," he said to Walter.

"What are you lookin' at me for?" Walter asked blandly.

"Because you did it."

"I did not."

"You did, too."

"You're a liar."

"Who's a liar?"

"You are if you say I did it."

Danny stepped forward, and Walter retreated. Billy Morris moved between the two of them and said that they were in his house. He looked scornfully at Danny. Billy's mother was disturbed, and asked the boys please not to start a fight and break any of her furniture.

Outside, the kids would not allow them to fight. They haggled and argued.

"Regan'll kill you," Dick said.

"Come on an' let him try."

"Why, you're goofy. Look at how much bigger than you Regan is," Ralph said.

"Listen, he's goofy. You can't hurt him. What's the use of fighting with a guy like that?" Andy Houlihan said.

Danny closed in towards Andy.

"You little shrimp."

Ralph, Walter, and Dick crowded in between Danny and the cowering Andy Houlihan.

"Come on, Regan. I'll take you an' Houlihan."

"I gotta go home. I can't be hanging around fighting somebody who's as goofy as you."

Danny clenched his fists and went for Walter, but he was caught from behind by Ralph and Dick.

"Come on, Glenn, I can't be staying out all night to watch that roughneck start a fight. Take me home," Roslyn said.

Glenn and Roslyn started to leave. Walter and Andy joined them. Danny was crying as he shouted after them. He cursed Ralph and Dick, too. He crossed the street and went home alone.

He walked home slowly. The night was shivery and silent on Fifty-eighth Street. The moon was weird, like a witch. Danny cried and cursed.

VII

On the following Sunday, Danny went to a movie at the Prairie Theater at Fifty-eighth and Prairie Avenue with Fat Mulloy. Danny still felt humiliated about Billy's party. At school they had laughed at him.

After the show Danny and Fat stopped at a soda fountain next door to the show.

"Fat, do you like Regan?"

"No."

"I was wonderin'. I'm gonna get him."

Fat doubted Danny's ability to get Regan. Danny repeated that he would, and could, get Regan. He knew he could knock the hell out of Regan, but he was anxious. The bunch would all be with Regan. He was rich and could buy them sodas and candy. Sometimes he took them riding in his father's automobile. It was a big limousine with his father's initials on the door. Danny knew he would be out of the bunch if he fought with Regan. He knew he would lose any friendship that Glenn might have for him. Glenn was only a runt and even a sissy, but he was Roslyn's cousin. He loved Roslyn and thought he should remain friendly with Glenn. If he beat up Regan, he would be left out of parties, too. He would be lonely. But he had to get Regan. And he would.

Fat and Danny talked over their sodas. Suddenly Fat pointed out of the window and said, "There's Regan."

Danny turned to see Regan pass by. Danny was afraid.

"Here's your chance," Fat said.

Danny rushed out of the soda parlor and called after Regan in a mood of desperation.

"Listen, Regan, I want to see you."

"What for? I'm in a hurry."

Regan walked back slowly.

"What do you wanna see me for? I'm in a hurry."

"Commere an' I'll tell you."

Danny found himself calm now. He was calm and he hated Regan. He hated Regan so much that he wanted to keep punching him and watch his face bleed.

"You shoved me."

"I didn't."

"You're a liar."

"I'm not a liar."

"You are. Now, listen. Will you fight?"

"I'm in a hurry. Anyway, I could lick you."

"Are you yellow or will you fight?"

"I'm in a hurry, and I can't now. Anyway, I could lick you."

"You *can*?"

"Can't I, Fat?"

Slap! The back of Danny's right hand snapped against Regan's lip, causing a thick trickle of blood. Danny was thrilled by the sight of Regan's blood.

"Damn you, will you fight now?"

"I can't now. I haven't the time, I tell you. But I'll get even with you for this. I'll settle with you."

Regan walked away.

"Yellow," Danny shouted after him.

"Yellow belly," Fat yelled.

VIII

"Are you going to Roslyn's party tonight?" Ralph asked Danny.

It was an autumn-weary day in the middle of November. Ralph and Danny were walking together on Indiana Avenue.

"No. I'm not invited."

"I don't think anyone was especially invited. She saw Billy and all of us the other day and asked us to come. Said she couldn't go up to everyone separately and ask them. She said she'd feel kind of funny if she did."

"Well, she never invited me. I saw her a couple of times last week, and she never invited me."

"Well, I know she meant that everybody should come."

"No, she never invited me."

"Well, I think she meant everybody. I know I'm goin', and I'm gonna have a good time."

"Hooray—Hooray—Giddap—Giddap—Bang, Bang, Bang—Look out, here I come on Pinto, chased by the sheriff, Fat Mulloy. Bang, Bang, Bang."

It was Billy Morris. He galloped past them, turned around, galloped back, and walked along at their side.

"Billy, in a way you're goofy," Ralph said.

Billy didn't say anything. They stopped in front of his home, a three-story, gray brick building.

"Where you going, Ralph?"

"Nowheres."

"And you?"

"Same place."

"Let's all go together. Or let's just sit here and talk for a while."

They sat down on Billy's front steps.

"I gotta go upstairs and take a bath for the party in a little while," Billy said.

Danny didn't want to sit, talking with them. It was one of those days when he wanted to be alone. But he thought that he might get them to go over to Roslyn's home and take a walk down around that neighborhood. Then maybe they would meet Roslyn, and she might invite him to her party. He knew Roslyn liked him despite everything. It was just pride that made her act like she did. Glenn once told him that she cared for him.

"Let's go up and see Glenn," Danny said.

"Glenn's gone downtown to get some favors for the party," Billy answered.

"We ought to have a good time tonight," Ralph said.

"Yeah, I always have a good time if Natalie is around. Gee, but she's a pip. She's got wonderful legs, too," Billy said.

"Yeah, she has, all right," Ralph said.

"She's more than all right. She's a pip," Billy said.

Danny envied Ralph and Billy. He was jealous of the easy way in which they talked of girls, of their popularity, and of their invitations to Roslyn's party. He wished he could talk of, and to, girls as naturally, and that he could get along with them as well as Billy or Ralph did.

"Let's take a walk down and see Andy Houlihan. Maybe he'll have a good bonfire going in the prairie next to his house," Danny said.

Andy lived one block away from Roslyn. Maybe they would see her if they went around that neighborhood.

"It's too far. I gotta get ready for the party," Billy said.

"So do I," from Ralph.

"We don't have to stay long," Danny said.

"Helen Scanlan's going to be at the party tonight, isn't she?" Ralph asked.

"Yeah. Say, you kind of like her, don't you?" Billy asked.

"Yes, she's a nice kid," Ralph said.

"She's another pip, all right. She's got legs almost as good as Natalie's," Billy said, getting enthusiastic.

"Yes, she has."

"I wouldn't mind playing post-office tonight. Oh, boy! . . . with Natalie tonight. With some girls, too, but not Natalie, you can get 'em in the dark and cop a couple of feels," Billy said.

"Well, I wouldn't mind, either."

Danny wanted to protest against something, but he couldn't find any word that would tell him what that something was. He wanted to protest, because somewhere there was unfairness. He wanted to know why Ralph and Billy got along so much better than he did, and why people liked them better. He wanted to know why they should be invited to the party and not he. He could do almost everything better than either of them. He could fight, wrestle, play football better than they. They didn't even know the first thing about basketball. He got better marks in school, too. All Billy could do better than Danny was dance and make wisecracks. There was something unfair in the world somewhere, and he wanted to protest about it.

"Natalie and Helen are the best lookers in school," Billy said, and Danny but half heard the remark. He sat pitying himself. There was something unfair, and he was being hurt because of unfairness and he wanted to fight, even though he was afraid of fighting.

"Yeah," Ralph said.

"Roslyn used to be, but she fixes her hair up funny now, and she's got skinny legs," Billy said.

Danny hated Billy for this remark. He looked at Billy, thinking of Billy's own toothpick legs, his ugly peanut of a head, his dirty brown skin. He hated Billy, and told himself that Roslyn was an angel.

"Billy, didn't Roslyn mean for everyone to come to her party?" Ralph asked.

"I guess so. Why?"

"I was telling Danny that, and he said it didn't mean him."

"She said she wanted everyone, but, then, she doesn't like him."

"Who wants to go to her damn party?" Danny said.

"I do. I expect to have some fun," Billy said.

A few minutes later Danny left, determined that Ralph, Billy, and Roslyn, too, could all roast in the hottest part of Hell. But he was glad the kids didn't know that he was so much in love with Roslyn. If they did, they'd never stop ragging him.

He had intended to go home. He walked down to Sixty-first and South Park and proceeded to go around the block several times. Each time he passed a lace-curtained window on the second floor of an ornate building in the middle of the block, he stopped and gazed up, as if interested in the stars that were just coming out.

A passer-by might have noticed that he was wistful as he gazed up past the lace curtains.

IX

Danny heard all about Roslyn's party. He was told that it was the best party ever given. They had played spin-the-bottle, post-office, wink, and tin-tin. Roslyn's father had played with them, and the kids said he was a regular fellow. And there had been all kinds of eats, too. Roslyn had called Andy Houlihan to the post-office a number of times, and Helen Scanlan had been sweet to Ralph. Glenn had copped off Natalie. He was a devil with the women. Billy Morris had been a scream. Every time he talked, he had made the whole party laugh. It had been a scream when he plopped the peanut into Dick's coffee.

And there were half-whispered conversations of what had been said and done in the post-office.

X

Danny met Ralph one afternoon about a week after Roslyn's party. He hadn't been playing with the bunch of late and was lonesome. He was glad to see Ralph and wanted to talk to him about a lot of things, particularly about Roslyn and her party. She had spoken to him, asking him why he hadn't come. He knew she liked him. He was glad to see Ralph, too, and wanted to talk about Roslyn.

"Hello, Ralph, how are you?"

"All right," Ralph answered with self-conscious casualness.

"Where you going?"

"No place."

"Let's go together," Danny said.

Ralph didn't answer. They walked slowly.

"You're kind of droopy. Do you know it?" Ralph said suddenly, following his remark with a scornful laugh.

Danny looked at Ralph.

"Yes, you're dizzy. How do you get that way?" Ralph asked, muffling his anger. "Yes, you're dizzy."

"Well, what if I am?"

"Nothing. Only you're dizzy and a droopy drawers."

"Supposing I am?"

"Nothing."

Ralph laughed again.

"Yes, you're an old droop. Look at the way you walk."

"No, I'm not. I just walk—slow."

Ralph laughed again.

"You're not any too fast or straight when you walk," Danny said.

"I'm not a droopy drawers," Ralph said.

He laughed again.

"You're worse."

"I am?" Ralph asked. He was angry, and his voice throbbed.

"Yes, what are you gonna do about it?" Danny asked, arrogant.

"I am worse than a droopy drawers?"

"Yes."

"Well, what am I?" Ralph asked menacingly.

Danny couldn't think of anything more to say. He answered that Ralph was—just worse than a droopy drawers. That was all. He was worse.

They glowered, and Ralph cried slightly, from anger.

"Take that back," he demanded.

"Not unless you do."

"Take it back."

"No."

"I beat you once."

"That was in the fifth grade. But you can't do it again," Danny taunted.

"I beat you once. I punched the crap out of you. I can do it again if I want to."

"You're afraid to try it again."

"Remember that time you socked Billy Morris? Well, I licked you, didn't I?"

"Yes, but you can't now. Go get Morris, and I'll take the two of you."

"You know I can lick you if I want to."

"Wanna fight?" Danny asked.

"I licked you once. You just be careful about saying that I'm worse than an old droopy drawers."

"Then you watch what you say."

"Suppose I don't?"

"Then I won't."

"Don't forget that I beat you once."

"I can take you and Billy together now."

"You think you're tough, don't you?"

"No, but I'm tougher than you are," Danny said.

They walked for a block, silent. Then Ralph repeated that he once licked Danny, and Danny repeated that he could lick Ralph. Ralph repeated and Danny repeated.

"I can't play with you any more," Ralph suddenly said.

Danny ignored Ralph.

"I can't play with you any more, because my mother knows there's swearing in your house, and your aunt gets drunk."

"It isn't so," Danny said hotly.

"It is," Ralph said. "I don't care. My mother told me not to play with you any more. She says you'll grow up to be a bad influence."

"Well, don't walk with me," Danny said.

"You started walking with me," Ralph said.

"I'm walking this way, and I'm gonna keep walking," Danny said.

"So am I."

They strolled on side by side, without any further conversation.

XI

Walter Regan, Ralph, Billy, Dick, Glenn, Andy Houlihan, Fat Mulloy, a kid nicknamed Blackie, new at St. Patrick's, and Danny were all standing in front of school.

"Diz here is goofy," Dick said.

"He's crazy. Crazy people always have dreamy eyes like he got. You know, eyes that are always asleep," Billy said.

"What if I am?" Danny answered.

"No if about it," Dick said.

"Shut up, Buckford!"

Dick grinned foolishly.

"Gee, you're a hot-headed Irishman all right," Billy said.

"Well, Dick gives me a pain. If he wasn't yellow, I'd bust his mush for him."

"He's goofy with an ivory head. He's the kind of a guy you can't hurt. You keep hitting him until you get tired. He's got an ivory head," Dick said.

Glenn and Billy started poking each other in the ribs and wrestling. Then they ran around in circles, chasing each other, and shouting. Soon they were on the ground, wrestling. Walter Regan and Dick joined in with a whoop. Danny moved to do likewise.

"Who asked you in?" Walter asked.

"None of your damn business."

"It is, too, my business who I play with."

"And mine, too," Glenn said, getting up.

"And I don't wanna play with a roughneck Irishman who is always lookin' for a fight. Why, you're worse than the Germans," Walter said.

"Yes, and my mother told me to have nothing to do with him because there's always a lot of swearin' and cursin' goin' on at his house," Ralph said.

"Yes, and he hasn't any breeding. He's like a Hun, throwing peanuts at parties and starting fights in other people's houses," Billy said.

"He's goofy about my cousin, and she hates him," Glenn said.

They laughed at him.

The remarks had come so swiftly that Danny was without a reply. He stuttered in anger. Walter Regan invited the bunch to go with him, and they all accepted.

"You can't come," he said to Danny.

"Who wants to play with a yellow belly?"

"You can't."

They all left, laughing back at Danny, who stood, tearful and defiant, shaking his fists at them.

XII

Danny remained in front of the school for about five minutes. He was hurt and angry. Then he headed east along Sixty-first Street, planning to go for a walk all the way to Jackson Park. He was lonely and, whenever he felt that way, he took a long walk. He usually walked in Washington Park, but today he'd walk in Jackson Park. As he drooped along, he planned scenes bloody with the revenge he would wreak. When he grew up and became a great basketball player and a greater fighter than Benny Leonard, he would snub them. And the next time they needed him in a scrap, he wouldn't stick with them. He was through with them, and he could wait for his revenge until he became great. He was through with them, and all winter he would remain at home, reading.

He thought of Roslyn. He wondered if Glenn had told the truth. Did she hate him? If she did, well, the hell with her, too. Some day she, all of them, would feel sorry. If he met her he would snub her. He did meet her. She opened her mouth to speak. Danny didn't look at her. In fact, he didn't see her. After she passed, she turned around and yelled, "Funny face."

He came to his senses with a start and turned around.

"Funny face," she repeated.

"If I'm a Funny Face, you're one, too," he said.

She stuck up her small nose, turned her head pertly, and walked away.

He felt like a fool. He was sorry, and angry. He told himself that she could go to the devil, and for an entire block he imagined her burning in Hell.

When he came to Jackson Park, his mood changed. He became moody and lost in a vaporous sadness. There was a sadness about the park, half mellow with autumn, half bare with the wounds of the early winter winds. The park seemed to console him. He forgot all about the raggings he received from the bunch. He imagined himself alone, away from the world, a Robinson Crusoe on some distant sphere. Things seemed strange to him. He imagined that he was a soul in Purgatory, a soul cast there willy-nilly.

He walked. The park seemed bare, cold, strange, lonely; dusk covered it like a robe. Overhead, a frosty moon had blown the sun out of the sky, sinking it in the oblivion of another day. He saw etched against the distant sky the vague outlines of a human figure. He watched it approach slowly. It was bent and familiar. He looked at it, and then at the moon, alone and companionless in a sky empty of stars. He remembered all that had hurt him in the past weeks. He was lonely. The figure was upon him.

"Hello, Danny," it said.

"Hello, Jim."

"What are you doing here?" Danny asked.

"Oh, taking a walk," Jim said.

"So am I. I like Jackson Park better than Washington Park," Danny said.

"So do I," Jim said.

Danny wished he lived in the Jackson Park neighborhood and knew a new bunch of kids.

"Goin' home? It's late and it'll be a long walk."

"We can get a hitch on a truck," Danny said.

"Where were you going?" Jim said.

"Over to the lake."

Jim seemed moody, too. They walked on to the lake in silence and looked at it.

"Looks rough today," Jim said.

"It's always rough at this time of year. It's kind of cold, and the wind is coming up," Danny said.

"Yes, it is," Jim said.

"It's gray and kind of dirty," Danny said.

"Oh, boy, what whitecaps," Jim said.

"I like the noise it makes. I like it kind of wild," Danny said.

"I don't. You couldn't swim in it this way," Jim said.

"I'd like to. I'm going to try and swim in it against those waves some time."

"I don't believe you."

"I will some day," Danny said.

The two boys stood before the lake in the gathering darkness looking at it, listening to the wild monotony of its slashing waves. Danny looked far, far out and saw the dark horizon. He looked and looked. He wanted to see the seagulls today, flying and crying in the darkness over the rough lake. He thought of Roslyn as a seagull. But he saw none. There was nothing but gray water, gray water and waves and foaming whitecaps on the lake. And there was no one around, no one in sight, only himself and Jim. They stood looking at the lake.

"Yes, it's better this way than when it's calm," Danny said.

They turned and walked back.

"Yes."

They walked along together.

"Where were the kids today?" Jim asked.

"I had a quarrel with 'em. They give me a pain, and none of them would fight."

"I don't like them either," Jim said.

Danny didn't answer.

"Was Glenn with 'em?" Jim asked.

"Yeah."

"Does he still tease his cousin?"

"He ought to. She's an old Funny Face. Worse than he is."

"I thought she was a nice girl."

"She gives me a pain."

"I kinda think she's all right," Jim said.

Danny changed the subject to baseball. And he had enough money to pay for both their carfares. They talked baseball all the way home on the car. They got off at Sixty-first and South Park. Danny looked up at Roslyn's window. It was lit up. He wished she'd look out and see him. They walked on.

Just as they were parting at Fifty-first and South Park, Danny said, "Listen, Jim, you come over to my house after school tomorrow?"

"Sure," Jim said.

"Danny, was that true what you told me about Rube Waddell?" Jim called after him.

"Yeah. I'll show you his records in the Spaulding and Reich guides tomorrow. I like a guy like him."

"So long, Danny."

"So long, Jim."

[1929, 1930-47]

The Wake of
Patsy McLaughlin

I

Patsy McLaughlin always said to himself and to others that he wanted
to die in harness with his boots on. This was but one of the many reasons
why the sunny day in June, 1929, when he retired as Superintendent of the
Vehicle Department of the Continental Express Company, was one of the
saddest of his life. His doctor had insisted on his retirement. Besides a
cardiac condition, he had high blood pressure. He was sixty-two, and he
knew that he wasn't the man he used to be. Driven around to the depots
every day, he would puff and grow tired, and when he got home at night
he would feel dull and weary. Even the White Sox ball games, which he had
always enjoyed so fully, fatigued him. He had become a weary, heavy, white-
haired man, whose rough and wrinkled ruddy face was blotched with darkening clusters of broken blood vessels. His manner had always been gruff,
but in his dealings with the men under his supervision he'd been direct.
He valued his word highly, and he had never broken it. He had bawled out

many a teamster and chauffeur, given layoffs and fired men, but most of the men on the wagon loved and respected as well as feared him. Around the garages, stables, and depots he was called "Patsy," "Old Patsy," and "The Old Man." On his last day, many of the wagon men were sad and regretful. The old-timers, especially, knew that they were going to miss him. He had once been one of them, and when he'd gone up the ladder he hadn't changed. In his heart he was still an old-time teamster. He always remembered the men when he'd run across them, and he would call them by their first names and would ask some of them about their families. They forgot the times he had been harsh and thought only of when he'd been lenient and given a man a break.

The dispatchers and route inspectors, too, felt much as the vehicle men did. Like Patsy, with very few exceptions they had once been on the wagons. They, as well as he, could remember how they'd once felt, getting a load of fish, working long hours during the Christmas rush, or being out on icy days in winter. Many of them had changed more than he after their promotions. He would call them in on the carpet and give them tongue-lashings the way they did their drivers and helpers. But on the day of his retirement such matters were forgotten. Work went on, and they were in the depots as early as usual, getting out the wagon loads. They were conscious that this was Patsy's last day. They had thought of growing old themselves, of retiring, and of one day dying, but somehow they hadn't thought of the day Patsy would go. In relationship to the Old Man they were like children who cannot clearly think of their father dying. On Patsy's last day they were a nervous, jumpy, saddened group of men. Many of them had strange, sad, and dark feelings they could not clearly describe to themselves—the kind of feelings and moods that caused them to think or remark that they needed to change their luck. And Patsy's retirement was full of forebodings for them. With Patsy over them, they had been secure. Most of them, at least, couldn't think of Patsy firing them. He'd been their boss for years now. They had a settled feeling about their jobs and the Company. Now and then, big muckety-mucks from the Main Office, and even from the East, and Efficiency Experts, too, had introduced or tried to introduce changes in the casual and inefficient way in which the Department functioned, but their new-fangled schemes had never really taken hold. Patsy could have changed no more than they. Tough as he occasionally had been, Patsy nevertheless had been anything but a really hard boss. They felt that he understood them and that he also had been a shield for them against the muckety-mucks. And they took pride in him. He knew the big-shot politicians, important police officials, dignitaries of the Church—the kind of men they would like to mingle with and would know if they got as far up the ladder as Old Patsy had.

They were a bit lost on this day. Cooper, who had been Superintendent of the Depot Department, was coming in to fill Patsy's shoes. They all knew that Cooper could never take Patsy's place. Some of them privately had called the new boss Gumshoe Cooper, and they were fearful as to how they'd fare under him. There would be shifts, and no one knew where he would end up. A couple of the Dispatchers and Route Inspectors even feared they might be sent packing back on the wagons or trucks, and that would be raw. Working all these years, they had come to feel at home on the job, and the Company had seemed less big and impersonal than it really was. Much as they now and then loafed and complained, they had come to like their work, and to see Old John Continental as something friendly and accessible. Sometimes when they referred to the Company as Old John Continental, they would even think of Patsy. And now the Old Man was retiring. They felt themselves to be less than they had been a week ago, as though they had shrunk in height.

Patsy had become part of their life, of their memories. His Ford coupé, sliding in and out of the depots, his grunts and coughs in his office, his gruff voice, his gentle, gray eyes, his heavy-footed walk, his slightly slouched shoulders—all this was so familiar. They had begun to feel the weight of time in their own lives, but now that that weight had fallen on Old Patsy, they felt it more heavily. They were very, very lonely on Patsy McLaughlin's last day.

Patsy himself seemed gradually to have accustomed himself to the idea of his retirement. Besides his pension, he had enough savings and investments to assure his security. As the time of his retirement approached, he had many moments when he thought this would be a good thing for him, and he looked forward to spending his last years in ease, free of all the strains and tensions of responsibility. He fancied how he and Mrs. McLaughlin would do some traveling, and would spend the remaining winters of their life in Florida or California. There would be ball games and friends, and he could take up gardening. Time would pass in quiet happiness until he was called. But he never could fully believe in his own plans and dreams. And on his last day he had to force back a flow of feelings which frightened him. He didn't want to retire. He didn't want to accept the fact that all his years, all his life as an expressman had come to an end. So much was gone, so much he had taken for granted. During all these years he had never wanted to have long vacations, and many times on a Sunday he'd run down to his office or around the depots just to be doing something. Now he would have nothing to do. He was retiring in order to try and enjoy the grace and quiet of a happy death. He felt weak and even powerless. The authority he had had would end with this day. He would walk out of his office for the last time, and then he would be respected and liked, but he wouldn't have authority and responsibility. Instead of being a Superintendent, he would merely be an old man. What he said or did on this last day wouldn't mean much because it could be undone in the morning. He had never really thought of how much his job meant to him, and on his last day he didn't think clearly about this or reason out what his retirement meant. But it was clear to him that his job had, as it were, become part of himself, and that he and his job as Superintendent of the Vehicle Department of the Continental Express Company had seemed to be inseparable. His job and his Department and the Company itself had all become part of his life.

Now part of his life was to be taken away, severed. This was like a foretaste of death. Retirement was a form of dying. He looked at the large office, saw Route Inspectors and Dispatchers, dictated a few letters, accepted and listened to greetings, congratulations, and expressions of good wishes, but all of this only left him with the feeling that he wasn't quite understood. And his pride was hurt. He had to retire because he wasn't the man he once was. Father Time had taken hold of him. And this was almost as though he had lost a vital part of his manhood. He concealed all this and tried to act like the same Patsy McLaughlin he'd always been. He talked of plans with Wade Norris, his Chief Clerk, and with some of the inspectors. He talked for a while with Joe Leonard, one of his assistant superintendents, telling Joe that he would go up to one of the Wisconsin lakes this summer and get in a lot of fishing. He thanked everyone for the gifts he had received. But he felt as though he might even be dreaming. All this didn't seem to be quite true, quite real. It was too soon to realize what was happening, that after today he wouldn't be here any more. It would take him time to get used to his retirement. He had been a superintendent for over twenty years. Days and months and years had passed, his hair had turned white, he had gained a little weight, and his old ticker had started skipping a beat here and there, and this all seemed to have happened in such a short time. He had gone on acting as though he'd be the boss here forever. And now he was leaving. He didn't know how to say what he felt. He couldn't even say it clearly to himself.

And when the day passed, he left his office for the last time. He said good night to Wade Norris for the last time. He walked out of the office for the last time. He was driven home in the Company's Ford coupé for the last time. And he was very sad and very lonely.

II

Patsy died in September. The summer had passed slowly for him, and he had been bored and irritable. He hadn't known what to do with himself. He and his wife had spent a month in Wisconsin, and he had enjoyed the fishing. That had been the best part of his short life in retirement. At home, he had had nothing to do. He had sat for hours, reading newspapers, listening to the radio, or merely sitting, with his mind vague, recalling at random incidents from his years as an expressman, thinking of the days when he had driven a single wagon, of men who had passed away, like his cousin, Jim O'Neill, and others. He had been saddened to be old and childless, and had imagined himself with sons and daughters who would now be married and have made him a grandfather. He'd puttered about the house. Over and over again he had announced that he would take up gardening, but he never had. He often had sat on the back porch in the shade and fallen asleep. He had come to want sleep, but he'd slept badly at night, and he came to dread each night. He had suspected old friends of thinking he wasn't the man he'd once been, and he had begun to lose interest in them. He had had nothing to do and had become very irritable because of his boredom.

Patsy died peacefully after having suffered severely from a heart attack. The doctor had thought that he had a good chance to survive the attack, but just as he seemed to be on the way to recovery, he passed away in his sleep.

Patsy was waked for three nights. He had had many friends, and the house, on a quiet North Side street near Evanston, was filled each night. Politicians, policemen, friends, express company officials, supervisors from his old department, and wagon men all came and paid their last respects. When the men from the Vehicle Department came, they looked at his corpse with awe and with regretful eyes, knelt down to say a few prayers for the repose of his soul, and hurried out to sit in the kitchen in the rear of the house. The kitchen was large and on the last night of the wake it was almost filled with expressmen. They sat there as though they wanted to huddle together, and a number of them seemed to be uncomfortable in their

Sunday clothes. The Route Inspectors saw one another every day, and many of the wagon men present also saw one another almost daily. In their encounters at work, they were usually talkative; they needled and ragged and insulted one another. Here, they were shy and diffident, and some of them were even a little solemn. Even dead, Patsy awed them. The sense of their difference from him remained even though his corpse lay in the casket surrounded by flowers in the front of the house. They sat on camp chairs and stood in corners, and now and then someone would say something about death, or about how Patsy had gone fast. A distant cousin of Patsy's passed cigars, and everyone took one, as though it were a ritual. Then Gashouse McGinty nudged Mike Mulroney and said that Willie Collins had snatched three cigars, but Mike hadn't picked up the joke. And no one picked up Willie's retaliatory jibe about how McGinty had long since beaten all comers in the contest to become champion cigar-snatcher at wakes. There were small flurries of talk, but they seemed to die out quickly, and the men sat in solemn silence.

While in the back of the McLaughlin home, most of these supervisors and wagon men were thinking, at one moment or another, that their day, too, would come, just as Patsy's had. His death spanned the working lives of most of their lives. He had been the man who had taken McGinty, Collins, Father Bryan, Heinie Mueller, and many of the others off the wagons and made them dispatchers and inspectors. He had singled them out from among hundreds of others, and he had kept them in their present jobs. Their lives had been changed because of his decisions. For years, day after day in their work, they had thought of him and had gone along thinking they were doing things for him, and that if they fell down on their jobs they would be letting Patsy down. They had gone on in the same way under his successor, Gumshoe Cooper, but it hadn't been the same. They hadn't become used to Cooper, as they had been to Patsy. Just as they had felt hurt and lost when Patsy had retired, so now did they feel hurt and lost, only their feelings were sadder, and they all repressed their own fright and fear. Smoking, talking, tapping their feet, and making many little nervous movements, these men all were troubled with thoughts and fears and memories they dared not express. There were thoughts as to who would go next, who would live longest. They thought of past wakes, and of endless little episodes in their lives in which Patsy was involved. Willie Collins confessed that he might go down to work tomorrow and even think the Old Man was still in the front office, and said that Patsy had always stood by him. McGinty said that Patsy had always been fair and had stood by any man who kept his eyes on the ball. Heinie Mueller declared that Patsy had been as square a man as anyone he ever knew. Mike Mulroney said no man could ever have had a better friend. The talk would break out like this, and then there would be moments of silences, and the men would quietly watch one another. Tomorrow, and for many days and years to come, they would talk and kid about this wake, but now, while attending it, they were strangely quiet. It meant something to them, something very tragic which they did not clearly put into words. It meant that a long period of their lives, the best period, had come to an end. It meant that one of the props for their feeling of belonging to the Continental had been destroyed. It brought them sadly back to the days when, as teamsters, they had been young and strong. Now they were middle-aged or old. Some were fat. Some had their hair beginning to gray, or even white hair. They felt a personal loss. They felt strangely uneasy to think that the Old Man was gone and that they were actually sitting in his kitchen and paying their last respects to him. One by one, or in small groups, they left, taking a last look at their dead boss, saying a last prayer, a last word of condolence to his gray-haired widow. Most of them would have cried had they dared to. Patsy was the man they would like to have been. He was gone. They would never be able to sit in his shoes, and no one who ever did sit in his shoes would be quite the same. The Company wouldn't be the same, either, or at least not for a long, long time. Burying him was like burying John Continental himself. It was like burying years of their work for the Company. They all went back to their homes saddened, and they went to work the next day, still saddened. They had lost something, something of themselves and of their own lives.

[1931, 1932–48]

The Fastest Runner
on Sixty-first Street

I

Morty Aiken liked to run and to skate. He liked running games and races. He liked running so much that sometimes he'd go over to Washington Park all by himself and run just for the fun of it. He got a kick out of running, and he had raced every kid he could get to run against him. His love of racing and running had even become a joke among many of the boys he knew. But even when they gave him the horse laugh it was done in a good-natured way, because he was a very popular boy. Older fellows liked him, and when they would see him, they'd say, there's a damn good kid and a damned fast runner.

When he passed his fourteenth birthday, Morty was a trifle smaller than most boys of his own age. But he was well known, and, in a way, almost famous in his own neighborhood. He lived at Sixty-first and Eberhardt, but kids in the whole area had heard of him, and many of them would speak of what a runner and what a skater Morty Aiken was.

He won medals in playground tournaments, and, in fact, he was the only lad from his school who had ever won medals in these tournaments. In these events he became the champion in the fifty- and hundred-yard dash, and with this he gained the reputation of being the best runner, for his age, on the South Side of Chicago.

He was as good a skater as he was a runner. In winter, he was to be seen regularly almost every day on the ice at the Washington Park lagoon or over on the Midway. He had a pair of Johnson racers which his father had given him, and he treasured these more than any other possession. His mother knitted him red socks and a red stocking cap for skating, and he had a red-and-white sweater. When he skated, he was like a streak of red. His form was excellent, and his sense of himself and of his body on the ice was sure and right. Almost every day there would be a game of I-Got-It. The skater who was *it* would skate in a wide circle, chased by the pack until he was caught. Morty loved to play I-Got-It, and on many a day this boy in short pants, wearing the red stocking cap, the red-and-white sweater, and the thick, knitted red woolen socks coming above the black shoes of his Johnson racers, would lead the pack, circling around and around and around, his head forward, his upper torso bent forward, his hands behind his back, his legs working with grace and giving him a speed that sometimes seemed miraculous. And in February, 1919, Morty competed in an ice derby, conducted under the auspices of the Chicago *Clarion*. He won two gold medals. His picture was on the first page of the sports section of the Sunday *Clarion*. All in all, he was a famous and celebrated lad. His father and mother were proud of him. His teacher and Mrs. Bixby, the principal of the school, were proud of him. Merchants on Sixty-first Street were proud of him. There was not a lad in the neighborhood who was greeted on the street by strangers as often as Morty.

Although he was outwardly modest, Morty had his dreams. He was graduated from grammar school in 1919, and was planning to go to Park High in the fall. He was impatient to go to high school and to get into high-school track meets. He'd never been coached, and yet look how good he was! Think of how good he would be when he had some coaching! He'd be a streak of lightning, if there ever was one. He dreamed that he would be called the Human Streak of Lightning. And after high school there would be college, college track meets, and the Big Ten championship, and after that he would join an athletic club and run in track meets, and he would win a place on the Olympic team, and somewhere, in Paris or Rome or some European city, he would beat the best runners in the world, and, like Ty Cobb in baseball and Jess Willard in prize fighting, he'd be the world's greatest runner.

And girls would all like him, and the most beautiful girl in the world would marry him. He liked girls, but girls liked him even more than he liked them. In May, a little while before his graduation, the class had a picnic, and they played post office. The post office was behind a clump of bushes in Jackson Park. He was called to the post office more than any other of the boys. There was giggling and talking and teasing, but it hadn't bothered him, especially because he knew that the other fellows liked and kind of envied him. To Morty, this was only natural. He accepted it. He accepted the fact that he was a streak of lightning on his feet and on the ice, and that this made him feel somehow different from other boys and very important. Even Tony Rabuski looked at him in this way, and if any kid would have picked on him, Tony would have piled into that kid. Tony was the toughest boy in school, and he was also considered to be the dumbest. He was also the poorest. He would often come to school wearing a black shirt, because a black shirt didn't show the dirt the way that other shirts did, and his parents couldn't afford to buy him many shirts. One day Tony was walking away from school with Morty, and Tony said:

"Kid, you run de fastest, I fight de best in de whole school. We make a crack-up team. We're pals. Shake, kid, we're pals."

Morty shook Tony's hand. For a fourteen-year-old boy, Tony had very big and strong hands. The other kids sometimes called them "meat hooks."

Morty looked on this handshake as a pledge. He and Tony became friends, and they were often together. Morty had Tony come over to his house to play, and sometimes Tony stayed for a meal. Tony ate voraciously and wolfishly. When Morty's parents spoke of the way Tony ate and of the quantity of food he ate, Morty would reply by telling them that Tony was his friend.

Because he was poor and somewhat stupid, a dull and fierce resentment smoldered in Tony. Other boys out-talked him, and they were often able to plague and annoy him, and then outrun him because he was heavy footed. The kids used to laugh at Tony because they said he had lead, iron, and bricks in his big feet. After Morty and Tony had shaken hands and become pals, Morty never would join the other boys in razzing Tony. And he and Tony doped out a way that would permit Tony to get even with kids who tried to torment him. If some of the boys made game of Tony until he was confused and enraged and went for them, Morty would chase the boys. He had no difficulty in catching one of them. When he caught any of the boys who'd been teasing and annoying Tony, he'd usually manage to hold the boy until Tony would lumber up and exact his punishment and revenge. Sometimes Tony would be cruel, and on a couple of occasions when Tony, in a dull and stupefied rage, was sitting on a hurt, screaming boy and pounding him, Morty ordered Tony to lay off. Tony did so instantly. Morty didn't want Tony to be too cruel. He had come to like Tony and to look on him as a big brother. He'd always wanted a brother, and sometimes he would imagine how wonderful it would be if Tony could even come to live at his house.

The system Morty and Tony worked out, with Morty chasing and catching one of the boys who ragged Tony, worked out well. Soon the kids stopped ragging Tony. Because of their fear, and because they liked and respected Morty and wanted him to play with them, they began to accept Tony. And Tony began to change. Once accepted, so that he was no longer the butt of jokes, he looked on all the boys in Morty's gang as his pals. He would protect them as he would protect Morty. Tony then stopped scowling and making fierce and funny faces and acting in many odd little ways. After he became accepted, as a result of being Morty's pal, his behavior changed, and because he was strong and could fight, the boys began to admire him. At times he really hoped for strange boys to come around the neighborhood and act like bullies so he could beat them up. He wanted to fight and punch because he could feel powerful and would be praised and admired.

II

Ever since he had been a little fellow, Tony had often been called a "Polack" or a "dirty Polack." After he became one of the gang or group around Morty, some of the boys would tell him that he was a "white Polack." In his slow way, he thought about these words and what they meant. When you were called certain words, you were laughed at, you were looked at as if something were wrong with you. If you were a Polack, many girls didn't want to have anything to do with you. The boys and girls who weren't Polacks had fun together that Polacks couldn't have. Being a Polack and being called a Polack was like being called a sonofabitch. It was a name. When you were called a name like this, you were looked at as a different kind of kid from one who wasn't called a name. Morty Aiken wasn't called names. Tony didn't want to be called names. And if he fought and beat up those who called him names, they would be afraid of him. He wanted that. But he also wanted to have as much fun as the kids had who weren't called these names. And he worked it out that these kids felt better when they called other kids names. He could fight and he could call names, and if he called a kid a name, and that kid got tough, he could beat him up. He began to call names. And there was a name even worse than Polack—"nigger." If Tony didn't like a kid, he called him a "nigger." And he talked about the "niggers." He felt as good as he guessed these other kids did when he talked about the "niggers." And they could be beat up. They weren't supposed to go to Washington Park because that was a park for the whites. That was what he had often heard.

He heard it said so much that he believed it. He sometimes got a gang of the boys together and they would roam Washington Park, looking for colored boys to beat up. Morty went with them. He didn't particularly like to beat up anyone, but when they saw a colored kid and chased him, he would always be at the head, and he would be the one who caught the colored boy. He could grab or tackle him, and by that time the others would catch up. He worked the same plan that he and Tony had worked against the other boys. And after they caught and beat up a colored boy, they would all talk and shout and brag about what they had done, and talk about how they had each gotten in their licks and punches and kicks, and how fast Morty had run to catch that shine, and what a sock Tony had given him, and, talking all together and strutting and bragging, they felt good and proud of themselves, and they talked about how the Sixty-first Street boys would see to it that Washington Park would stay a white man's park.

And this became more and more important to Tony. There were those names, "Polack," "dirty Polack," "white Polack." If you could be called a "Polack," you weren't considered white. Well, when he beat them up, was he or wasn't he white? They knew. After the way he clouted these black ones, how could the other kids not say that Tony Rabuski wasn't white? That showed them all. That showed he was a hero. He was a hero as much as Morty Aiken was.

III

Morty was a proud boy on the night he graduated from grammar school in June, 1919. When he received his diploma, there was more applause in the auditorium than there was for any other member of the class. He felt good when he heard this clapping, but, then, he expected it. He lived in a world where he was somebody, and he was going into a bigger world where he would still be somebody. He was a fine, clean-looking lad, with dark hair, frank blue eyes, regular and friendly features. He was thin but strong. He wore a blue serge suit with short trousers and a belted jacket, and a white shirt with a white bow tie. His class colors, orange and black ribbons, were pinned on the lapel of his coat. He was scrubbed and washed and combed. And he was in the midst of an atmosphere of gaiety and friendliness. The teachers were happy. There were proud and happy parents and aunts and uncles and older sisters. The local alderman made a speech, praising everybody, and speaking of the graduating boys and girls as fine future Americans. And he declared that in their midst there were many promising lads and lassies who would live to enjoy great esteem and success. He also said that among this group there was also one who not only promised to become a stellar athlete but who had already won gold medals and honors.

And on that night, Morty's father and mother were very happy. They kept beaming with proud smiles. Morty was their only son. Mr. Aiken was a carpenter. He worked steadily, and he had saved his money so that the house he owned was now paid for. He and his wife were quiet-living people who minded their own business. Mr. Aiken was tall and rugged, with swarthy skin, a rough-hewn face, and the look and manner of a workman. He was a gentle but firm man, and was inarticulate with his son. He believed that a boy should have a good time in sports, should fight his own battles, and that boyhood—the best time of one's life—should be filled with happy memories.

The mother was faded and maternal. She usually had little to say; her life was dedicated to caring for her son and her husband and to keeping their home clean and orderly. She was especially happy to know that Morty liked running and skating, because these were not dangerous.

After the graduation ceremonies, the father and mother took Morty home where they had cake and ice cream. The three of them sat together, eating these refreshments, quiet but happy. The two parents were deeply moved. They were filled with gratification because of the applause given their son when he had walked forward on the stage to receive his diploma. They were raising a fine boy, and they could look people in the neighborhood in the eye and know that they had done their duty as parents. The father was putting money by for Morty's college education and hoped that, besides becoming a famous runner, Morty would become a professional man. He talked of this to the son and the mother over their ice cream and cake, and the boy seemed to accept his father's plans. And as the father gazed shyly at Morty he thought of his own boyhood on a Wisconsin farm, and of long summer days there. Morty had the whole summer before him. He would play and grow and enjoy himself. He was not a bad boy, he had never gotten into trouble, he wasn't the kind of boy who caused worry. It was fine. In August there would be his vacation, and they would all go to Wisconsin, and he would go fishing with the boy.

That evening Morty's parents went to bed feeling that this was the happiest day of their lives.

And Morty went to bed, a happy, light-hearted boy, thinking of the summer vacation which had now begun.

IV

The days passed. Some days were better than others. Some days there was little to do, and on other days there was a lot to do. Morty guessed that this was turning out to be as good as any summer he could remember.

Tony Rabuski was working, delivering flowers for a flower merchant, but he sometimes came around after supper and the kids sat talking or playing on the steps of Morty's house or of another house in the neighborhood. Morty liked to play Run, Sheep, Run, because it gave him a chance to run, and he also liked hiding and searching and hearing the signals called out, and the excitement and tingling and fun when he'd be hiding, perhaps under some porch, and the other side would be near, maybe even passing right by, and he, and the other kids with him, would have to be so still, and he'd even try to hold his breath, and then finally, the signal for which he had been waiting—Run, Sheep, Run—and the race, setting off, tearing away along sidewalks and across streets, running like hell and like a streak of lightning, and feeling your speed in your legs and muscles and getting to the goal first.

The summer was going by, and it was fun. There wasn't anything to worry about, and there were dreams. Edna Purcell, who had been in his class, seemed sweet on him, and she was a wonderful girl. One night she and some other girls came around, and they sat on the steps of Morty's house and played Tin-Tin. Morty had to kiss her. He did, with the kids laughing, and it seemed that something happened to him. He hadn't been shy when he was with girls, but now, when Edna was around, he would be shy. She was wonderful. She was more than wonderful. When he did have the courage to talk to her, he talked about running and ice skating. She told him she knew what a runner and skater he was. A fast skater, such as he was, wouldn't want to think of skating with someone like her. He said that he would, and that next winter he would teach her to skate better. Immediately, he found himself wishing it were next winter already, and he would imagine himself skating with her, and he could see them walking over to the Washington Park lagoon and coming home again. He would carry her skates, and when they breathed they would be able to see their breaths, and the weather would be cold and sharp and would make her red cheeks redder, and they would be alone, walking home, with the snow packed on the park, alone, the two of them walking in the park, with it quiet, so quiet that you would hear nothing, and it would be like they were in another world, and then, there in the quiet park, with white snow all over it, he would kiss Edna Purcell. He had kissed Edna when they'd played Tin-Tin, and Post Office, but he looked forward to the day that he got from her the kiss that would mean that she was his girl, his sweetheart, and the girl who would one day be his wife just like his mother was his father's wife. Everything he dreamed of doing, all the honors he would get, all the medals and cups he dreamed of winning—now all of this would be for Edna. And she was also going to Park High. He would walk to school with her, eat lunch with her, walk her home from school. When he ran in high-school track meets for Park High, Edna would be in the stands. He would give her his medals. He wanted to give her one of his gold skating medals, but he didn't know how to go about asking her to accept it.

No matter what Morty thought about, he thought about Edna at the same time. He thought about her every time he dreamed. When he walked on streets in the neighborhood, he thought of her. When he went to Washington Park or swimming, he thought of Edna. Edna, just to think of her, Edna made everything in the world wonderfully wonderful.

And thus the summer of 1919 was passing for Morty.

V

Morty sat on the curb with a group of boys, and they were bored and restless. They couldn't agree about what game to play, where to go, what to do to amuse themselves. A couple of them started to play Knife but gave it up. Morty suggested a race, but no one would race him. They couldn't agree on playing ball. One boy suggested swimming, but no one would go with him. Several of the boys wrestled, and a fight almost started. Morty sat by himself and thought about Edna. He guessed that he'd rather be with her than with the kids. He didn't know where she was. If he knew that she'd gone swimming, he'd go swimming. He didn't know what to do with himself. If he only could find Edna and if they would do something together, or go somewhere, like Jackson Park Beach, just the two of them, why, then, he knew that today would be the day that he would find a way of giving her one of his *Clarion* gold medals. But he didn't know where she was.

Tony Rabuski came around with four tough-looking kids. Tony had lost his job, and he said that the niggers had jumped him when he was delivering flowers down around Forty-seventh Street, and he wanted his pals to stick by him. He told them what had happened, but they didn't get it, because Tony couldn't tell a story straight. Tony asked them didn't they know what was happening? There were race riots, and the beaches and Washington Park and the whole South Side were full of dark clouds, and over on Wentworth Avenue the big guys were fighting, and the dark clouds were out after whites. They didn't believe Tony. But Morty said it was in the newspapers, and that there were race riots. The bored boys became excited. They bragged about what they would do if the jigs came over to their neighborhood. Tony said they had to get some before they got this far. When asked where they were, Tony said all over. Finally, they went over to Washington Park, picking up sticks and clubs and rocks on the way. The park was calm. A few adults were walking and strolling about. A lad of eighteen or nineteen lay under a tree with his head in the lap of a girl who was stroking his hair. Some of the kids smirked and leered as they passed the couple. Morty thought of Edna and wished he could take her to Washington Park and kiss her. There were seven or eight rowboats on the lagoon, but all of the occupants were white. The park sheep were grazing. Tony threw a rock at them, frightening the sheep, and they all ran, but no cop was around to shag them. They passed the boathouse, talking and bragging. They now believed the rumors which they themselves had made up. White girls and women were in danger, and anything might happen. A tall lad sat in the grass with a nursemaid. A baby carriage was near them. The lad called them over and asked them what they were doing with their clubs and rocks. Tony said they were looking for niggers. The lad said that he'd seen two near the goldfish pond and urged the boys to go and get the sonsofbitches. Screaming and shouting, they ran to the goldfish pond. Suddenly, Tony shouted:

"Dark clouds."

VI

They ran. Two Negro boys, near the goldfish pond, heard Tony's cry, and then the others' cry, and they ran. The mob of boys chased them. Morty was in the lead. Running at the head of the screaming, angry pack of boys, he forgot everything except how well and how fast he was running, and images of Edna flashed in and out of his mind. If she could see him running! He was running beautifully. He'd catch them. He was gaining. The colored boys ran in a northwest direction. They crossed the drive which flanked the southern end of the Washington Park ball field. Morty was stopped by a funeral procession. The other boys caught up with him. When the funeral procession passed, it was too late to try and catch the colored boys they had been chasing. Angry, bragging, they crossed over to the ball field and marched across it, shouting and yelling. They picked up about eight boys of their own age and three older lads of seventeen or eighteen. The older lads said they knew where they'd find some shines. Now was the time to teach them their place once and for all. Led by the older boys, they emerged from the north end of Washington Park and marched down Grand Boulevard, still picking up men and boys as they went along. One of the men who joined them had a gun. They screamed, looked in doorways for Negroes, believed everything anyone said about Negroes, and kept boasting about what they would do when they found some.

"Dark clouds," Tony boomed.

The mob let out. They crossed to the other side of Grand Boulevard and ran cursing and shouting after a Negro. Morty was in the lead. He was outrunning the men and the older fellows. He heard them shouting behind him. He was running. He was running like the playground hundred-yard champion of the South Side of Chicago. He was running like the future Olympic champion. He was running like he'd run for Edna. He was tearing along, pivoting out of the way of shocked, surprised pedestrians, running, really running. He was running like a streak of lightning.

The Negro turned east on Forty-eighth Street. He had a start of a block. But Morty would catch him. He turned into Forty-eighth Street. He tore along the center of the street. He began to breathe heavily. But he couldn't stop running now. He was outdistancing the gang, and he was racing his own gang and the Negro he was chasing. Down the center of the street and about half a block ahead of him, the Negro was tearing away for dear life. But Morty was gaining on him. Gaining. He was now about a half a block ahead of his own gang. They screamed murderously behind him. And they encouraged him. He heard shouts of encouragement.

"Catch 'em, Morty boy!"

"Thata boy, Morty boy!"

He heard Tony's voice. He ran.

The Negro turned into an alley just east of Forestville. Morty ran. He turned into the alley just in time to see the fleeing Negro spurt into a yard in the center of the block. He'd gained more. He was way ahead of the white mob. Somewhere behind him they were coming and yelling. He tore on. He had gained his second wind. He felt himself running, felt the movement of his legs and muscles, felt his arms, felt the sensation of his whole body as he raced down the alley. Never had he run so swiftly. Suddenly Negroes jumped out of yards. He was caught and pinioned. His only thought was one of surprise. Before he even realized what had happened, his throat was slashed. He fell, bleeding. Feebly, he mumbled just once:

"Mother!"

The Negroes disappeared.

He lay bleeding in the center of the dirty alley, and when the gang of whites caught up with him they found him dead in dirt and his own blood in the center of the alley. No Negroes were in sight. The whites surrounded his body. The boys trembled with fear. Some of them cried. One wet his pants. Then they became maddened. And they stood in impotent rage around the bleeding, limp body of Morty Aiken, the fastest runner on Sixty-first Street.

[1948]

Johnny's Old Man

Johnny walked home quickly, carrying the can of foaming beer. In his mind there was a confused picture of the Wentworth Avenue saloon: the sawdust floor, the men, big men, at the bar with the brass railing, one of the men drunk and calling Heinie Zimmerman of the Chicago Cubs a thick-headed Dutchman, the smiling Irish bartender who had told him to help himself at the free lunch counter, and the small man who had said, "So you're Jack Collins's kid, huh?" and had given him a nickel. Something about the saloon, about the language, the tough voices, the size of the big men at the bar made him awfully afraid, and he was always glad to get out of it, even though the bartender was nice to him. He hurried home, because his old man usually cursed him and gave him a sock on the ear when he didn't come straight back from the store, especially when he had been sent for a can of beer. He walked fast, but he was careful, so as not to spill any of the beer. He remembered once how his old man kicked the living hell out of him when he had spilled a can of beer.

The Collinses lived on Forty-fifth Street, just off Wentworth Avenue, in a rambling old wooden house with five dirty rooms, a leaky roof, an outhouse, a weedy back yard, and a damp, unusable cellar. The rent was ten dollars a month, but his old man was always cursing and complaining that the landlord was a lousy robber.

Johnny's mother was a fat, slovenly woman, the mother of eight children, all of whom were living. Johnny, thirteen, was the oldest. His mother always insisted that she could not take good care of the children and the house at the same time. When Johnny's old man was in a good-natured mood, he would tell her to let the house go and watch the kids, but when he was drunk, he'd tell her she was a goddamn old hag and clip her one on the jaw. When he punched her, she always retired to her dark, musty bedroom, to cry and to pray.

Johnny came home with the can of beer. His old man was taking it easy in his favorite chair, his back to the kerosene lamp; his feet, perspiring, with the toes sticking through the holes of stiff socks, lay comfortably on a crumbling davenport. Johnny gave his father the can. The father angrily complained it had taken him long enough. Johnny said that they were busy at the saloon and that he'd had to wait. The father said "yes" sarcastically; then he said he did not want his own son crapping him like that. Johnny retreated into a corner and cowered.

The mother screamed at the father, demanding that he stop abusing her son. He told her to shut up and take better care of her brats and of his house. She told him to earn more money. He told her to pray, because then St. Anthony or some other saint might leave some gold in the back yard. She told him not to be blasphemous. He told her to clean herself up, take care of the house, and not to go around always looking worse than a two-bit whore in a waterfront town. She told him he couldn't call her a whore and get away with it. He said she had better shut her goddamn trap. She picked up a stick from the woodpile in the corner and said that no sonofa-bitching, lousy, nonproviding husband was going to call her names. She waved the stick and called on God to testify that she was a good woman, who had protected her virtue by lawful wedlock. She reminded him that he'd married her because she had been good and had refused all of his dirty advances before he had put a ring on her finger. And then, turning up her nose, she said: "Maybe you wanted a whore?"

He said "Yeh" sarcastically.

She screamed and cursed.

Johnny still cowered in a corner of the room. He loved neither his father nor his mother. He became terribly afraid when they began to yell and fight, as they were now. He was afraid the old man might knock the mother out and someone would call the police, and then they would all be disgraced, and all the kids in the block would look down on him even more than they did already. He called out, "Please, papa," and "Please, stop, mama," but his appeals were lost in the shrill contest.

The father punched the mother in the ear, and she slumped into a praying heap in a corner. She moaned and sighed, called on Jesus, Mary, and Joseph, blessed herself innumerable times, and threatened to go out and get Father Corbett, the pastor of St. Martha's. He told her to go ahead, and that if the priest came around, sticking his long nose in Jack Collins's family affairs, Jack Collins would bust his nose, too. Then the father drank his beer and wiped the suds off his mouth with the opened cuff of his dirty, blue working shirt. The youngest baby woke up and started bawling. The mother hastened to feed it some milk. Then two other youngsters started bawling, and the father had to sing them to sleep for his own peace of mind. In about fifteen minutes, the house was calm; all the children were asleep except Johnny. He sat quietly by the parlor window, unnoticed. The mother and the father acted as if nothing had happened; he finished his beer. In a little while they went to bed. Johnny, tiptoeing past their closed room, heard the bed shaking, as if people were wrestling on it. Johnny knew what was happening.

He returned and looked out the window, where the black night was so beautiful and hid all the dirt and ugliness of the street. He cried, and he dreamed of what he would do when he grew up, of how he would go away and become a great man and never have nothing to do with his old man and his old lady. He knew that God commanded you to honor your father and your mother, but Sister Maria at school said that God also wanted your parents to be good to you. He thought of how, when he grew up, he would have all the things he wanted. He would have ice cream, and cake, and all the mashed potatoes he could eat, at every meal. He would have a season box at the White Sox games, and a chauffeur would drive him from his home on Grand Boulevard and call for him after the game. He would wear a new suit every day. He was going to get even, all right. He thought of how he would come back to the old neighborhood and scorn everybody. He would be a Rich Gentleman with a cane, like the men he saw in the movies two weeks ago. Everybody would look at him and try to be friendly, and he wouldn't have nothing to do with them. No, sir, he would fix them all, and especially the McNulty kids, who always laughed at him because his old man drank and his old lady was dirty. Two days ago Billy McNulty had said that his mother said he shouldn't play with Johnny Collins, because in the Collins's house they were always blaspheming, and scandalizing, and drinking and cursing, and that old man Collins was always beating the old lady. Johnny knew it was all true, but he didn't like people saying so, and it hurt a whole lot when they did. But he would get even.

He kept looking outside at the dark. The dark was mysterious, and houses, posts, blocks of wood, holes in the street that Johnny knew so well now looked so strange and different. He looked out the window, his eyes full of terror. He tried to imagine good things, but he was too afraid. Footsteps and other street noises menaced him. Every time he heard them, he grew afraid and wondered if they signaled the approach of a robber come to kidnap him and who would kill him because there would be no ransom money. He sat, and his eyes were fastened on the awesome street. He shuddered. He did not like his father, but it was warm-like and comfortable to know that his old man was in the house when he got afraid like he was now. But someday he was going to be big and brave. Then the husky, strange men who passed with loud footsteps would not make him timid and afraid. But now he was afraid, and not a big great man.

His father came out of the bedroom to go outside to the toilet. He saw Johnny. Johnny was relieved from his fear. He could not be hurt by robbers now.

The old man looked at him.

"Jesus Christ, ain't you in bed yet?" he said, giving Johnny a kick.

Johnny scurried into his bedroom. It was filthy, with dirty, unopened windows, and smelly, the air fouled from the unwashed, perspiring bodies of his three younger brothers. He curled up without removing his clothes, and cried. He cried until he fell asleep and dreamed of a big man with a cane, who wasn't afraid of anything.

[1930-50]

Norman Allen

One spring afternoon many years ago I came out of the University bookstore and encountered a group of friends. There were about eight of us. We chatted for a while and then went our various ways. This scene returns to me in memory because Norman Allen was one of that group.

Tall and brown-skinned, Norman always dressed neatly in the latest style. He liked light-gray suits and bright ties. Norman had high cheekbones, a lean face, restless brown eyes, and lips that were just a bit thick. You might be talking with him about a problem of philosophy or about the weather, and a meaningless smile would cross his face. He used to smile with no reference to what was being said and when nothing in a conversation called for it. His was a cold, impersonal smile that came and went like a shadow. It would distract and mildly disconcert you, and you would wonder why he smiled that way. What was the joke? You didn't get it. But then you would forget this and go on talking or listening to him. But again the disconcerting smile would flicker on his brown face. We sometimes discussed Norman, but I do not recall anyone ever speaking of his smile. Now across the years that separate me from youth and the days when I first knew him, that smile comes back to mind and remains fixed in my memory as one of his most significant traits. It was in a way more important than almost anything I recall having heard him say.

But I want to dwell for a moment on that casual scene of a sunny afternoon in May, over twenty-five years ago. Even though those were the days of the Depression, the future seemed open to us. Economic prospects were bleak, but in our group we did not talk and think merely of the Depression. We expected to go on pursuing our intellectual interests. All of us had either intellectual or artistic ambitions. The future seemed like an adventure in art, ideas and living. We were what is perhaps best characterized by the phrase "liberal-minded." In our group Norman seemed to feel at ease. He interested us because of his intelligence and his brilliant promise in philosophy, and not because he was a Negro. He was a protégé of Dr. Dwight of the Philosophy Department; he had studied under Whitehead at Harvard, and was an ardent admirer of Dewey and Mead. He had a fellowship in the graduate school and was working on his doctoral thesis. Big things were expected of him.

On that particular afternoon, we talked for only a few minutes. There was then a plan afoot for the publication of a magazine to which both white and colored students and Chicago young people would contribute. The prospective editor was a jolly but erratic young colored man named Dennison who had graduated and who bragged of knowing Jack Johnson, former heavyweight champion of the world. He claimed he was writing a biography of Johnson, but the book has never been published and was probably never finished. Dennison asked us all to contribute to the proposed magazine.

"We'll have Jack Johnson, philosophy, and advance-guard aesthetics," he said with a laugh.

"Good," Norman said. "I'll write an article on Whitehead and the Negro problem."

I was not the only one who was struck by the apparent inappropriateness of this remark. I remember that Carter, who was considered a very brilliant student, laughed at it when he and I were talking later.

"Allen is always making remarks like that," Carter observed. Anyway, Dennison promised to accept and feature Norman's proposed article in the first issue. A few moments later I left the hatless group of young men and went to Harper Library.

One afternoon shortly after this, I ran into Norman and we walked to the campus together and then eastward along Fifty-seventh Street. I did most of the talking. During this period I planned to write articles of literary criticism from the standpoint of philosophy. I held then that you cannot only and solely interpret literature from the standpoint of itself, but that you need to bring ideas to bear on works of literature in order to render them more understandable. Norman was or at least seemed to be quite interested in my remarks.

"It's wonderful to look forward to writing like that," he said.

My talk clearly implied a faith about the future. And as I spoke eagerly and with enthusiasm, I assumed that Norman felt as I did.

Today this casual meeting takes on more meaning than it had at the time. The students strolling about, the coeds in their colorful spring dresses, the sight of so many young people, gave the scene an almost poetic freshness. On the campus was the possibility of learning and joy, and young minds and hearts could fill with hope, eagerness, a sense of the wonder of life and rich promises of tomorrow. The University and its campus was an island, green and quiet, amidst the tragic turbulence that was Chicago. And for a while Norman and I were youths who could be on that campus. Ideas and truths could be more important to us than anything else in the world.

We talked amiably and seriously as we walked. "Yes, how fine it is," he said, "to know what you are going to do in the future."

His remark, made a second time, seemed a bit singular to me. I believed that he also knew what he wanted to do with his life and where he expected to go. But my surprise quickly vanished. We continued talking about literature and philosophy for several blocks and then parted.

Norman worked as a janitor. He had little money and the circumstances of his life were hard, harder than I then realized. Later I was told of an incident in his life by Pete, a Greek studying at the University who knew Norman very well. Norman had told his friends that he was going to live at the home of a professor and give up his job as a janitor, although he would perform a few chores around the professor's home. His friends were all pleased to hear this news. It meant that he would be more comfortable and would have more time for study. And it seemed like a welcome example of the absence of race prejudice on the part of the professor. But one evening Pete visited Norman at the professor's home on Kimbark Avenue. Pete said Norman took him through the basement entrance and led him to a part of the basement close to the furnace. There was a dim electric bulb overhead, a small cot set very near the furnace, a scarred old dresser, and a few shelves on the wall for books. This was where Norman lived and sometimes wrote or studied. Pete had been shocked. He also said that Norman had been embarrassed.

Norman was exceptionally well-read for his age. He was then, in 1930, only twenty. But he was already firmly grounded in philosophy. He had been influenced by Nietzsche as well as by Dewey, Mead, Dr. Dwight, and Whitehead. He knew the thought of Hegel and Kant, and had also read the Greeks. In addition he was more informed, more interested in, and more sensitive to literature than most of the graduate students I knew at the University. And among the writers he had read and admired were Dostoevsky, Joyce, Proust, Thomas Mann, and T. S. Eliot. His reputation for brilliance was rapidly spreading about the campus, and many already considered him a genius.

There was a little theater, the Diagonal, located at Fifty-seventh and Stony Island near the University campus. Pete had founded it and was its maestro. One of the students, Joan, a plump, handsome, black-haired girl with shining dark eyes, directed plays there. Joan was intelligent and kind as well as attractive. She put on a series of one-act Negro plays. These were well acted by an all Negro cast and received much publicity in the Chicago press. Norman went around with the young Negro actors and actresses, most of whom were students. One of the group was his cousin, Sarah, an extraordinarily beautiful girl with lovely light-brown skin. Another of the group was Madeline, to whom Norman was engaged. She was a small, quiet, friendly, and extremely pretty girl with a light-brown skin. She and Norman made an attractive couple. Everybody thought that they were very happy.

When the Negro plays were put on, a number of parties were held. At one of them Norman met Joan and fell in love with her on sight. You could tell that he was in love with her even though no one ever mentioned it, for whenever he saw her he would become intense and nervous as he stared and gaped like a schoolboy. At times he would seem to try and consume her with his eyes. He would be unaware of and blind to everyone else, and Joan's presence rendered him uncommunicative. And just as Norman was attracted to Joan, similarly some of the white young men were entranced by the colored girls, especially by Sarah and Madeline. There was mixed dancing and some flirting, but nothing more serious than this happened, even though most of the group were free-loving Bohemians.

Insofar as anyone could observe, Norman's infatuation for Joan did not cause any friction in his relationship with Madeline. Charming and poised, she seemed sure of herself. Norman was attentive to her. Their devotion and sweetness to one another were frequently commented upon. But once he saw Joan, Norman ignored Madeline and everyone else.

While very sympathetic to Norman, Joan was firm in her refusal to have a love affair with him, and she told him this as gently as she could. He became disturbed and, at times, disconsolate. He would take long walks alone and late at night, tramping and prowling the streets of the South Side until dawn. And in a number of small ways, his conduct became unpredictable. He stalked silently out of groups for no apparent reason, and made remarks that seemed strange or odd because of their irrelevancy.

For a number of months after the summer of 1930, I did not see him. Then I left Chicago. However, I heard that he had completed his doctoral thesis, received his degree, married Madeline, been appointed to a faculty post in the Department of Philosophy of a Negro university, and was launched on a promising career. I believed that he was happy and that he would go on to do important work in his field. Once or twice when I met mutual friends, I inquired about Norman and was told that he was getting on well, and also that Madeline had given birth to a son.

It seemed as though Norman were moving forward to a productive and brilliant future and would have a happy personal life.

One day in New York a couple of years later, I met a friend from Chicago who told me that Norman had had a nervous breakdown and was recuperating in a private sanitarium. Then about three months later, I learned that he had been released and was again teaching. Six months after this I heard that he had been placed in a government mental hospital, but I was unable to get any information about his condition.

In 1935 I was in Washington. Carter, who worked there, had seen Norman, knew something of his illness, and told me he was in bad shape. Late one night just before he had been committed, Norman had gone out on the street wearing a top hat but, for the rest, stark naked. Carter also said that when Norman had been examined by psychiatrists he had been brilliant. Carter had visited Norman several times at the hospital, but then had stopped going because Norman wouldn't talk to him. It was pointless to see Norman, and Carter added that the poor fellow was gone.

From time to time after this meeting I heard chance bits of news about Allen. In 1937, for instance, Joan told me that Norman had been given insulin shock treatment and that there was hope that he would even be cured and released from the hospital. I read a few news stories about insulin shock treatment, and I believed that a cure for insanity had been found and that Norman and many others like him would be restored to society. The news pleascd me. While I had never been an intimate friend of Norman's, I liked him and wanted him to do well in life, especially since he was colored. Now and then in the old days in Chicago, I had passingly thought and imagined that Norman would, by his expected success, help to disprove notions and biased claims about the lack of capacity for abstract thought on the part of Negroes. But Norman did not recover. More years went by. Occasionally I still heard that Norman was in the hospital, and that there had been no change in his condition.

In 1945, accompanied by two doctors in residency at the hospital, I visited Norman. He was a patient of Dr. Strauss, who was young, thin and bespectacled and in his second year as a resident psychiatrist. The other doctor, Dr. Arnold, was also young, but was on another service at the hospital.

It was the end of a June day, and the sun had begun to sink as we drove to the ward building. The hospital grounds were large and attractive, and they had the aspect of a campus. In the automobile Dr. Arnold said: "Allen has become what's called a backward patient."

"Has he ever been your patient, Doctor?" I asked.

"No, but Abe Strauss here is his doctor. I've heard Allen discussed a lot around here and I know that a fortune has been spent trying to cure him."

"Who spent it?" I asked.

"Foundations and universities."

"He's been examined," Dr. Strauss said, "by a number of the most able and important psychiatrists in America." He then mentioned the names of several famous or well-known psychiatrists who had been brought in on Norman's case.

"What happened?" I asked.

"Nothing," Dr. Strauss answered. "Nothing has helped."

"Isn't there any hope for him?" I asked.

"The prognosis is poor," Dr. Strauss said.

"Wouldn't electric shock treatment help him?"

"No, I don't think so."

"What's wrong with him exactly?" I asked.

"He's a paranoid schizophrenic," Dr. Strauss answered.

We parked in front of the ward building. It was old and of a dull red brick. Seeing it in the fading light, I had an overpowering feeling of dreariness and hopelessness, and also of sordidness. I knew that this would be a sad experience. Getting out of the automobile, a state of awe came over me. I had already seen enough of this institution and of its inmates to be deeply touched and inexpressibly saddened by the spectacle of wholesale insanity. Unlike the doctors accompanying me, this was still new and unfamiliar. I had heard the wild, shrill, angry and frightened screams and curses of the inmates echoing through the pleasant green grounds. I had talked with some of these patients. And now I was going to see Norman Allen and he was one of them.

It had been years ago, in my youth, that I had last seen him. We had talked about the ideas of Dewey and Whitehead and about the future. I recalled that once on campus he had told me that, after receiving his degree, he planned to teach. And I had said I would write literary criticism and, somewhat shyly, that I was writing a novel. And the novel that I had then been writing had made me somewhat famous. And then, after many years, there was I, entering the dreary building where Norman was confined.

"He probably won't even recognize you or know you," Dr. Strauss told me as we walked toward the building entrance.

I had the vain and excited hope that Norman would recognize me, and the even more vain and naive hope that somehow my visit would touch and move him and would help him a little to recover.

The interior of the ward building was clean but dimly lit. The walls of the corridor had been recently painted in white and the waxed floors gleamed. Several inmates stood in the first-floor corridor, along the walls or in front of opened room doors.

"How are you?" Dr. Arnold asked one of the patients. He was a big black man, and he had tied and wound many old rags about his chest and shoulders. The inmate mumbled something to Dr. Arnold that I did not catch.

"What do the voices say?" Dr. Arnold asked.

The inmate grinned foolishly.

"What are these for?" Dr. Arnold asked, pointing at the old rags on him.

"To keep the voices out," the inmate answered.

I heard several wild shrieks—loud, piercing, not quite human, throbbing with pain and violent with anger. We continued along the corridor. Some of the inmates ignored us; others stared.

We entered a large ward room on the right. Six inmates were sitting or lying on the beds. A man in pajamas howled. The five others paid no attention to him. On the bed nearest the door lay a lean, brown-skinned man staring at the ceiling with fixed eyes. I recognized Norman instantly.

But he was changed. He was thinner than he had been fifteen or so years ago. His cheeks were hollow, giving more prominence to his high cheek bones. And his eyes were sunken and there were hollows around them. He wore a nondescript pair of unpressed gray trousers and a white shirt.

As we approached his bed he lay motionless; his eyes were dull and glazed and there was a mad, absent look in them. We stopped at the side of his bed. His eyes lit up in surprise, came to life, and for a few seconds his face lost its masklike rigidity.

Imagining that he had recognized me, I was flattered. But if he had recognized me, I wouldn't have known it. Who and what I was and represented in his distorted mind will remain, along with many of his fears, secrets, hopes, and thoughts, a mystery never to be unraveled.

"Hello, Norman," I said, speaking gently and softly. He lay in a catatonic state, staring at the three of us.

A kinky-haired madman on the bed next to Norman's let out a violent shriek. I told Norman my name, but he did not respond; he fixed me with dull, glazed eyes.

"Do you remember me, Norman?" I asked.

Again the kinky-haired madman shrieked. He made loud, angry cries, but none of the patients looked at him or in any way revealed that they heard him. He was in his forties and there were touches of gray in his tangled black hair. He paused for a moment and then, as though with a fresh energy, he yelled again. I saw through the window behind him that it was twilight and when he again paused, I heard the chirping of birds.

"Don't you remember me from Chicago, Norman? Do you remember Joan? And Carter?" I still spoke softly and gently. And he continued to fix me in a rigid stare.

Dr. Strauss called an attendant, who came to us quickly. He was medium-sized and plump. Dr. Strauss instructed him to give Norman an injection of sodium amythol.

The kinky-haired madman continued yelling. Dr. Strauss told him to be quiet. Ignoring the doctor, he screamed with increased intensity and violence.

"He's always like that. Tell him to be quiet," said a patient sitting on a bed to my left. He was a young Negro with dark skin.

The madman howled. Dr. Strauss told me that he was from a very rich merchant family on one of the Caribbean islands. The attendant came back to our group carrying a needle, a bottle of alcohol, and a piece of cotton. As he leaned down to give the injection, rubbing Norman's arm with alcohol, Norman let out a low growl. Then he trembled as the attendant jabbed the needle in, but quickly he looked up with pained submissiveness.

In a few moments he said to me: "I know you." However, his face did not become very expressive. He rolled his eyes and pointed to Dr. Arnold whom he had never seen before.

"But I don't know you. You're not in the picture." Then he pointed to Dr. Strauss. "I know you."

"Norman, remember . . ." I began. The kinky-haired madman shrieked. "Do you remember me, Norman?" I asked. The kinky-haired madman shrieked again.

Norman rolled his eyes, glanced at the howling inmate, and smiled briefly in pleasure. He turned toward me, and I saw on his face the same smile I had seen years ago on the University campus.

"He's in trouble," Norman said, referring to the howling madman.

"How are you, Norman?" I asked, hoping that by speaking softly and gently I could reach him.

"Be quiet! I hear you," Dr. Strauss told the madman. He quieted down. Dr. Strauss spoke with Dr. Arnold and the attendant about taking Norman to a room where it would be easier and more convenient to talk with him. The attendant said that there was a vacant room down the corridor.

"Come, Allen, we'll have a talk," Dr. Strauss said. Norman allowed the attendant to help him get off the bed. He walked at a careless, shuffling gait as we left the ward room.

In the corridor the inmate with rags bound about his chest greeted us with foolish grins. Behind me I heard babbling talk. Norman shuffled at my side with his eyes on the floor. His shoulders drooped.

We used a small room. Norman sat facing us, with his back to the open window. The hospital bed was on his left. Through the open window I could see a hedge of rich green bushes, and their fragrance floated in through the open window. The persistent song of insects, the natural perfume of the shrubbery, and the thickening blue sky, all spoke to me of another world than this small one of mania. Norman could not walk alone by those bushes, nor could he stand alone under that sky. Did he ever yearn to or want to, or was the open sky another of the terrors that made him shiver with fear? Did that blue open sky symbolize a freedom too terrifying for him even to contemplate?

After we were seated, I took out a package of cigarettes.

"Give me one," Norman said.

I offered him an opened pack. He pulled out a cigarette and immediately tore it to bits which he let drop in an ash tray. Then he ground and squashed the tobacco and played with it as a small child might.

He stared at me as though I might be a meaningless object. Sitting there a few feet away from me, he could have killed me, and not for anything I had done or would do to him, but rather because of his own fears. And these were no different from the fears that could terrify and destroy us all, were they to rage unchecked in our nature as they must have in Norman's.

He was not quite human. He was a shell with all the form that humans possess. My regret, my sadness, my awe was deep. And I felt about him something of what I should have felt about myself had I been so stupidly and stupefyingly drunk as to have destroyed all consciousness and self-control. I saw in him the most tragic of all kinds of waste, the waste of human emotion and thought.

I hoped Norman would talk sensibly. There, in that small room as twilight spread beyond the window, I hoped Norman would come back from his dream world.

"Don't you remember me, Norman? Don't you remember when we would sometimes talk?"

"I remember you," he answered flatly. "I met you at State and Madison. But him—" Norman pointed at Dr. Arnold, "—he's Himmler. I met him with Himmler at State and Adams. Himmler, Hitler."

"Allen, do you know that Hitler's dead?" Dr. Arnold asked him.

"Yes, the Fourth International killed him. It's June, 1953. The Fourth International killed him in Cuba."

This was very painful. But my feelings were also qualified by curiosity. I had seen madmen and madwomen on streets, and I had talked with some of them here at the mental hospital. But it had been different from sitting there with Norman and remembering him fifteen years before when he had been so different, and had been known as a brilliant student and possibly a genius.

"Do you know what year it is?" Dr. Strauss asked him.

"1945. My son is older now."

"Yes, that's true. It is 1945," Dr. Strauss said.

"There are houses out there," Norman said, pointing stiffly at the open window through which no houses were visible.

"What do you think about all day, Allen?" Dr. Strauss asked.

"I hear them."

"Do you hear voices?"

"White women. Their voices are very sweet. They talk to me like music. They talk to me. I compose symphonies . . ."

He reached for another cigarette, and I gave him one. Immediately he crushed it and played with it in the ash tray. He stared at me as though he had never seen me before.

"Do you remember Dr. Dwight?" I asked.

He laughed at me quietly and as though he had played a joke on me.

"Do you remember, Norman? Do you remember how we talked about Dr. Dwight's papers, and about Whitehead?"

He played with the broken cigarettes and the tobacco in the ash tray. He swept me with a haughty look.

"Allen, why did you play with your feces in the toilet bowl the other day?" Dr. Strauss asked.

"To find contentment in the womb," Norman answered with a suggestion of contemptuous laughter in his voice.

Norman seemed hopeless to me, but still I was not ready to give up. I wanted him to recognize me. I was convinced that he did, even though he would not say so. I wanted him suddenly to become more sane and rational, and I believed that he could if he would only take the step.

I looked out of the window at the fading twilight and I heard the insect chorus as something fresh, a call to feel and love the world and life. And the dark green bushes seemed so verdant. For a moment, I felt myself alone and set apart, and I listened to the chirping insects. It was like a call to and a celebration of some beautiful world which existed somewhere out there beyond the window and under that sky which was now a deep rich blue. Then I realized, as if anew, where I was. Again I saw Norman, the two doctors, and the hospital room—a small drab room with bare green walls, a hospital bed, simple chairs, a table, and a stand. It was the kind of room in which one could die alone.

I thought of how madmen must have been confined to this room and lain on that bed, and of how they must have screamed and shrieked in their traumatic fears, terrors, and angers, fighting unseen foes and assailants and filling their minds with strange and distorted dreams and visions.

I looked at Norman again. There was a shadow of coldness across his face, an unchanging stare in his eyes, and a smirking suggestion of a smile on his lips. I told myself what I knew—that Norman was mad, mad, unalterably and hopelessly mad. I tried to reach him with a friendly gaze. He met it with a chill and unrecognizing look. I smiled. His face did not change.

"Norman, don't you remember . . ." I began.

"I remember those houses," Norman interrupted in his flat voice.

"Where are the houses?" Dr. Arnold asked.

"Right out there beyond the window. You live in them."

"Don't you know, Allen, that there are no houses right out there beyond the window?" Dr. Arnold asked.

"I see them. It's May, 1945. Those houses, there they are."

"Do you know where you are, Allen?" Dr. Arnold asked.

Norman nodded affirmatively.

"Do you know what kind of place this is?" Dr. Arnold asked.

Norman grinned foolishly.

"What do the voices say?" Dr. Strauss asked after Norman had failed to answer Dr. Arnold's last question.

"They are sweet and soft."

"Why are you here?" Dr. Arnold asked.

"I am happy here. I like it."

Norman's talk became incoherent and disjointed. I did not pay close attention to it. I thought he had probably told the truth when he had said that he was happy in the hospital.

"The houses are green. Green houses. Carter. Marya Carter."

"Marya is Carter's wife," I interrupted. "Do you remember Carter at the University, Norman?"

"I met him at State and Madison with Himmler there." Norman looked at Dr. Arnold. "Hess wasn't there. I don't know Hess. I like it here. I am perfectly happy. The green houses aren't happy. I compose beautiful symphonies. White woman never slept with me."

"Why do you say that, Allen?" Dr. Arnold asked.

I leaned forward, eager to hear his reply. I could not help believing that he was better oriented in the present situation than would seem the case, judging from his conduct and his conversation.

"I don't like him," Norman said.

"Do you remember the University and Dr. Dwight, Norman?" I asked.

"Dr. Dwight. They don't sleep with me. They talk to me. Voices soft, sweet." He spoke as though everything he said were self-evident.

"Allen, why do you think white girls won't accept you?" Dr. Strauss asked.

Norman grinned at the doctor as though he were an idiot.

"There are men of your race who have married white women," Dr. Arnold said.

"They only talk to me. All day. I compose. They talk sweet."

"Why do you sit masturbating in the ward, Allen?" Dr. Strauss asked.

"For them, when they talk to me."

"What do they tell you?" asked Dr. Strauss.

"Life. There's life in the houses, life in the green houses. But they won't let me in."

"What houses, Norman?" I asked.

"Out there. Out-houses, green houses. They go there and sing to me."

"Allen, even if white women won't accept you or sleep with you," Dr. Arnold said, "is there any reason why you should be here? Do you know where you are?"

"In a comfortable place and they talk to me like songs. Sweet, soft music . . . Schumann."

"Don't you want to go out into the world again and teach?" Dr. Strauss asked.

"Outside, somewhere outside, I hear a wild cry, a shriek," Norman said.

"Why don't you talk more, Allen? Why do you lie in bed all day, silent?" Dr. Arnold said.

"I talk to myself. Yourself, myself, you're good company to myself. Voices like music, soft voices, speaking music."

"You don't have to be afraid to go out into the world, Allen," Dr. Arnold said. "You can make your own way and be a brilliant person."

A cold smile came over Norman's face.

"Norman, do you remember one day on campus when we talked of Whitehead?" I asked.

He looked at me with a face as close to being expressionless as a human face could be. "Hegel wrote the dialectic. Yes, no, no, no, no, no, no, Nora, nobody no white heads for me."

"You studied under Whitehead. Don't you remember, Norman? You wrote your doctoral thesis about his thought," I said.

"Bridgeheads to the moon, did you ever think of bridgeheads to the moon? The moon will come up. I can never build bridgeheads to the moon with Professor Bridgehead."

"Don't you know, Allen, that you aren't talking sense?" Dr. Arnold asked.

"On the moon, you have supersense, surrealism."

"Norman, you were a pragmatist in your thinking, I remember," I said.

"Allen, what is a pragmatist?" Dr. Strauss asked.

"Pragmatism is the ascertainment of meaning," Norman answered.

Struck by his ready definition, I said:

"And the pragmatic theory of knowledge, Norman, what is it?"

His eyes wandered vacantly about the room. His face did not change.

"What is the purpose of life, Norman?" I asked.

"To create the ideal inner self."

"Can you create it here, Allen?" Dr. Arnold asked.

"I'm going good. Good, better, best."

"Could you do better outside in the world, Allen? Is anything worse than being here in your condition?" Dr. Arnold asked.

"Doing good, better, west. Go west young man. The wester you go, the wester you are. Yes, I like it here."

The two doctors looked at one another knowingly.

"You won't get anything out of him," Dr. Arnold said.

Dr. Strauss nodded in agreement.

They both rose, and Dr. Strauss left the room. I looked at Norman, trying to think of something more to say, but my mind went blank. I felt deep sorrow. But I was still convinced that Norman knew more, recognized more and remembered more than he would admit or reveal to us.

The attendant entered the room, and Norman rose and docilely followed him into the corridor. Dr. Arnold and I followed.

"Good-by, Norman," I said.

He did not answer.

I watched him shuffle along the dimly lit corridor. An inmate in one of the rooms screamed. We left the building.

Driving away as it grew darker, Dr. Arnold said: "Yes, he's like a shell of a human being."

"I think he knows more than he will admit," I said.

"Possibly," Dr. Strauss said. "But there's no way of reaching him."

"He seems to me to be incurably sick," Dr. Arnold said.

We got out of the car in front of another building. I heard a woman screaming from behind a barred window. From other buildings the plaintive, shrieking chorus of mad men and women cut the spring night.

Two years after I had visited Norman, I heard that he had gouged out one of his eyes. Then, a year or two later, I learned that he had died of pneumonia.

[1947, 1948–57]

Kilroy Was Here

I

Standing at the parlor window, Danny looked out at Washington Park; it was bare under the heavy autumn sky. He had never imagined he would do this again, but here he was, and there was the park. Below him was South Parkway, and on the opposite side of the street the tennis courts, and the shrubbery without leaves, and the park, bleak and grassless, and in the distance the lagoon and a fragment of the boathouse.

The apartment was near Fifty-seventh Street. Years ago, his family had lived a block away. At $5816^1/_2$ he had so often stood by the parlor window, brooding as he stared out at the park: in those days he had so lacked confidence in himself. He had seen Washington Park in all seasons, when it was green and when it was dreary, as it was now. It had become the source and stimulation for the brooding of others, of other boys, boys of another color.

He lit a cigarette. Bryan, a gentle colored lad in his twenties, stood quietly behind Danny. Danny imagined that Bryan was trying to guess what his feelings and thoughts were now.

"I never thought I would stand by a window on South Park Avenue and look out on Washington Park again."

"Has it changed?" Bryan asked.

Danny shook his head and sat down on the sofa. The parlor was clean; the heavy furniture polished. There were framed pictures of flowers on the wall, and books in a bookcase at one side. Work and pride were represented in all the furniture; it expressed a will to dignity.

As he and Bryan talked, Danny thought of his trip out here from the Loop. He had got on the subway—there had been no subway in Chicago in the old days—and then had ridden out on the El, shooting along the express tracks, looking out at the same old deteriorating buildings of the Black Belt, the yards full of junk and rubble, the back porches, the dirty-looking stone and wooden tenements, the junk yards, the narrow streets. There were so many of the nameless dead who had produced all this that was Chicago, and here, in this old neighborhood, he thought of all those who had built these streets and buildings. And of those who were dead but who had once lived and looked out at that park, and walked in it, and seen him and talked with him in it. He remembered a day when his eyes had ached, and he had lain in the grass of Washington Park, rejected and dispir-ited, thinking of the Middle Ages and of a Beatrice who had rejected him, and he had read Swinburne's "The Garden of Proserpine" aloud. That had been on a summer day many years ago.

He sat back relaxed and comfortable and said to Bryan: "Just after we left this neighborhood, you moved into it. You went to the same grammar schools as I did, Crucifixion and St. Patrick's."

"Yes, I did."

"Do you like this neighborhood?"

"No, but it's home. It's always been home to me. I lived in New York, but I came back here. It's been my home. Has it changed since you were here, Danny?"

"Some of the streets are dirtier."

"I've seen that happen."

"It's overcrowded now, isn't it?"

Bryan told Danny of conditions of life in the neighborhood. The col-ored people were charged high rents, and most of the landlords had split up the apartments in order to get more rent.

"One of my brothers," Danny said, "was delivering a package out to the old building on Calumet Avenue where he used to live—it's the building where my father died. In the basement there was an old storeroom without any windows. They made an apartment out of it. That's where he delivered the parcel."

"I know. And the people are cynical and dissatisfied. They're cheated, and they don't care. Most of them know they'll never get anywhere. They don't care. They spend everything they get because they're cynical and they don't care."

"The people who lived around here in my day," Danny said, "did care, and it didn't do many of them any good."

"The colored boys are as tough as the boys were in your days."

"They weren't such tough boys."

"These boys are afraid, so they have to be rough and tough," Bryan said. "If they aren't tough and cynical, where will they belong? That's the way they are. They gamble and play the numbers. My brother works in the post office, and he knows he can't ever do anything else. He's cynical, too."

"Are you?"

"No."

"Why?"

"I'm not. I'm sorry my mother is working today. I wanted you to meet her. She's heard about you. I think she understands what I want to do. I think you'd like her."

"My mother died—not so far away from here, either. It was last January. She lived over past Wentworth Avenue near Garfield Boulevard. She didn't want to live anywhere else. That's the boundary line now."

"Danny, I don't want to have to think I'm colored, a Negro. I want to think that I'm myself, another person, a poet, with my own feelings."

"Was growing up in this neighborhood too rough on you?" Danny asked Bryan.

"I don't know," Bryan answered thoughtfully. "I don't know what to say. I didn't like it. I don't know how I could like it, any more than you did. It all seems like your books. They were the same kind of boys that you knew. And I guess I just wasn't the same kind, that's all. You understand me, don't you?"

Danny nodded.

Bryan's aunt called them to lunch. They went through the hallway to the dining room in the rear of the apartment. The rather large, square dining room was very clean. There were dishes in a cupboard on one side. The big round table was carefully set, and the dishes were beautiful. Danny was touched by the display and by the abundance of food. He realized this was a gesture of pride and friendliness. Bryan introduced Danny to his two aunts. They were both gray-haired and wore clean bright aprons. One was small and plump; the other was tall and fleshy but not fat. Like Bryan, they had tannish-brown skin. They looked maternal, and both glanced with tenderness at their nephew. Danny spoke with them about the neighbor-hood, mentioning that he had formerly lived here, and he told them a lit-tle about his grandmother and his mother.

He and Bryan sat down to eat, and the two women served them. The women were friendly but dignified, and with pleasure they accepted his thanks for the lunch they had prepared and told him how glad they were that he liked it. Looking around the table with so much on it, the special dishes, the plate of rolls, the bowl of salad, the shining silver, the linen cloth, Danny was touched again, and he thought of how all this also represented work, hours and hours of work. And this dignity of tablecloth and silver and dish-es had been bought with the pride of those hours of work. This was obvi-ous, and yet he remembered how there had been a time when he wouldn't have thought of this and he wouldn't have been as touched as he was now.

Bryan was telling Danny how glad he was to have him out.

"I don't know whether or not I feel strange, being back here, Bryan. You know, it's really the same neighborhood it always was, it's the same neighborhood in many ways."

"I know it is. The colored boys were no different than the white boys. I've seen them grow up, and they don't care. They don't care about much of anything, anything that you and I would care about."

"There's something more important than their not caring. They don't know. That's the point about the boys I grew up with—they didn't know. I ran into a fellow I knew around here when I was a boy. I met him on the I. C. the other day. Do you know what he does every night in bed before he falls asleep?"

"What?"

"He lies in bed and thinks of Fifty-eighth Street. He remembers every building on Fifty-eighth Street between South Park and Calumet Avenue. To him there never was a neighborhood like this one. It's his boyhood."

"You fought this neighborhood, Dan."

"That doesn't express it. I didn't know, either, but I wanted to know. The beginning of knowing, of finding out, was right here when I lived on South Park Avenue."

"I want to know, too, Danny."

There was something appealing but soft in Bryan. He was sensitive and gifted, but something in him had been hurt. Danny wondered what had hurt Bryan most in life. Bryan kept mentioning his mother, how she worked so hard, and how she wanted him to become somebody. Nearly everyone else told Bryan he was wasting his time trying to get out of all this. It couldn't be done, they said. But his mother understood. Danny wished he had met her.

"Do you know what I mean, Danny?"

"About what?"

"Cynicism. How do you feel about cynicism and pessimism?"

"Pessimism signifies a lack of confidence in yourself and others. Cynicism is an extreme form of pessimism."

"I want to get out, I want to go back to New York, but then I think of my mother. She doesn't have much in life; she never did have. She always worked hard, mostly for me. If it weren't for my mother, I wouldn't go on. I was away in New York. I liked it. But I came back here because of my mother and because I thought perhaps I could write better. I lost four years in the army."

"Did you like the army?"

"I don't know. Can any Negro like the army? Most of them don't. Danny, I think there are a lot of them around here who'll never go to bed thinking about Fifty-eighth Street the way your friend does. America is different to them, especially after they fought for it. That's why they're cynical. I don't like it at all—I don't want to think I'm just a Negro. I don't want to have to think I'm just a Negro poet. I want to think I'm—I guess it's just as well to say American as anything."

"A human being?" asked Danny.

"Yes—a human being. That's what my mother wants me to be, and that's what she wanted to be herself. She is that, and I know it, but hardly anyone cares if she's a human being or not. That's what they all want to be, and they're not, they're cynical."

"I don't think they want to be cynical."

"I don't know—maybe they don't. But you can't get them to read much or care much. If I tried to convince my brother, he'd only laugh. He was in the army. He laughs at me and says it was Jim Crow and it's a Jim Crow world, and what's the use. That's the way they are in this neighborhood now."

"I can well understand," Danny answered.

One of Bryan's gray-haired aunts poured them second cups of coffee, and Danny thanked her.

"The problem of writing poetry is principally the problem of feeling, of living," Danny said.

Bryan nodded in agreement, but yet the expression on his face was such that Danny didn't think Bryan really understood. Danny talked on, in a slow and quiet manner.

"How much feeling and hope they have to have to break out of this cynicism and despair! Because, Bryan, it is despair."

"My mother doesn't despair. I guess I don't, either. I just don't like to be the way many of the colored boys around here are, that's all. That's why I want to write," Bryan said.

II

Danny and Bryan left the apartment. There were some spots of dirty snow along the dark patches of earth by the sidewalks, where scraps of paper were blowing about. A jitney taxicab passed, and some colored people walked by them on the street. Danny looked at the flat buildings between Fifty-seventh and Fifty-eighth Streets.

"I've walked this block, Bryan, perhaps as many times as you."

"I wouldn't doubt that."

"And yet it was a different street we walked—this same block between Fifty-seventh and Fifty-eighth on South Park."

"It's South Parkway now."

"I've been around here often since I left Chicago. Every time I see those buildings and this neighborhood, it's different. These stones, the stones of all these buildings change for me. Sometimes they are like ghost houses and sometimes they are merely dead and lifeless stones."

"What are they like now?"

"I'm trying to fix them in my memory. I knew a boy who lived in this place," Danny said, pointing to a red-brick, three-story building. "His name was Lenny Bernstein. He was a rich boy and had soft, flabby flesh. He used to try and lay every maid his mother hired. He always bragged about laying colored maids. He's a playboy now, and I see his name in gossip columns occasionally."

They were near Fifty-eighth Street now. More Negroes had passed them on the street. Danny had not seen another white person.

It was a warm muggy day with a threat of rain in the air.

"There are a lot of men on the streets. Is there much unemployment in this neighborhood?"

"Many of them work nights, and some of them have small rackets. Maybe I'll be able to point out some of the neighborhood pimps to you. One boy I went to St. Patrick's with, Doxey Dugan, has become a pimp. He dresses in loud, flashy clothes and hangs around Fifty-eighth and Prairie."

Danny glanced across the street at the park entrance. He was slowly beginning to invest everything he saw with something of his own emotions and his own past. He thought of himself, lonely and brooding and, at times, filled with sorrow for himself, entering the park across the street. In those days these streets, the park, were a big world in which he had been lonely and out of place. They seemed bigger to him then than the entire world now seemed, and he had been more afraid in this smaller world than he could ever be in the bigger world. How big was this neighborhood world in Bryan's mind? He pondered the question as he and Bryan turned the corner at Fifty-eighth Street and South Parkway.

"This street has changed. It never used to be this dirty," Danny said.

He looked around him. The sidewalks were littered and upswept. There were eight or ten colored persons on the street. Under the dark sky, it looked like a dreary slum.

"Bryan, I walked here so many times, but now all this is dead. And yet I momentarily catch the illusion that somewhere around here the past is lodged as though it possessed substance, as though it were a material thing."

"I sometimes feel that, too."

"That alley—the number of times I went down it," Danny said, pointing across the street at the alley entrance. "Let's go and look at my old back yard."

They crossed the street and entered the alley. It, too, was littered; papers, tin cans, rubbish lay everywhere. The alley had never been like this in the old days.

"God, it's dirty now," Danny said.

"Yes, it is."

"There's nothing to make them care, so they litter up the alleys and the streets. That's what you mean by cynicism, isn't it, Bryan?"

"I guess so."

They stopped at the back yard of the 5816½ building. The back fence was gone.

"There used to be a fence," Danny said. "And you can see that grass hasn't grown here in a long time."

The yard was cluttered with more rubbish. Danny thought of the back yards he had seen from the elevated train while riding out here to the South Side. He looked up at the old back porch. He thought of his Airedale dog, Lib. She was dead so many years. Behind that porch, inside the door of that flat, so much of his life had been lived, and all that life with its agonies and fears and worries had gone into making him what he now was. Once he used to think of the agonies of those days. Now he realized that inside that flat on the second floor he had dreamed, and his ambition had flourished.

"Up there," Danny said, pointing, "in the rooms behind that back door on the second porch, I became a writer. That's where I was living when I resolved to write."

"I admire you. I've often thought of you around here, as I would walk these streets."

"We're walking them together this afternoon," Danny said, thinking that he, however, was no longer involved here but that Bryan was.

They turned to walk out of the alley, and they continued on over to Fifty-eighth Street.

"There's still a drugstore here, and there's still the same drugstore at Fifty-eighth and Prairie."

"Yes, and the young colored fellows hang out at the corner of Fifty-eighth Street."

"Across there, there used not to be stores in some of those basements," Danny said, pointing toward the south side of Fifty-eighth Street.

There were a great many colored people on Fifty-eighth Street, and a number of the men were flashily dressed.

"Most of the stores have changed, of course," he told Bryan.

"I've seen changes in my time here, too. I was hoping I could see neighborhood characters to point out to you, Dan, but I don't see any. It's too bad you haven't more time. We could go around and we could meet people. I could show you what the insides of some of these houses look like now. Most of the flats are overcrowded."

"Bryan, compare the clothes of the people with their surroundings. The clothes tell a story. The war of all vanities against all other vanities is to be seen in these loud suits."

They walked all over the neighborhood. Danny's eyes darted one way and another, acquisitively taking in the streets, the people, the buildings.

The fireplug still stood at Fifty-eighth and Prairie Avenue. Once it had seemed big to him, but in reality it was a low plug, painted a brownish red, and it had once been painted black. A group of colored men stood in front of the Walgreen drugstore. Bryan commented on them. They hung around here regularly, and some of them were tough characters.

"Are you afraid of them?" Danny asked.

Bryan was taken aback by the question. He didn't answer immediately. They crossed Prairie Avenue and Danny knew that they were followed by the eyes of the group on the corner. In his day, it would have been white boys and men whose eyes would have followed a black and a white walking along here.

"I remember when that theater was being built. I used to play around the foundation of it in 1916," Danny said, pointing to the theater down from the corner on Prairie Avenue. "It used to be called The Prairie."

They walked on along Fifty-eighth Street.

"That was before I was born," Bryan said.

Danny wondered about the changes in this neighborhood. Was it that there were more changes in the neighborhood or in him? The time between the present, when he was walking along Fifty-eighth Street, and the past, when he had walked along here, seemed dense and full and rich. It seemed to have been such a long time ago, and in such a different world. The realization that there was a connection between himself of then and himself of the present moment seemed to him singularly strange. He glanced about, observing store fronts and faces of the colored people he passed. He didn't speak to Bryan for a while, and they turned into Indiana Avenue and stopped on the sidewalk before the vacant lot near Fifty-eighth Street. It seemed smaller and narrower than it had in his boyhood.

"You used to play here?" Bryan asked.

"Yes, I used to play indoor ball here, and touch football. Touch football wasn't as developed and as popular a game then as it is now."

"I want to write about this neighborhood and describe the way life went on here after you left. It's the same in many ways as you described it. You licked this neighborhood. I want to."

They walked on along Indiana Avenue toward Fifty-seventh.

"It wasn't the neighborhood that I licked; it was some of the fears in myself."

The old familiar houses, the old familiar homes, the building where Dan Donoghue had lived, the gray old stores where the Scanlans and Johnny O'Brien had lived, and the buildings on the corner where he had lived, and also where Andy Le Gare had lived. Danny thought of these houses. He wondered what life was going on inside them now, and he briefly closed his eyes and imagined Indiana Avenue peopled with the kids of his boyhood. He told Bryan briefly of those kids, of himself dreaming in those days, and Bryan said:

"I wanted something when I was a boy around here and I didn't know what I wanted."

"This neighborhood was a world to me; now it's only so many streets," Danny said.

"They're sad to me. The people underneath are sad."

"They look at it differently from us. I'm looking at it now from the outside. You're looking at it half from the inside and half from the outside. They're looking at it pretty much from the inside."

"I guess so. You escaped. I want to escape."

They walked around. The alley between Michigan and Indiana was as dirty as that between South Park and Calumet. The old play house in the Shires' yard was gone. Michigan Avenue was cleaner and better kept up than most of the other streets. A wall of one of the red store buildings at Fifty-eighth and Michigan attracted Danny's attention. A boy had scribbled with chalk:

KILROY WAS HERE BUT LEFT
BECAUSE THE PLACE STANK.

They walked on and saw other streets, and Danny and Bryan stood before the building between Fifty-ninth and Sixtieth on Calumet Avenue in which Danny's father, Jim O'Neill, had died. He was sad but in a restrained way. He was over forty now. They wandered on for almost a half hour.

Then they left the neighborhood to go over and around the University. In the present, as in the past, he was going away from the neighborhood in the same direction.

[1948]

Prairie State Books